WORLD
FUTURES

BARRY B. HUGHES *is a professor in the Graduate
School of International Studies at the University of
Denver. His many publications include three books,*
The Domestic Context of American Foreign Policy,
World Modeling, *and* Evaluating Transnational
Programs in Government and Business.

WORLD FUTURES

A Critical Analysis of Alternatives

BARRY B. HUGHES

The Johns Hopkins University Press
Baltimore and London

To my wife, Marilyn

© 1985 by The Johns Hopkins University Press
All rights reserved
Printed in the United States of America

The Johns Hopkins University Press, Baltimore, Maryland 21218
The Johns Hopkins Press Ltd, London

The paper in this book is acid-free and meets the guidelines for permanence and durability
of the Committee on Production Guidelines for Book Longevity of the Council on Library
Resources.

Library of Congress Cataloging in Publication Data

Hughes, Barry, 1945–
    World futures.

    Bibliography: p.
    1. Forecasting.   2. Economic forecasting.
3. Technological forecasting.   I. Title.
H61.4.H83 1984   003'.2   84-47964
ISBN 0-8018-3236-5
ISBN 0-8018-3237-3 (pbk.)

Contents

Figures

Tables

Preface

This book appears a little more than a decade after a small group at The Massachusetts Institute of Technology released a report containing the first set of global forecasts for multiple issues (food, population, economics, resources) ever to capture the attention of a wide public. For a variety of reasons, reviewed here in the first chapter, many other reports, some of them mutually contradictory, have followed and have received comparable attention.

The clash of prophets over the last ten years has been dramatic. Images of even the fairly near future vary sharply. As a researcher and teacher in the area of futures, and as a contributor to the public debate, I have felt my own need to impose some organization on the controversies gradually grow. It is not likely that any of the groups or individuals producing different images of the future monopolize understanding of how the world works. And yet they often write as if they do. There has frequently been a messianic fervor, a desire to convince the public so strong that authors flesh out their own views and make their own cases almost without serious consideration of alternatives.

This book seeks to aid others who share a sense of frustration at this confusing array of possible futures. It attempts to convey how the bases of difference arise from alternative world views, from competing methodologies and theories, and from contradictory evidence. It neither coins new catch phrases nor promulgates its own image of the future.

The work is fundamentally synthetic and as wide in scope as the futures studies it reviews. Academics often exhibit a reluctance to undertake analysis with great breadth. They fear leaving out important variables or failing to make their research and argument sufficiently rigorous. And social scientists are notably cautious about using their theories to make forecasts. Given the quality of much of their theory and the success rates of those who have made forecasts, their caution has basis. But forecasting or pre-diction is the ultimate test of theory, and broad social theories do underly competing global futures images. Thus, as an academic and social scien-tist, I feel that analysis of the last decade's debate can advance theoretical work. And as a futurist, I feel that a more social scientific approach is overdue. This book tries to bridge a wide canyon.

Foremost among my intellectual debts is that to Mihajlo Mesarovic, who introduced me to modeling and forecasting and provided me with an opportunity to participate directly in the public debates. For that I will always be grateful. My direct indebtedness to his concepts and ideas is obvious throughout the book. This work would not have been done, how-ever, were it not for the gentle urging by Harold Guetzkow to maintain a social scientific perspective and to impose it on the forecasting exercise. That, too, I appreciate greatly.

This work began at Case Western University Reserve and was con-cluded at the University of Denver. Both institutions have been very sup-portive, and classes at both universities and at the Foreign Service Institute have provided valuable feedback to ideas and arguments. The manuscript received partial or full reviews by Frank Beer, Peter Brecke, Herman Daly, Garrett Hardin, Dennis Pirages, and Joseph Szyliowicz. Their comments have been of great help, although I have failed to heed all of their advice. Research assistance by Merouane Lakehal-Ayat and Terrance Peet-Lukes is also gratefully acknowledged.

I always smile when I read prefaces in which the author attributes a book's completion to the support of a spouse. My own wife, Marilyn, to whom this book is dedicated, provides tremendous personal support, but makes completion of manuscripts exceedingly difficult. For both I thank her.

1. Introduction: The Proliferation of Futures Studies

Is global population growing faster than our ability to feed it? Or are we slowly bringing world food problems under control? Do we face increasing scarcities of energy and other raw materials? Or does new technology promise ever greater abundance? Are we increasingly polluting our environment and thereby threatening our health and our food supply? Or are we now creating cleaner, healthier environments for most inhabitants of the earth? Can the economic gap between the rich and poor countries of the world be closed? Or is it unbridgeable? Should we expect economic growth to characterize the rest of the century for the wealthier countries? Or is stagnation our future?

These questions about the future, and many others like them, are interrelated. It is difficult to attempt to frame answers for almost any of them without at least considering many of the others. The interdependencies among issues like population, food, energy, and economic growth have become as great as those among the geographic regions of the world. Disagreements concerning the correct answers to these questions are intense. That should not surprise us, because the "facts" are poorly understood and the stakes are enormous.

Many books have put forward definitive answers to these questions. This book does not. Instead, it has two purposes. The first is to place such "definitive" answers, very contradictory ones, into a structure—to allow us to understand better the key positions on these issues and how they relate to one another. The second is to provide background information necessary to any serious consideration of the questions. Such information includes "facts" or "data"; but, as important, it includes theories and models about how the world works. Instead of providing answers, this book seeks to assist in an informed search for them.

Although never denying the importance of efforts to better comprehend our futures, I have retained a skepticism concerning our ability to forecast.

1

We have not progressed as far as we might like, or as far as some might believe, beyond the time when Cicero suggested to the Roman Senate: "It seems to me that no soothsayer should be able to look at another soothsayer without laughing" (reported in Augustine 1982). Although the arguments for forecasting are strong, we still must be careful not to take our forecasts too seriously.

THE INCREASED INTEREST IN GLOBAL FUTURES

During the 1970s, there was an explosion of interest in global issues and global futures. More specifically, the interest has been in global issues other than the cold war—issues such as the rapid acceleration of population growth, the uncertainty of food sufficiency, the degradation of environmental quality, the shortages or crises of resource (especially energy) availability, and the persistent gap between the global rich and poor. (For useful reviews, see Marien 1976; Ferkiss 1977; Fowles 1978; Markley 1983; and recent issues of the *Futurist*.)

Many factors help explain the intensity of interest. First, a decade of decreased conflict along the East-West dimension of global politics allowed other issues to be given greater attention. In both the United States and Western Europe, public attention and political activity have returned to a considerable degree in the early 1980s to the issues of the cold war: military spending levels, nuclear and conventional military strategies, relationships of foreign policy and external domestic crises to superpower conflicts, and arms negotiation possibilities. It seems safe to posit, however, that the issues mentioned above will continue to share the stage and will even, in all probabilty periodically dominate it.

Second, these "other" issues may have become absolutely, not just relatively, more important. Global population growth attained rates in the early 1970s (nearly 2 percent annually) exceeding any in mankind's recorded history. Threats to the environment have grown with our ability to exploit it. Resource scarcities (especially of energy) appear more threatening than any we can remember. And the hopes generated in the developing countries when they achieved their independence from colonizing countries (primarily in the 1940s and 1950s) were often dashed by the realities of continued economic inferiority (some would say subservience) and a gap between rich and poor nations that simply refuses to close.

Third, we have systematically gathered an increasingly global data base related to these issues. It allows much better assessment of our current situation and patterns of change than we have ever had before. The efforts of the League of Nations between World War I and World War II initiated this improvement in global data. The post–World War II efforts of the United Nations, the Organization for Economic Cooperation and Development (OECD), the World Bank, and the International Monetary Fund (IMF), to mention only the most important of many organizations, have succeeded in establishing and refining a post-1950 global data base far more comprehensive and detailed than anything preceding it. The image mankind sees of itself collectively in that data base may be analogous to the first images individuals once saw of themselves reflected in still pools—superficial and sometimes distorted, but of profound importance.

Fourth, we have only quite recently developed the methodological skills, not only to maintain, improve, and analyze the growing data base but also to make estimates about the future based upon it. Application of the techniques often profits from and, in some cases, requires the availability of computers, themselves a recent phenomenon.

Fifth, theoretical understanding of these global issues and their interrelationships has grown rapidly, in part in response to the perceived importance of the issues and the availability of data. Theoretical perspectives guide the organization and interpretation of the data (and direct further data collection), providing a basis for projections into the future.

Finally, the proliferation of futures analyses almost certainly has been affected by the approach of a new millennium in the Christian calendar. There is a psychological attraction to the year 2000, and it is far from coincidental that so many futures analyses have ended their forecasting period with that year.

THE ISSUES

The issues addressed by most of these studies are those of what has been called the "world development system" (Mesarovic and Pestel 1974b). Attention to the world or global development system centers on the size, distribution, and growth rate of the global population and economy. Attention extends, however, to the physical and biological support systems of populations and their economic activities: to the availability of land and its food production capacity; to the sufficiency of raw materials, especially fossil fuels; and to the absorptive capacity and self-cleansing abilities of the air and water envelopes of life on earth. Attention also extends to the factors that organize and direct mankind's demographic and economic systems: to the value systems that motivate and shape behavior and to the political and social organizations that coordinate activity. Figure 1.1 represents the global development system as a hierarchy of subsystems (see also Mesarovic and Pestel 1974, 50; Daly 1980, 9). The organization of this book is based on that hierarchical structure. Higher layers of the hierarchy in many respects seek to control lower layers; our values shape our political institutions, which intervene in our economy, which organizes our technology. Lower levels serve as constraints on higher ones; resource levels

FIGURE 1.1.   *Components of the Global Development System*

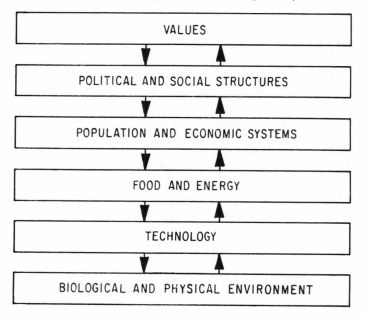

Source: Adapted From Mihajlo Mesarovic and Eduard Pestel, *Mankind at the Turning Point* (New York: E. P. Dutton, 1974), 29.

constrain energy availability, which affects economic growth, which may determine levels of political freedom. To understand one aspect of the global development system, one must at least consider the influence of all others.

The breadth of the issues addressed encompasses the interests, concerns, and expertise of numerous academic disciplines and professional occupations. The integrative thrust of futures studies constitutes, in fact, one of their most distinctive characteristics. And they are *integrative*, not just encompassing. "Systems thinking," popularly defined in the expression "everything is connected to everything else," has characterized most futures work. The concept of global interdependence has been dramatically extended. It has long been a cliché to speak of a "shrinking world." The cliché was given new and concrete meaning in the 1970s by OPEC's humbling of the United States and by the famine in North Africa (the Sahel), linked to the 1972–73 crop failures in India and the USSR. Realization of the second important interdependence—that among issue areas—has come a little more slowly. We now attribute, however, much of our global economic malady in the 1970s and early 1980s, stagflation, to oil prices and many of our environmental problems (and sometimes solutions) to economic growth. We know that the malnutrition and short life expectancies in Africa and Asia are tied to population growth rates, as is the ability of those countries to grow economically.

Thus, study of global development system futures has evolved into the study of the interconnected operation of a multitude of subsystems. The Club of Rome, with an often bleak image of the future, has labeled this nexus the *problématique,* or predicament. More optimistic forecasters, such as Herman Kahn, write of a global transition to a far wealthier and relatively problem-free future, but still emphasize the interconnectedness of the issues.

DIFFERENCES OF OPINION

If the global futures studies largely agree in identification of the key subsystems, their prognostications fail to extend that agreement. One of the most obvious and, for someone interested in the study of forecasts, disconcerting features of the supposedly scientific futures literature (as opposed to science fiction) lies in its extreme diversity. It is not difficult to find diametrically opposing viewpoints on almost any issue. This can be illustrated by quotations from some of the best known futurists.

With respect to general, long-term prospects for global population and economic systems, contrast Kahn and Meadows:

> The scenario presented, elaborated, and tested in this book can be summarized with the general statement that 200 years ago almost everywhere human beings were comparatively few, poor and at the mercy of the forces of nature, and 200 years from now, we expect, almost everywhere they will be numerous, rich and in control of the forces of nature. (Kahn, Brown, and Martel 1976, 1)

> If the present growth trends in world population, industrialization, pollution, food production, and resource depletion continue unchanged, the limits to growth on this planet will be reached sometime within the next one hundred years. The most probable result will be a rather sudden and uncontrollable decline in both population and industrial capacity. (Meadows et al. 1972, 23)

Differences extend to all the major support systems. They may be most dramatic with respect to food:

> The famines which are now approaching will not, in contrast [to historic ones], be caused by weather variations and therefore will not be ended in a year or so by the return of normal rainfall. They will last for years, perhaps several decades, and they are, for a surety, inevitable. Ten years from now parts of the underdeveloped world will be suffering from

famine. In fifteen years the famines will be castastrophic and revolutions and social turmoil and economic upheavals will sweep areas of Asia, Africa, and Latin America. (Paddock and Paddock 1976, 8).

Indeed, there are signs that the food problem may unfold during the eighties as dramatically as the energy problem did during the seventies. . . . Just as Middle Eastern oil is being depleted, so too are North American soils. At the existing intensity of cultivation, every ton of grain exported leads to the loss of several tons of topsoil. (Brown 1981, 7)

The primary reason why we have failed to achieve the degree of international food security now possible relates not to nature but to man. And the aspect of man responsible for this failure is not man as farmer or scientist or extension worker or grain marketer or food retailer—but man as politician. I use the term politician very broadly to include all who influence decisions that affect production, prices, and trade of food. (Johnson 1980, 185)

Yet there is little reason to believe that, in the foreseeable long run, additional people will make food more scarce and expensive, even with increasing consumption per person. It may even be true that in the long run additional people actually *cause* food to be less scarce and less expensive, and cause consumption to increase. (Simon 1981, 69)

Nor, of course, do the futurists agree on the availability of raw materials and energy or the need to conserve them:

The geologic, economic, and demographic evidence indicates that no physical lack of resources will seriously restrain our economic growth for the next quarter century and probably for generations thereafter. Judging by past trends, the estimates of most reserves will increase; for the few cases in which crustal exhaustion is remotely likely, there will be sufficient warning adjustments. (National Commission on Supplies and Shortages 1976, x; cited in Hamrin 1980, 57).

The history of economic exploitation of nonrenewable resources over the past 200 years is, in general, one of decreasing costs and increasing reserves. However, the direct energy or work costs of recovery have been rising, slowly for a long while, more rapidly as the number of tons of ore required to produce a ton of refined metal has started to rise more steeply with decreasing ore grade. . . . Now that energy resources themselves are beginning to cost more in work, now that the efficiencies of energy conversion appear to be nearing limits dictated by the strength of materials and the laws of thermodynamics, and now that the work costs of recovery, at least for some resources, are moving up the steeper parts of exponential curves, the nature of the limits to exploitation of nonrenewable resources is beginning to be recognized. (Earl Cook, in Daly 1980, 97)

We would hardly expect agreement on the environment:

For unlike the threats posed by population growth or war, there is an ultimate certitude about the problem of environmental deterioration that places it in a different category from the dangers we have previously examined. Nuclear attacks may be indefinitely avoided; population growth may be stabilized; but ultimately there is an absolute limit to the ability of the earth to support or tolerate the process of industrial activity, and there is reason to believe that we are now moving toward that limit very rapidly. (Heilbroner 1974, 47)

I do believe, however, that if concentrations of CO_2, and perhaps of aerosols, continue to increase, demonstrable climatic changes could occur by the end of this century, if not sooner; recent calculations suggest that if present trends continue, a threshold may soon be reached after which the effects will be unambiguously detectable on a global basis. Problematically, by that point it may be too late to avoid the dangerous consequences of such an occurrence, for *certain proof* of present theories can come only *after* the atmosphere itself has "performed the experiment." (Schneider 1976, 11)

For regions in which the maximum standards of abatement were applied, total costs (including investment and current costs) of abatement procedures included in the study amounted to 0.7–0.9 per cent of gross product. . . . Thus the findings of the study are that although pollution is a grave problem for humanity, it is a technologically manageable problem, and that the economic cost of keeping pollution within manageable limits is not unbearable. (Leontief et al. 1977, 7)

Both the probability and the desirability of technological solutions to problems are debated:

Thus science and technology—which in Western civilization removed poverty, illiteracy, hunger, frequent and severe disease, and short life spans for the majority of people and created for them instead relative affluence, improved health and medical care, longer life expectancy and a sense of increasing power—now appear to some groups to raise a general threat to the continuation of our civilization. . . . But we maintain that on balance, and with some exceptions (for example, nuclear proliferation) the arguments are heavily against deliberate policies to halt or slow down the basic long-term technological trend. (Kahn, Brown, and Martel 1976, 164)

Can there be "forbidden"—or as I prefer, "inopportune" knowledge? Could there be knowledge, the possession of which, at a given time and

state of social development would be inimical to human welfare—and
even fatal to the further accumulation of knowledge? . . . [if so, one
must] consider such issues as: the possible restriction of the rate of
acquisition of scientific knowledge to an "optimal" level relative to the
social context into which it is brought. (Sinsheimer 1980, 146–47)

When we turn our attention to the "higher" human systems, both of
individual values and of political organization, we again encounter conflict. On values:

Needless to say, wealth, education, research, and many other things are
needed for any civilization, but what is most needed today is a revision
of the ends which these means are meant to serve. And this implies,
above all else, the development of a life-style which accords to material
things their proper, legitimate place, which is secondary and not primary.
(Schumacher 1973, 278)

Underlying those "limits-crises" is a gap between man and nature which
is widening at an alarming rate. To bridge that gap man has to develop a
new attitude to nature based on harmonious relationship rather than
conquest. (Mesarovic and Pestel 1974, 153)

We believe strongly that greater control over the environment (which may
or may not lead to greater happiness) is a good indicator of
modernization. We also believe it is greatly to be desired. Economic
affluence and technological advancement are essential to modernization.
(Kahn 1979, 44)

With respect to general domestic political directions:

All this suggests that it may be time to view the faults of the U.S.
capitalist economic system from the vantage point of a socialist
alternative—to debate the relative merits of capitalism and socialism.
Such a debate is now the central issue of political life in Europe, and it is
perhaps time for the people of the United States to enter into it as well.
(Commoner 1976, 26)

The one thing that capitalism and socialism have agreed upon is the
importance of economic growth. Both have accepted the criterion that
whichever system can grow faster must be better, and each strives to win
the growth race. The notion of an SSE [steady state economy] is rejected
by both. Both systems suffer from growth mania, and the SSE presents as
much a challenge to Big Socialism as to Big Capitalism. (Daly 1980,
367)

Coercion is a dirty word to most liberals now, but it need not forever be
so. As with the four-letter words, its dirtiness can be cleansed away by
exposure to the light, by saying it over and over without apology or

embarrassment. To many, the word coercion implies arbitrary decisions of distant and irresponsible bureaucrats; but this is not a necessary part of its meaning. The only kind of coercion I recommend is mutual coercion, mutually agreed upon by the majority of the people affected. (Hardin and Baden 1977, 27)

Americans should not be fearful about the capacity of American society to adapt to fundamental changes; our society is adaptable and resilient. . . . We should keep faith with ourselves, with democracy, and with our basic ideals. (Richardson 1982, 5)

And with respect to general international directions:

The most urgent need is for the programme of large-scale transfer of funds from North to South to be stepped up substantially from year to year during the final two decades of this century. Such an effort effectively directed towards the solution of the major problems discussed in this Report will benefit the South and turn back the rising tide of world poverty; it would also provide important benefits to the North. (Brandt 1980, 237)

One may be deeply concerned about the economic development of the Poor countries and still support a policy in some cases of benign neglect because one fully recognizes that they really have to do it themselves. Outside interference can sometimes be counterproductive. (Kahn 1979, 496)

It should be stated immediately that the above quotations were, of course, selected to illustrate extremes of opinion and that many of the above authors have taken pains to qualify somewhat or weaken the full force of their words (others, like the Paddocks and Simon, are quite consistent throughout). There is also a publicity value in extreme statements which did not go unrecognized by many of those quoted.

I am not so cynical as to attribute most of the vast differences in forecasts to their publicity value. Nor will I, as some have done, attribute views largely to conscious and self-serving "class interests" of forecasters (although cultural and economic bases are important, including the inherent bias many government officials have toward active public policies). Instead, the central purpose of this work is to clarify the intellectual bases of alternative world futures.

THE BOOK

Readers of futures studies generally fall into two major categories. Many are "believers." They have adopted one particular position—a limits-to-growth or a technologically optimistic view, for instance—and generally reject the writing and forecasts of the "opponents." They vary greatly in their sophistication. Some have an empathetic understanding of alternative viewpoints, truly comprehending major premises and arguments, while others merely believe, critiquing other positions superficially.

Another large category contains the "confused." They also vary greatly in their sophistication and the extent of their knowledge of forecasts. The most widely read may have become convinced agnostics, no longer anticipating that anything but the future itself will resolve the disagreements. But many find themselves swayed or even convinced by the last report they have read. They may feel that there is little or no value in reading more "science fiction."

This book is directed at all those still interested in these critical issues, both the believers and the confused. It should have something to say to all but the most sophisticated of the believers. For the intent of this work is to examine the bases for alternative world futures. The argument here is that the bases can be seen at three interconnected levels: world views, theories, and evidence.

At the highest or most complex levels are *world views*. World views provide highly integrated images (some would say models or paradigms) of the way in which the global development system functions. World views normally also incorporate quite explicit value systems and, therefore, related images of the way in which the global development system *should* function. World views have important historical bases and serve to structure not only images of the global development system but images of national and local community systems and even models of individual behavior as well. Certainly not everyone has a well-articulated and explicit world view, much less recognizes and understands competing ones. Sophisticated "believers," as discussed above, do have them. Most people acquire world views at early ages by being immersed in a culture or subculture dominated by a particular wordview and socialized (often with little independent thought) to accept the view. Sometimes experiences in later life, including study, will lead to replacement of a world view; more often they do not. World views to be discussed in subsequent chapters are those of the classical liberal, the internationalist, the radical, the neotraditionalist and the modernist. It will be argued that there are two primary dimensions that structure these world views. Some individuals can be classified on both, but one dimension dominates the thinking of many.

World views often shape the selection of alternative *theories,* the second level on which we will analyse alternative world futures. For instance, competing theories of the dynamics of the economic production process— some focusing exclusively on the accumulation of capital, others emphasizing the growth and education of a healthy labor force—are tied in important ways to world views. We shall see, for instance, that it is no accident that the former theory was used in the construction of the *Limits to Growth* model (Meadows et al. 1972) and that the latter was the basis for one by a Latin American group (Herrera et al. 1976). Similarly, basic concepts, the building blocks of theory, vary in ways tied to world views. For instance, definitions and measurements of the concepts ''scarcity'' and ''North-South gap'' vary among futurists.

By no means, of course, are all concepts and theories closely tied to specific world views. Some are inherent parts of several; other theories stand largely alone. They, too, shape forecasts, and we will discuss how they do so. For instance, the relationship between an individual's income and the portion he spends on food is largely (not entirely) free of linkages to specific world views. So, too, is a method for projecting population called cohort-component analysis.

In an important sense, *evidence,* or data, the third level of our analysis, does not exist outside of a theoretical context. That is, our concepts (names of both concrete and abstract phenomena) are the tools with which we structure data, and most of our concepts are imbedded in theoretical structures. Thus, our discussion of basic evidence or data with respect to the evolution of the global development system will be shaped by our world view and theory. But for many readers, this is the level at which some very important questions shaping choices among competing world future images must be addressed. For instance, what exactly is the level of global oil reserves? How dependent is agricultural production on fertilizer prices? How fast is the population of Africa growing relative to its grain production?

Obviously, no one can hope comprehensively to analyze competing views of the future on all of these levels. Nor can the views of any author be divorced from an analysis of this type. A start can be made, however, and a serious effort can be made at an even-handed and objective presentation.

In the next chapter I review some of the key futures studies of the 1970s. Then I turn to a general presentation of major world views and how they shape future images. Succeeding chapters will proceed by issue area (population, economics, food) to examine in more detail alternative forecasts for the evolution of the world development system. In each I shall look specifically at how theoretical structures and selection and interpretation of evidence buttress forecasts. Finally, I shall return to the general and basic issue of this book, ''What are we to believe about the future?''

2. Competing Images of the Future

As outlined in Chapter 1, the futurist literature presents radically varying images of the manner in which the global development system is most likely to evolve. This chapter reviews some of the studies of the 1970s and early 1980s which have attracted the most attention. Such a review will assist the subsequent efforts to elaborate on the bases of the disagreements among reports.

The literature upon which we could draw here is huge, with books numbering in the hundreds and articles in the thousands. Magazines such as *Futures, The Futurist, Omni,* and *Discover* have arisen to support the market. In fact, the volume of the literature, combined with its great diversity and internal dissension, have given rise to a whole new meaning to the phrase "future shock." Instead of Toffler's meaning (1970)—bewilderment, confusion, disruption, and even alienation resulting from a world in which technology, economics, and society are changing at high speed—many otherwise well-informed and intelligent individuals are suffering a sense of bewilderment, confusion, disruption, or even alienation in response to the literature itself. One writer has even referred to "Future Shuck." He points out that "the nice thing about future shucking is that, by 2001, or even by the end of the week, nobody is going to remember . . . to contradict the most outrageous futurizing. . . . It is just scifi with a Ph.D." (Nachman 1982, 9). Much of the literature is, in fact, flimsy and unsystematic speculation about dramatic technological developments and their possible social impact.

The primary focus here is on a more serious and studied body of work. I have restricted my examination largely to work of the 1970s and early 1980s (simply because of the significant increase in both writing and interest in that period) and have selected primarily studies that have attracted considerable public attention, ignoring others that are as worthy of attention. Most importantly, I have focused on analyses of the wide spectrum of issues surrounding the global development system: population, food, energy and raw materials, economic growth and the North-South gap, and the environment. This decision is not arbitrary because our primary interest in this volume is the system as a whole. Later chapters will draw attention to the work in individual areas which supports these general studies.

A Review of Recent Futures Studies

The best known and most widely read forecast for the global development system was presented with much fanfare by the Club of Rome in 1972 under the title *Limits to Growth.* The Club of Rome is an informal international association of about one hundred individuals (scientists, businessmen, authors, scholars, and public officials) who share an interest in the global development system and an unease about its future prospects (Peccei 1977). Established in Rome during 1968, the club cast about for approaches to global futures analysis and decided that the development of a computerized model of the global development system capable of projecting trends and analyzing the interaction of subsystems far into the future represented one such tool.

The result was the decision to sponsor and publicize (Volkswagen Foundation provided the financial support) work done at the Massachusetts Institute of Technology, first under the leadership of Jay Forrester (1971) and then under the direction of Dennis and Dana Meadows. *Limits to Growth* was the public report released by this project team; it was supported by two technical volumes (Meadows et al. 1974, 1976).

Limits to Growth, as indicated by a quotation in Chapter 1, portrayed a very gloomy future for the world. In fact, the basic conclusion of the analysis, involving many alternative computer runs of the model, was that unless global population *and* global industrial output are quickly stabilized at levels very near those prevailing today, major systemic collapses resulting from shortages of resources, land, or pollution absorption capacity are inevitable in the 21st century. In sharp contrast, no demographer has forecast population stabilization at less than twice current levels. Moreover, Third World leaders have naturally argued that they cannot even slow, much less cease, their economic growth, and First World leaders seem very unlikely to suggest a redistribution of their own wealth to the poorer countries. Since the report's conditions for avoiding collapse cannot be met, the report all but said that collapse is inevitable.

Limits to Growth was not, of course, the first or only study to draw largely negative conclusions about global futures. For instance, Pirages and Ehrlich (1974) sketched roughly the same portrait at almost the same time. The Meadows team had several advantages in spreading its message. First, their book is very well written, making computer analysis meaningful to nontechnical readers, and it relates a highly integrated, logically presented "story." Second, the Club of Rome proved to be an incredibly capable press agency. The message went out nearly simultaneously around the world, reported by the highly regarded club members. Third, the release of the report was uncannily timely. Poor monsoons in 1972 and 1973 reduced crops in Africa below the Sahara (the Sahel region) and in South Asia. Simultaneous crop failures in the Soviet Union and internal political decisions not to cut back meat production pushed that country into the international grain market as never before. Much of the traditional U.S. surplus was purchased by Soviet trading agents before even most commodities experts in the U.S. food market knew what was happening. Results were higher food prices globally and the reduced ability of South Asia and the Sahelian countries to import.

Almost simultaneously, the late 1973 Mideast war and the resulting oil embargo by Arab petroleum exporters, coming at a time of an already tight international oil market, forced oil prices upward by a factor of four or five and created panic concerning oil availability in many localities. Both the energy and food "crises" came at the end of a period of rapid global economic growth which had already put pressure on the supplies of a number of other raw materials (Fried 1976).

It is thus not so surprising, although still impressive, that *Limits to Growth* became a best seller. It should also have surprised no one that criticisms of the report surfaced almost immediately and were scathing. Criticisms have come from many directions. Some have been generally skeptical of forecasts. They have pointed out how past forecasts of population and economic growth, or of resource availability, have more often been wrong than right. For instance, the Reverend Thomas Malthus had reached almost identical conclusions a century and a half earlier (1798–1803), prior to the most dramatic growth in population and economic well-being in mankind's history. A group of scholars at Sussex University relied on this line of criticism, among others, in a book called *Models of Doom* (Cole et al. 1973).

Others have criticized the study methodologically. For example, *Limits to Growth* employed a modeling methodology called "systems ·dynamics," developed by Jay Forrester. It allows models to be constructed without an extensive data base, relying upon general theory and even common sense. The Meadows group was quite open in admitting that only a very small fraction of the data desirable in constructing a world model is in fact available. Economists, in particular, rely heavily upon data in their own highly developed modeling methodology, econometrics, and were quick to criticize the report's methodology. Economists have often also argued that omission from the model of prices, the key variable in assuring adequate supply in economic models, invalidates the analysis. In addition, some have argued that the treatment of the world as a whole, when some of the problems analyzed appear to be largely regional (e.g., pollution, food availability) is a major weakness.

Many of these criticisms miss the central, simple, and almost tautological argument of *Limits to Growth*. That argument is that exponential growth of any process in a closed system will eventually reach the inherent limits of that system and will be abruptly stopped. Those criticisms that have been more on target have thus directly attacked the assumptions explicit in that argument.

For example, one can argue that the system is not closed. Belief in the probability of expansion of human economic activities beyond earth (e.g., satellite solar stations or asteroid mining) is a dramatic illustration of such arguments. More mundane is the argument that the Meadows report vastly understated the natural resource base by underestimating technological developments (or even materials availability with current technology) and similarly discounts too heavily our abilities to control pollution. Such a line of argument does not deny the ultimate limits. Only mankind's reliance on infinite or completely renewable resources (and not even the sun is infinite or indefinitely renewable) would eliminate ultimate limits. But the argument can push limits forward into a much more distant future. Or one can argue that there are already processes at work which will operate to slow and then stop exponential growth in population and industrial production, an argument that in combination with less constraining limits effectively eliminates any reason for concern. These arguments are thus the ones that will merit most attention in subsequent chapters.

A number of studies of global development system futures which followed *Limits to Growth* in the 1970s were in significant part responses to it. Among the earliest was another report sponsored by the Club of Rome and authored by two members, Mihajlo Mesarovic and Eduard Pestel (1974). *Mankind at the Turning Point* generally accepted the conclusions of *Limits to Growth* with respect to resource scarcity and environmental fragility, but argued that the limits were not so near that collision with them was inevitable. Instead, appropriate political and social action was possible to avoid them. (It should be pointed out that this was also the actual conclusion of the Meadows group book—it is simply difficult to see how it could be reached from their analysis.) The second book argued that it is critical to maintain growth in industrial and food production in the Less Developed Countries (LDCs), although not completely along the highly resource intensive and polluting lines of historical developed country growth. The report argued that it is necessary simultaneously to reduce global population growth, especially in the LDCs; to reduce or stop industrial country growth in the use of raw materials and in pollution generation; and to assist the LDCs in closing the gap between themselves and the developed countries through markedly increased international transfers.

This report was also based on a computer model, but one with a great deal more detail in structure than the *Limits to Growth* model, including a division of the world into ten regional groupings of states. The goal of the project team was to develop a computerized tool for assisting policy analysis with respect to the issue areas of the global development system. Work has continued on that tool, including the development of national level detail and structures specific to particular policy areas (Hughes 1980).

Mankind at the Turning Point elicited neither the level of popular attention nor the level of criticism which the first report to the Club of Rome had. Most responses to it, both supportive and critical, were parallel to those for *Limits to Growth*.

Two years later still another computer model-based futures analysis was released. The authors were a group located in Bariloche, Argentina, and it came to be known as the Bariloche, or Latin American, model. *Catastrophe or New Society?* (1976) was very much a reaction against *Limits to Growth,* particularly against the implication that LDCs would need to abort their economic development processes to avoid global catastrophe. Again, the Meadows' conclusion that industrial growth must be halted globally, combined with the improbability of significant sharing of wealth by the developed countries, was justifiably interpreted by many as carrying that implication, even though it was denied by the Meadowses.

The Bariloche team specifically rejected the ecological limits perceived by the Club of Rome. To the degree that resource scarcity or pollution are problems, they were attributed to overconsumption by the rich, a conclusion largely shared by the Club of Rome reports. The Bariloche group, however, did not even include resource or environmental variables in their model.

The group specifically identified the principal interacting problems as the economic condition and the political and social structures of the Third World. They argued that radical restructurings of the political and social systems so as to emphasize satisfaction of basic human needs (food, shelter, education) and equality of distribution are needed. They structured their model so that three of the four regions represented were Third World regions. Whereas economists traditionally divide the economy into sectors such as agriculture, materials, manufacturing, and services, this model identified sectors like nutrition and housing. Instead of emphasizing aid or trade as mechanisms of economic development in the Third World, the Bariloche model instead severed all economic linkages among regions, thus representing autarkic development patterns. And instead of emphasizing population control measures as necessities to avoid food shortages, the Latin American group argued that reduction in fertility will follow from improved living standards. The researchers did not view population policies by themselves as useful tools.

The conclusion of analyses undertaken by the group was that dramatic improvement was possible in Latin America, Africa, and Asia in the meeting of basic human needs, given effectively equal distribution of goods within the regions and a considerable increase in investment rates. This could in fact be interpreted somewhat pessimistically, inasmuch as the changes argued to be prerequisites of the improvements, especially the distributional ones, are not likely to be made. Moreover, the group found that South Asian success was not assured prior to a time point at which population overwhelmed food production and made success impossible.

The major criticisms of this report drew a descriptive/prescriptive distinction. The book presents a clearly prescriptive view of the future, in contrast to the more descriptive efforts of the Club of Rome. In doing so, it opened itself to the criticism that "we can't get there from here"—that its prescriptions are politically unrealistic. Many, of course, also were unhappy with where the authors wanted to go, that is, with their clearly socialist outlook.

At almost the same time as the Latin American report, another report was issued which attracted considerably greater attention. Herman Kahn, best known to many for his earlier work on nuclear war, directed a group at the Hudson Institute in the preparation of a report called *The Next 200 Years* (1976). This was not a computer model-based analysis, but the argument was nonetheless a highly integrated study of the global development system.

The major difference between it and the literature discussed to this point was its conclusions. Barring a catastrophe such as nuclear war, the report argued that the future should be superior in almost all respects to the present. It denied any significant resource limitations on economic growth, citing, for instance, abundant energy supplies, including very high levels of usable fossil fuels. It pointed to improvements in several areas of environmental performance and argued that the cost of improvements in other areas would be quite manageable. These conclusions were not softened by statements about overconsumption by rich countries, as in the Latin American group report. The report argued that economic growth even in rich countries can continue at high rates for a long time.

The Hudson Institute study did not go so far as to conclude that economic and population growth globally could and would continue indefinitely without constraints. In fact, a central part of the argument is that both will gradually level off over about the next two hundred years (as they gradually accelerated in the last two hundred), reaching levels perhaps three and one-half times above current ones for population and fifty times higher for gross world product. But the transition to a relatively steady state, at least temporarily, was not seen as a forced one, but rather as one that would occur as the result of more natural (if not too clearly specified) causes.

These conclusions directly and strongly challenged those observers who perceive important and near-term limits to global growth. They responded with as much enthusiasm (if not outrage) as had the critics of *Limits to Growth*. The categories of criticism have been roughly parallel.

First, some critics have simply felt that such forecasts are totally incredible. They point to the energy and food crises of the 1970s as precursors of worse to come. And they question what these relatively unspecified processes are that will lead to a natural and quite painless slowing and eventual cessation of economic growth. For instance, are there actually levels of consumption at which individuals are satiated? If not, of course, then continued growth in per capita output, resource use, and pollution would eventually (and with exponential growth eventually comes quickly) reach the most optimistic upper limits.

Others have criticized the study methodologically. The absence of a formal model has bothered some analysts. It is more difficult without a mathematical structure to assure consistency of assumptions and arguments from one issue area to another and to integrate the argument fully. It has been pointed out, for instance, that the authors often seem to argue in a circular fashion. In particular, the conclusion that in two hundred years the global average economic product per capita will reach $20,000 (in 1975 real dollars) is used to suggest that even if energy or food prices go up somewhat there will be no difficulties in affording the commodities. Critics have reasonably asked how such high incomes could be attained if costs of primary products rise.

But realistically, both the *Limits to Growth* and *The Next 200 Years* present circular arguments insofar as they argue that the various subsystems of the global development system are interconnected. In an interconnected system with any one subsystem in major crisis, others will experience crises as well. But in one in which no subsystem has major problems the success of other subsystems will benefit any experiencing minor difficulties.

The key difference between the two approaches, and the one toward which analysis must be directed, lies in the perception and representation of constraints. Even in the two Club of Rome models the subsystems initially support each other—industrial growth boosts agricultural production potential, which, as it improves diets, allows diversion of industrial production to other uses, such as energy production or luxury goods. A somewhat minor "set-back" in one system, such as reduced acreage used in agricultural production, can be more than offset by progress in another area. But in the two computer models, the constraints on ultimate land availability and natural resource availability are simply much greater and assumptions about technological potential are much less than in the Kahn report. Comparative examination of such assumptions thus proves much more productive than methodological criticism, and I shall examine in detail the assumptions in subsequent chapters.

It was noted earlier that economists were among those most critical of the *Limits to Growth*. Thus, it may have been only a question of time before a more traditional economic world model was created to challenge the Meadows' work. It was done by a team working with Nobel Prize-winning economist Wassily Leontief, and the major report of the project was called *The Future of the World Economy* (1977). The United Nations sponsored the effort.

The structure of the computer model centered on input-output matrices of the economies of fifteen global regions, a technique pioneered by Leontief. The matrices represent the inputs required from all other sectors of the economy (or from imports) in the production of any given sector. Thus, given a scenario about future growth in an economy, including assumptions about how that will affect demand in each sector, it is possible to calculate total required inputs. By extending the technique a little one can also calculate labor requirements and pollution generation.

Leontief's group investigated the potential for the LDCs to grow sufficiently quickly to narrow the gap considerably (in ratio terms) between their per capita incomes and those of the more developed countries. Specifically, they tested a U.N. target of reduction by the year 2000 to seven to one in per capita income ratio, down from twelve to one in 1970. The authors concluded that it could in fact be done, assuming among other things considerable increases in foreign aid from the wealthy countries and quite dramatically increased investment rates (the portion of GNP directed toward increasing capital stock) in the LDCs. They also examined the requirements for agricultural land, yield increases, and resource inputs resulting from the scenarios and concluded that no food or resource constraints need be encountered. Similarly, they concluded that pollution generation was no problem because a relatively low percentage of GNP directed at pollution control efforts would control it (see p. 7, above).

This report received somewhat less public attention and analysis than others discussed here and thus also less criticism. Besides its less sensational conclusions, the failure of its release to coincide with any major changes in the global system (like an energy crisis), and a style less suited for the layman than other reports, people might well have been tired by this time of global model–based studies. Again, however, methodological criticisms can be made. The failure of the project explicitly to address resource availability levels, for instance, makes the authors' conclusions that there are no constraints a bit weak. For instance, their forecasts indicate that global petroleum consumption in 2000 will be 5.2 times that of 1970 (Leontief et al. 1977, 5), a figure exceptionally high in comparison with even optimistic assumptions. Similarly, they compute that LDC-region foreign debt will climb sharply in most variations of their basic scenario. Many observers would certainly argue that if they had "closed the loop," i.e., had constrained the growth of the debt to what might be considered more reasonable levels, the growth of the LDCs would be significantly reduced.

Not to be outdone, another international organization, the Organization for Economic Cooperation and Development (OECD) followed the United Nations with its own global futures study. The Interfutures project of the OECD released *Facing the Future* (1979). It based this report in part on the results of analyses with a computer model named SARUM (SARU 1977), although the analyses went well beyond results from the model. In general, they relied on the scenario technique, i.e., the development of alternative, well-integrated images of the future.

This study reached rather more "middle ground" conclusions than most of those discussed to this point. Most of its analysis extends to the years 2000 or 2025, and up to the latter point they foresee no significant problems with respect to physical limits on agricultural production or materials availability. But problems may arise, the authors of the Interfutures project argue, from inadequate agricultural investment capability in some regions and from lack of access to resources. In short, they see socioeconomic constraints, but not physical ones. However, they do believe that upward trends in real prices of raw materials are likely, and they do feel that governments must develop policies (especially greater research) to avoid problems in climate, energy, and soil erosion.

OECD also forecast slowing economic growth in OECD countries, although they attribute it largely to managerial problems, many of which are tied to institutions created for achievement of social objectives. With respect to the Third World, the Interfutures project emphasized the great diversity that has emerged with respect to growth prospects, both within and between major geographical regions. Prescriptively, the group recommends increased aid and increased Third World access to loans and technology.

This report did not draw the attention of a large audience, especially in the United States, where in general there has been less attention to all of these studies than in Europe. Among the reasons for the relatively lower interest in the OECD work must be the relatively unexciting nature of its analysis, style of presentation, and conclusions. It is not difficult to imagine, however, the nature of the criticisms that it would attract from adherents to the positions of the reports outlined above.

Another and only slightly later government-sponsored study, *The Global 2000 Report to the President* (CEQ 1981) did attract a great deal of attention. This report was requested by President Carter of the Council on Environmental Quality and Department of State. The analysis and forecasts are predominantly a collection prepared by various U.S. governmental agencies and departments (but also some international organizations). In spite of this, the project director, Gerald Barney, presented it as the result of the U.S. government's "world model." The reason for doing so was to emphasize that all such future analyses and policies based upon them, or upon less detailed forecasting, actually do involve models of the world. Such models may not, of course, be as clearly articulated and highly integrated as those represented on computers, but they shape forecasts and conclusions as strongly. Barney went a step further in "model development" by taking the initial forecasts produced with almost complete independence by the agencies and asking the agencies in a second pass at forecasting to consider those produced by each other. This process of "closing the loops" did result in a methodology more similar to those of the global development system studies discussed above than is typical in a governmental study.

The conclusions of the report were strikingly similar to those of the first two reports to the Club of Rome. It sketched a future in which scarcity of food and raw materials and environmental degradation were highly probable. It called for strong governmental responses to current and potential problems. The release of the report had the advantage of roughly coinciding with the period of the second oil shock, when the Iranian revolution and the Iran/Iraq war reduced global supplies and pushed up prices, rekindling debates over longer-term energy and raw materials futures. The report attracted the same mixture of acclaim and sharp criticism that the earlier pessimistic reports had done.

Another widely read study of global futures was released near the same time. Alvin Toffler's *The Third Wave* (1980) is difficult to compare with other books discussed here. It does not focus on the global development system. For instance, it says little or nothing about demographic futures, makes no statements about economic growth rates, almost fails to mention distinctions between rich and poor countries (it really focuses on the rich), and barely touches on issues of the environment and natural resources. Policy recommendations are almost nonexistent, consisting only of rather vague calls to develop institutions based on three principles: minority power, semidirect democracy, and decision division (greater decentralization of decision-making to greater numbers of political and economic institutions).

Yet the book, like Toffler's earlier *Future Shock* (1970), attracted a wide readership. The book merits attention here in spite of, and perhaps because of, its totally different approach to futures analysis;—furthermore, it helps illustrate the distinctiveness of those works that do focus clearly on the global development system.

Toffler's focus is on the nature of economic relationships, social patterns, and their interaction. Much of his basic argument parallels one developed by others, namely, that our economic structures (at least in the First World) are increasingly postindustrial or service-oriented (see, for example, Bell 1973). He offers both elaboration of this theme and some variation. The most important variation is his argument that the new economic structures will result in a reunion of producer and consumer roles, a unity characteristic of the first wave (agricultural society), but lost in the second wave (industrial society). This theme of the "prosumer" interacts with a strong technological optimism and the earlier *Future Shock* concept of increasing diversity of both consumer roles and potential use of increased leisure time, to provide the economic background upon which Toffler sketches his image of evolving social relations.

Although he foresees a reorganization of energy systems on the principle of renewable energy, no energy or raw materials shortages, economic conflicts, or environmental problems mar Toffler's future. Thus, in many respects, the vision shares a common set of basic assumptions with the scenarios of the Hudson Institute. Although the futures built on those assumptions differ considerably, the Hudson Institute describes a quaternary sector economy, based on information, which it distinguishes from the traditional services of the tertiary sector. Had Toffler called his book *The Fourth Wave*, the similarities would be stronger.

The Third Wave, as a popular book rather than one in the ongoing and somewhat more academic debate on the global development system, has not drawn the same kind of critical analysis which the scholarly literature has received. Toffler's style is both synthetic (drawing together bits and pieces of information, ideas, and literature) and somewhat loose and anecdotal. In many respects it titillates and excites the reader with an avalanche of ideas and information, rather than inviting serious analysis. Many readers probably fail to come away with the ability to summarize the argument, but instead complete the book with a sense of having been entertained and informed.

More recently, John Naisbitt's *Megatrends* (1982) has had much the same kind of public impact, and is in fact a very similar book. Again, Naisbitt neither explicitly treats issues such as food and energy availability or environmental quality nor abstracts for the reader a cohesive image of social/political futures. Instead Naisbitt presents ten trends designated as most significant for the United States on the basis of "content analysis" of newspapers.

The methodology is subject to question with respect to how the researchers established trend categories. For instance, all the trends are generally positive, and one wonders how growing concern with armaments and war and how asocial and violent behavior, from terrorism to rape to drug abuse, managed to be excluded. The public was certainly ready for an upbeat book, but the news that the researchers subjected to content analysis seldom seems so positive. The methodology is also open to question concerning the degree to which the identified trends represent the passing fashion of press and public attention (for instance, civil rights, the environment, and the Vietnam War would presumably have appeared in such an analysis from the 1960s). Nevertheless, the trends identified are of interest. Among them are the economy's transition from manufacturing to information and the growing importance of "high tech." In addition, and again like Toffler, Naisbitt emphasizes decentralization and participation (as opposed to representation) in social/political structures. The overall portrayal of our future is an attractive one.

The last two works I shall discuss here are in the mainstream of analyses of global development system studies. Lester Brown's *Building a Sustainable Society* (1981) and Julian Simon's *The Ultimate Resource* (1981) were released at almost the same time and invite simultaneous analysis; both received considerable attention. Lester Brown has written several books with the same focus and, in fact, with considerable overlap in content. He is quite well known for his earlier work and for his role as founder and director of the Worldwatch Institute, which publishes short reports on global issues. Julian Simon, an economist and student of population growth, was much less well known prior to release of his book; that work came out with much fanfare and almost instantly made Simon's reputation.

The two works agree on practically nothing. Brown's book is in the tradition of the first two Club of Rome reports. Neither his nor Simon's work relies on computer models; Brown's is very different in approach and focus from the computer-based reports. Brown emphasizes the threat mankind's activities pose to three ecosystems: forests, grasslands, and fisheries. He is particularly concerned with soil erosion and its implications for our ability to sustain agricultural productivity in many areas of the world, including the United States.

Much of Brown's book—and that which most distinguishes this one from his prior work—is devoted to suggesting what can be done to build a sustainable society. Brown argues that global population should be held to 6 billion (as I noted earlier and shall discuss in Chapter 4, this is effectively impossible) and presents various policy recommendations, including proposals for reforestation and increased solar energy usage. He also discusses the important role of market forces, such as those which have increased the efficiency of energy use.

Simon's book is altogether different. He argues that there is in fact no scarcity of raw materials, nor will there be one in the foreseeable future. He cites long-term decreasing resource prices and share of individual budgets spent on raw materials as evidence of the dominant trend, in contrast to what he sees as the temporary increases that occurred during the 1970s. He argues that far from degrading soil quality, farmers globally have upgraded it and will continue to do so. And, in contrast to studies that deplore population growth, he argues that in the longer run population growth will spur technological innovation, create infrastructure and economies of scale, and generally improve living conditions for all. Simon also attaches a positive value to the existence of additional human lives, even if population increase somewhat diminishes average living conditions, something he does not believe will happen. This acceptance and even support of population growth separates Simon from others (such as scholars at the Hudson Institute) who anticipate improved futures and has been the least well received of his arguments. Simon does argue, however, that economic growth will automatically reduce fertility levels through individual choices to have fewer children.

With respect to prescriptions, Simon relies heavily upon market mechanisms. He advocates reduction of the role of government, especially with respect to population control policy.

Simon's book raised a storm of criticism from those who believe limits to growth exist and favor strong action to mitigate the effects of these constraints. In addition to rejecting the values Simon adopted, most criticism has focused on the evidence he marshalled to support his arguments. And critics have expressed strong disagreement with Simon's effective rejection of the concept of finite natural resources (Daly 1982, 39). Simon argued that ultimate oil resources are not measurable and hence "not meaningfully finite."

Simon and Kahn collaborated in 1982–83 to produce a book (unfinished at the time of Kahn's death in mid-1983) directly responsive to *Global 2000*. The edited volume, *Global 2000 Revised* will undoubtedly reignite many of the ongoing controversies.

GENERALIZATIONS

We should attempt to mine these selected futures studies for some generalizations. What has a decade of controversy produced? Are we any closer to an understanding of the operation of the global development system? Are there any clear trends in the literature?

The most obvious conclusion must be that there is little or no evidence of a convergence toward a middle ground (or toward one extreme, since truth does not always lie in the middle). Images of the future—even images of the year 2000, now only fifteen years hence—remain as diverse as they were a decade ago. Clearly, either basic data needed to understand where we are and where we are going are simply unavailable or analysts are talking past each other, proceeding on different assumptions and understanding and selecting the data according to different criteria.

The absence of some convergence is also surprising in light of the clearly reactive nature of many of the futures studies. *Limits to Growth* spurred other work: Mesarovic and Pestel questioned its utility for policy analysis; Leontief codified the methodological inadequacies perceived by many economists; the Bariloche group reacted to the book's perceived fundamental industrial country biases; and Herman Kahn attacked both the work's basic assumptions and its conclusions. Yet in spite of these criticisms, the *Global 2000* report and Brown's work hark back very much to the original Meadows work, and almost exactly ten years after the publication of *Limits to Growth* Julian Simon felt the need again to present a counter case. It thus appears that highly intelligent individuals, who presumably read each other's work and who appear to respond to one another, are not convincing one another—and perhaps are not even communicating.

One trend that has appeared in the work reviewed is that toward government involvement. The first studies were done without governmental support. By the late 1970s, international organizations (the UN and OECD) took a serious interest in futures studies. By 1981 the U.S. government was examining the issues for itself. That literature and research trend may well suggest a movement toward long-term forecasting and perhaps planning by governments, a corollary trend that other evidence supports. Some observers, such as believers in limits to growth, will applaud the trend. Other critics will fear the inefficiencies of government relative to the market and feel that government will exacerbate or even create the very problems it attempts to resolve.

I have not attempted to analyze any of the issues and controversies I have cited in this chapter. The purpose here has rather been to present the issues, in order to allow different images of the future to be categorized. This chapter thus provides a basis upon which different images of the future may be compared and contrasted. Inherent in each of the above synopses of work are elements of description (how the world works), forecasts, and prescription (introducing a value component). In some presentations, as in some of the work, these three elements are much clearer than in others. The next chapter undertakes the categorization.

3. Structuring the Images: World Views

The last two chapters illustrated the diversity of images futurists hold with respect to the future of the global development system. This chapter and the remainder of the book address the bases for the diversity. Unless we want to take on faith or on the basis of our prior dispositions claims that there will or will not be enough food or energy, and that LDCs will or will not develop economically, we must seek an understanding of the competing forecasts.

In this book, I seek to explain differences in images of the future at three levels: world views, theories and models, and evidence. World views affect approaches to theories, models, and evidence and must therefore be examined prior to examination of the other levels of explanation.

A world view is a comprehensive set of values, basic assumptions about the way the world works, and derivative "understandings" of complex events and processes. It implies as well derivative prescriptions with respect to individual, social, and political behavior. Some scholars have called this a "paradigm" (Kuhn 1970; Daly 1980). Other writers have preferred to talk about "prescriptive political theories" (see Breckling 1974). We could even use the word "ideology," although as Diesing (1982, 10) points out, that term often carries negative emotional connotations.

World view, paradigm, prescriptive political theory, and even ideology are, in fact, all closely related concepts and I shall not hesitate to use the terms interchangeably.

Here I examine two dimensions of world view called "political ecology" and "political economy." The phrase "political economy" is used widely and the discussion will be a review for some readers; the label "political ecology" has, insofar as I know, not been used in other literature, although general presentations of political ecology issues exist (see

Sprout and Sprout 1971; Pirages 1978). The existence of "political" in both names suggests the degree to which the two dimensions carry strong prescriptive elements with respect to policy.

Many of the forecasters discussed earlier explicitly recognize such dimensions and could place themselves on one or both of them. Other writers hold particular world views so strongly that even the existence of other coherent perspectives goes largely unrecognized. True understanding of alternative world futures requires, however, that we understand alternative world views.

POLITICAL ECOLOGY

A world view incorporates values and assumptions, as well as derivative understandings and prescriptions. Political ecology world views focus on the nature, both actual and ideal, of the relationships among humans, individually and collectively, and the biological and physical environment in which we live. Views with respect to this relationship differ widely and fundamentally. I shall call two vastly different viewpoints "modernists" and "neotraditionalists." Other writers might call them "optimists" and "pessimists." Lindsey Grant (1982) uses the terms "Cornucopians" and "Jeremiads"; Dennis Pirages (1983) has suggested "exclusionists" (seeing man as separate from the environment) and "inclusionists"; while Harman (1976) likes "New Naturalism" for what I call "neotraditionalism." All labels unfortunately carry some connotations that might incline a reader toward or against a given position; my reasons for using "modernist" and "neotraditionalist" should become clearer as we proceed.

It bears emphasizing that the world views presented in this chapter are ideal types. Although I associate individuals fairly closely with these ideal types, I must often qualify that association. Belief systems are generally more complex than the simplifications we produce to conceptualize them. Nevertheless, we require such simplifications in order really to grasp the structure of the arguments.

Introduction to the World Views

The dominant political ecology world view, or paradigm, of the last two centuries has been the modernist. Modernists have a strong belief in mankind's potential for mastery of its environment. This is a potential that has come to be recognized at an accelerated pace in the last few centuries. We are now, the modernist would point out, on the average better fed, better sheltered, and healthier than at any time in history. If there is any doubt about the beneficial aspects of modern technology, a glance at mortality patterns should dispel it. Global average life expectancy at birth is now sixty years. In the poorest forty-five countries, it is forty-eight years—in traditional societies it has seldom historically exceeded thirty (although many lived much longer, very large numbers died as infants or children).

Certainly there have been problems associated with the increasing demands that man has placed upon the environment. The same DDT that contributed so much to improvement of human nutrition and that helped eliminate dread diseases was also associated with health hazards. But in the United States we have been able to substitute other substances, and in parts of the Third World it is believed that the benefits of DDT justify the risks. Similarly, although air pollution from automobiles is obviously unhealthy, it is probably less so than horse manure in the streets. The infrastructure of the modern city would have been impossible without technological progress. Most importantly, modern technology has given us an increasing ability to cope with negative side effects of our environmental interventions and with naturally occurring threats (e.g., earthquakes or single bad harvests). Traditional and technologically primitive societies have often faced threats from the environment (e.g., changing climate or plague) and have sometimes succumbed. We may also succumb, but we are now better able to cope with unexpected threats than ever before.

The modernist recognizes that resources, both physical and biological, have always been a constraint on mankind's activities: civilizations have vanished because they exhausted the land. Yet the modernist argues that we are now better equipped to deal with shortages of almost all materials than we have ever been before. The resourcefulness on both sides during World War II in producing substitutes and synthetics illustrates our flexibility under extreme duress. Current energy and agricultural problems, to the extent that they are real, will be resolved by the same ingenuity. We already have more than enough options, and the issues are actually ones of political and social choice.

Modernists not only view history in terms of regular, if not uninterrupted, progress for mankind, but feel that the future will be characterized by continued technological and material advances.

At the opposite end of the political ecology spectrum are the neotraditionalists. The neotraditional world view has been steadily gaining adherents since the global oil and food crises of the 1970s; continued economic uncertainty inspires additional converts. Traditional peoples did not believe in their abilities physically to control the environment. In fact, gods were often personifications of the environment and could at best be manipulated only slightly, by ceremony and ritual. Neotraditionalists recognize our considerable ability to shape physical and biological worlds, but often doubt our ability to do so rationally. Much of our impact is entirely accidental (our fouling of lakes, for example). Even that which we try to plan, like major development in the Amazon, is likely to have secondary and tertiary consequences (like the creation of deserts or the extinction of valuable species) that we cannot anticipate and will not be able to control.

The most important recognition for the neotraditionalist is that because the magnitude of our impact is now so much greater than ever before (because of our numbers and our technology), our potential for harm is far greater than it was in earlier eras. We have already poisoned large lakes and much air—we may now actually be changing the oceans and the global climate.

As far as resources are concerned, we are rapidly exhausting highly desirable and irreplaceable fossil fuels. There are no comparable substitutes for oil and natural gas; environmental quality standards are under pressure in the United States as we try coal. The neotraditionalist feels that we must lessen our use of limited resources and reduce the damage we inflict on the environment by consuming and shifting to sustainable resources (like solar power) rather than limited ones.

Neotraditionalists also argue that we have neglected real improvements in the quality of life because we too often measure it in terms of consumption. A simpler, less materialistic life style is also valued for its own sake. This is, in fact, the main reason I have not referred to the neotraditionalist world view as a "limits" view and to the modernist paradigm as a "no limits" view, even though such terms may have more inherent meaning to many readers. There exists for many neotraditionalists a strong strain of moral rejection of growth because of its association with materialism, conflict, coercion, or other rejected values. Similarly, modernists often anticipate eventual barriers to further economic and demographic growth, or even look forward to some eventual "steady-state" in both, but argue that we have not yet reached such limits nor attained the conditions which can adequately provide for the material needs of humanity. These distinctions will become clearer as we look briefly at the long history of thought in both neotraditionalist and modernist world views.

The Political Ecology World Views Historically

It has already been noted, and it is implicit in the label, that many traditional peoples were the philosophic forefathers of contemporary neotraditionalists. They lacked a concept of economic progress and they took for granted that mankind was a part of the environment, rather than a conquerer of it. A letter purportedly written in 1855 by Chief Sealth of the Duwamish tribe to President Pierce illustrates this well:

> The great Chief in Washington sends words that he wishes to buy
> land. . . . How can you buy or sell the sky—the warmth of the land?
> The idea is strange to us. Yet we do not own the freshness of the air or
> the sparkle of the water. How can you buy them from us? We will decide
> in our time. Every part of this earth is sacred to my people. Every

shining pine needle, every sandy shore, every mist in the dark woods, every clearing and humming insect is holy in the memory and experience of my people.

We know that the white man does not understand our ways. One portion of the land is the same to him as the next, for he is a stranger who comes in the night and takes from the land whatever he needs. The earth is not his brother, but his enemy, and when he has conquered it, he moves on. He leaves his fathers' graves, and his children's birthright is forgotten. The sight of your cities pains the eyes of the redman. But perhaps it is because the redman is a savage and does not understand. (*Environmental Action*, April 1979, 9)

Clearly Chief Sealth not only had some concept of the modernist paradigm but could also intelligently appeal to its own self-doubts.

Turning to a long history of formal Western political theory, we can see in the thinking of two millennia the dominance of the "steady-state" or "no economic growth" view characteristic of the contemporary neotraditionalist. Plato did not explicitly develop a no-growth view because it was implicit in all of his thinking and work. For instance, in *Cratylus*, Socrates says:

Nor can we reasonably say, Cratylus, that there is knowledge at all, if everything is in a state of transition and there is nothing abiding; for knowledge too cannot continue to be knowledge unless continuing always to abide and exist . . . but if that which knows and that which is known exist ever, and the beautiful and the good and every other thing also exist, then I do not think that they can resemble a process of flux. (Plato 1937, 229)*

The perfect or ideal city developed at length in *The Republic* was argued to be one with limits on wealth and size and one in which people would have "no more children than they can afford in their care against poverty or war" (Plato 1956, 169).

Subsequent Christian philosophy explicitly denied the accumulation process that is at the heart of economic growth. Augustine advised:

Lay not up treasures for yourselves upon the earth where the moth and rust corrupt, or where thieves dig through and steal, but lay up treasures for yourselves in heaven, where neither rust nor moth corrupt, nor thieves dig through and steal. (Augustine 1947, 13)

Machiavelli, in fifteenth-century Italy, still reflected a period in which a perception of cycles in human civilization, including stages of deteriora-

---

*Many of the quotations from political philosophy cited here were identified by Breckling (1974). Although the absence of a concept of progress in Greek thought has been stressed by Bury (1932), it is disputed by Edelstein (1967).

tion, dominated thought. Instead of uninterrupted economic and demographic growth, Machiavelli argued that

> when countries become overpopulated and there is no longer any room
> for all the inhabitants to live, nor any other place for them to go to, these
> being likewise all fully occupied—and when human cunning and
> wickedness have gone as far as they can go—then of necessity the world
> must relieve itself of this excess of population . . . ; so that mankind,
> having been chastised and reduced in numbers, may become better and
> live with more convenience. (Machiavelli 1940, 298)

A strong sense of limits, both descriptively and prescriptively, on economic and population growth is a common thread in the thought of this
otherwise diverse set of philosophers. A look back at some of the quotations cited in Chapters 1 and 2 should identify the resurgence of such
thought in contemporary writing.

There is no need to pinpoint the change, but by the eighteenth and
nineteenth centuries, philosophers as diverse as Adam Smith and Karl
Marx had come to share a belief in the possibility of long-term economic
progress, even in the face of population growth.

Interestingly, Plato had discussed in great detail the proper division of
labor in his ideal but quite static city and the efficiency which that division
produced. Adam Smith, however, identified such a division of labor and
ongoing improvements in the technology of production as the bases of
continuing economic growth. For instance, Smith argued:

> The abundance or scantiness of [economic goods and
> services] . . . seems to depend more upon . . . skill, dexterity, and
> judgment . . . than upon . . . the soil, climate, or extent of territory
> of any particular nation. (Smith 1937, 13)

Marx, of course, identified clear stages of history which were steps of a
powerful, if not irreversible process:

> No social order ever disappears before all the productive forces for which
> there is room in it have been developed, and new higher relations of
> production never appear before the material conditions of their existence
> have matured in the womb of the old society. . . . In broad outlines we
> can designate the Asiatic, the ancient, the feudal, and the modern
> bourgeois methods of production as so many epochs in the progress of
> the economic formation of society. (Marx 1959, 44)

In fact, Marx specifically attacked the pessimistic views of Malthus, which
he felt were put forward to justify (as in fact they were) abandonment of
proposals for relief of working class poverty:

> The hatred of the English working class against Malthus—the
> "mountebank-parson" as Cobbett rudely calls him—is therefore entirely

justified. The people were right here in sensing instinctively that they
were confronted not with a *man of science* but with a *bought advocate,* a
pleader on behalf of their enemies, a shameless sycophant of the ruling
classes. (Meek 1953, 123)*

And consider the argument of John Stuart Mill, in contrast to the earlier
cited quotation from Augustine:

> That the energies of mankind should be kept in employment by the
> struggle for riches, as they were formerly by the struggle for war, until
> the better minds succeed in educating the others into better things, is
> undoubtedly more desireable than that they should rust and stagnate.
> While minds are coarse they require coarse stimuli, and let them have
> them. (Mill 1857, 319–20)

We must be quick to note that none of these writers believed that
economic (and population) growth would continue indefinitely. Adam
Smith, in fact, perceived an eventual, but far distant, end to the growth
process with an implication as stark as that of Malthus:

> In a country fully peopled in proportion to what either its territory could
> maintain or its stock employ, the competition for employment would
> necessarily be so great as to reduce the wages of labour to what was
> barely sufficient to keep up the number of labourers. (Smith 1910, 138)

Marx had a much happier image of the ultimate steady-state economic
destiny of man, the socialist state:

> The bourgeois relations of production are the last antagonistic form of the
> social process of production—antagonistic not in the sense of individual
> antagonism, but of one arising from conditions surrounding the life of
> individuals in society; at the same time the productive forces developing
> in the womb of bourgeois society create the material conditions for the
> solution of that antagonism. This social formation constitutes, therefore,
> the closing chapter of the prehistoric stage of human society. (Marx
> 1959, 44)

Mill, too, felt that an eventual economic and demographic steady-state
could be at a high standard of living. His perception of further progress at
such a time is reminiscent of Plato's notions of virtue:

> It is scarcely necessary to remark that a stationary condition of capital
> and population implies no stationary state of human improvement. There
> would be as much scope as ever for all kinds of mental culture, and
> moral and social progress; as much room for improving the Art of
> Living, and much more likelihood of its being improved, when minds
> ceased to be engrossed by the art of getting on. (Mill 1857, 147)

---

*Several of these quotations were identified by Pavitt (1973).

In spite of such recognition of the inevitability of a halt in economic growth processes, most modernist writers perceive constraints as becoming binding only in the distant future. Many writers, like Marx, have also felt that the steady-state would not result from ultimate resource or other environmental limits but rather from a satiation of economic needs or desires (the same notion appears in Kahn, Brown, and Martel [1976]).

A Summary of Political Ecology World Views

Table 3.1 reveals a summary of the two political ecology perspectives. It differentiates between them in three areas: important descriptive statements they make (strongly reflecting fundamental assumptions); typical forecasts offered by writers adopting the paradigm; and most common prescriptions (building on key values).

Descriptively, the modernist emphasizes mankind's increasing ability to control his environment—to produce food, to extract resources, and to limit pollution where so desired. Technological sophistication is generally the key to such control—neotraditionalists often attack modernists as suffering from a "technological fix" mentality. The modernist recognizes that some civilizations collapsed in the past because they were unable to deal with changes in their environment and that collapse of our civilization is not to be ruled out. Yet, it is argued, we are better able to deal with unforeseen threats now because of our technology, our economic strength, and even our numbers. Thus, although control of the environment is sometimes valued almost for its own sake, more often it is valued for its ability to ward off disaster. The modernist often defines progress, upon which high value is placed, in terms of economic growth; and Gross National Product (GNP) per capita is a favored indicator of well-being.

The neotraditionalist perceives the environment as much more fragile than the modernist does, and argues that mankind's attempts to control it have been largely destructive. Descriptively, the neotraditionalist believes that global environmental quality in many arenas (e.g., air, water) has been deteriorating for decades. The neotraditionalist emphasizes structural (interconnectedness) issues when attacking the modernist, arguing that even a "successful" technological solution in one area (e.g., scarcity of energy) will result in additional problems in another (e.g., the environment). The neotraditionalist perceives the impact of human systems on natural systems as much more significant than does the modernist.

The neotraditionalist also often places a value on aspects of the environment, such as protection of a species from extinction, which the modernist may perceive as irrational. The neotraditionalist defines progress not materially but rather in terms of esthetic values or the potential for individual human fulfillment.

Abraham Maslow's scale of human needs suggests that individuals

TABLE 3.1. *Political Ecology Paradigms*

	Important Descriptive Statements	Typical Forecasts	Prescriptions
Modernists	Mankind increasingly controls its environment.	Materially and technologically progress will continue.	A policy of *laissez innover* should be adopted with respect to most technology; active research and development programs should be sponsored.
	Technology is the key to a better future.	Environmental problems will be solved. Resource limitations will be overcome.	
Neotraditionalists	Environment is more complex and delicate than often believed.	Material and technological progress will prove unsatisfying.	Control and selectivity should be exercised with respect to new technologies.
	Lifestyles consistent with human values are the keys to a better future.	Environmental problems will appear faster than they can be addressed.	Economic "throughput" (input of resources and output of pollutants) should be minimized to conserve resources and limit environmental impact.
		Resource scarcities will intensify.	Control population.

direct attention in large part sequentially to survival, security, affection, self-esteem, and self-actualization needs, moving up the scale only as lower-level needs have been largely satisfied (Maslow 1970). In terms of this scale, the neotraditionalist clearly emphasizes the "higher-level" needs, in contrast to the modernist who focuses on lower-level needs. Not surprisingly, neotraditionalist thinking has tended to be a middle- and upper-class phenomenon of the economically advanced countries. In fact, non-Marxist modernists have directed at them the same critique that Marx aimed at Malthus—such thought is a tool of the wealthy in a battle to deny material well-being to the poor of the world (see, e.g., Kahn [1979]).

The forecasts that follow from the two paradigms flow logically from their descriptions of the current world situation. In each case the forecasts are largely extrapolations from the descriptive statements: the future is seen as a continuation of the past. The modernists argue that material and technological progress will continue. Because they believe that solutions to environmental problems have been developed, they anticipate continued technological progress. Similarly, modernists point to the steadily increasing availability and diminishing historical cost of raw materials (including energy) and forecast a continuation of those trends as well. The price increases of the 1970s are seen as temporary deviations from the longer-term trends.

The neotraditionalist reads history differently, believing that technological and material progress has proven unsatisfying in the past and will prove so in the future—if such progress should, in fact, continue. Placing great weight on the events of the 1970s the neotraditionalist argues that increases in resource (including food) prices during that decade are evidence of our having reached limits that were not hitherto binding, but will continue to be so in the future. Thus, we can anticipate further real price increases, intermittent physical shortages, and deteriorating prospects for economic growth. Moreover, environmental problems, seen by neotraditionalists as having been long intensifying, will become even more severe. Much of the rest of this volume will elaborate on the differences in the forecasts emanating out of the two paradigms and the bases for those differences.

Prescriptively, the modernist is generally satisfied with current policies. With respect to technology this attitude has been labeled "laissez innover" (McDermott 1972, 155). The modernist does not deny the existence of all environmental problems or of periodic resource scarcities but does argue that the economic resources for dealing with the environmental problems exist (Leontief et al. 1977). Moreover, an allocation of resources to the environment is in fact being made, at least in developed countries, so little or no change in policy is needed.

The neotraditionalist wants significant changes. That society should exercise selectivity with respect to technology is one clear prescription. But most neotraditionalists should not be considered "antitechnology," and many neotraditionalists would agree with the modernist criticism that mechanisms to screen technologies and to anticipate their consequences are difficult to establish. Technology assessment processes to seek advance warning of potentially negative consequences are nevertheless endorsed by many neotraditionalists.

The real emphasis of most neotraditionalist work is not on technology, however, but on economic and population growth. Limitation of population growth is probably the single most urgent prescription of neotraditionalist futurists. Even assuming strict population control, however, the neotraditionalist argues that the rates of resource use and environmental despoliation by the globe's wealthy are unsustainable. Thus, strenuous efforts must be undertaken to conserve resources and to minimize pollution. Many measures, such as maximizing the lifetime of goods, or cutting consumption viewed as frivolous, do both simultaneously.

There is considerable disagreement among neotraditionalists as to whether collective or individual action should be emphasized. Many neotraditionalists believe that changes in individual values and behavior must precede and establish the foundation for collective action (Richardson 1982); some neotraditionalists appear on the basis of their own "counter-culture" lifestyles to have opted strongly for individual or small group choice. Other thinkers (Hardin 1980) argue that such a strategy is doomed to failure since those committed to population and economic growth will simply become relatively more powerful and numerous if no-growth advocates opt out. Collective coercion is necessary. An intermediate strategy seeks wide-scale social action on the basis of grass-roots movements. For instance, the Hunger Project was established to direct attention and resources toward global food problems. Eschewing both collective action through government intervention and individual action, the project seeks to grow as a mass movement and eventually to succeed by the strength of collective voluntary effort.

Another aspect of the value-based and prescriptive differences separating the two world views lies in attitudes toward risk. Neotraditionalists suggest what is basically a "minimax" strategy in the face of the uncertainties associated with human impacts on other systems and with technological developments. That is, they prefer a relatively cautious, or risk-avoiding strategy, in which society sacrifices potentially superior material gains in return for a more assured outcome. Modernists perceive the risk associated with a more active, growth-oriented strategy to be lower and in fact, often posit that economic growth and technological development are our best guarantees of being able to meet unexpected future challenges, thus minimizing risk. In addition to perceiving less risk in growth, modernists may also be less risk adverse.

It should be noted that both modernists and neotraditionalists largely agree in characterizing the current world as modernist. This is implicit in both the modernist's approval of the status quo and the neotraditionalist's desire for major value and institutional change.

POLITICAL ECONOMY

Although differences in political ecology world views may have the longer philosophical history, in the last two centuries controversy over political economy world views has generated much more heat.

Introduction to World Views

Political economy perspectives, or paradigms, differ over the proper relationship between the political and economic systems and on the structure of each. At one end of the spectrum is the classical liberal position, which emphasizes the efficient and beneficial operation of a free market (this should not be confused with our contemporary use of the label "liberal"—I refer here to the classical liberals, such as Adam Smith, individuals often now called "conservative"). According to classical liberals, political interference with the market generally does more harm than good, often harming even those it was intended to help. Liberals recognize some of the problems I have identified above but believe that the market, if left to itself, will resolve them.

Classical liberals believe the principle of the free market applies not only to the industrialized nations but to Third World nations as well. LDCs, for instance, must proceed through much the same development processes that the currently developed countries endured earlier. Rostow has argued that this process contains several stages (Rostow 1971). In the earlier stages, changes in traditional thought patterns occur and some development of physical capital (ports, railroads, communications systems) and human capital (training of engineers, scientists, political leaders) takes place, but growth is slow. Thus, the gap between the more modern and the more traditional societies narrows slowly and may even appear to widen. Only once preconditions are satisfied can rapid growth begin. Even then growth will be initially concentrated in a few geographical areas and economic sectors so that inequality within the developing country will actually increase.

The very existence of the income gaps within and between countries, however, will cause the gaps to narrow. Lower average incomes mean plentiful and inexpensive labor, which may give the poorer countries a comparative price advantage in the goods they produce. As long as markets remain free and open, the developing countries will be pulled into equality by the already developed (Kahn, Brown, and Martel 1976).

The population problem, argue the classical liberals, will largely resolve itself as the income problem is solved. Having or not having children is, in considerable part, a rational choice. In rural areas where children can contribute to income and in countries without old-age security programs, it is rational to produce large families. In more modern societies, the costs of raising (including educating) children exceed the pecuniary benefits that children yield, so large families are no longer economically rational (Simon 1981).

In similar fashion, energy and agricultural problems are best left to the market and to natural development processes. In fact, it was interference in the free market by OPEC which caused the energy problem and interventionist government policies in the consuming countries (like price controls in the United States) that have prolonged the problem. The market will eventually provide substitutes for OPEC oil and may even undercut the cartel in the process. And it is well known that the world can produce much more food than it now does. Some calculations suggest that the globe could feed a population of 16 billion, even with current technology (Linnemann undated). U.S. food aid in the 1950s and 1960s actually may have hurt more than it helped, by keeping down food prices in recipient countries and thus discouraging investment in local agriculture. Well-intentioned but misdirected local government industrial development programs further weakened the agricultural sector.

Normally, the liberals would argue that international assistance programs are misguided. They not only foster dependence but they polarize life in the Third World by increasing the power and wealth of governments relative to the broader society (Bauer 1981, 103–4). There is no moral imperative behind such programs, because the poverty of the Third World is not a result of Western developed country behavior. In general then, liberals prescribe the maintenance of free international and domestic markets, the reduction in government interference, and time.

A second political economy paradigm can be called internationalist. Internationalists agree with much that the liberals say. They argue, however, that the very existence of more developed countries in the international environment of currently developing countries means that the development process will be significantly different from that which the United States and Western Europe went through. They argue that there are, as liberals suggest, some potential advantages to the LDCs in the current global setting, but that there are also significant disadvantages. Liberals pay too little attention to power issues. Rich countries and powerful multinational corporations (MNCs) are so much stronger than LDCs and their local enterprises that terms of bargains struck between them may not be equally advantageous. The internationalists say that the post–World War II deterioration in LDC terms of trade (the relative price of goods sold by the LDCs) illustrates this. Thus, LDC governments must intervene when MNCs enter the country and must regulate their behavior. Moreover, developed countries so dominate in manufactured goods that LDC entrepreneurs cannot compete. They need tariffs which protect their domestic market and initial preferential treatment in developed country markets.

Another problem is that most LDCs are very heavily dependent upon exports of one or two goods, often primary goods such as agricultural commodities (cocoa, coffee, cotton) or metals (copper, aluminum). Prices of these goods fluctuate wildly compared to those of manufactured goods, making rational development planning even more difficult. Thus, international policies to stabilize prices and demand levels would be highly desirable.

The wealthier countries ought to recognize the suffering of the poor in the LDCs and undertake to shorten the development process. Foreign aid can and ought to be increased. Thirty years' experience with loans and grants to the LDCs have improved our ability to administer such programs without the negative side effects liberals decry.

With respect to population, the LDCs are in a trap—modern medicine has given them the means to reduce mortality, but the resulting larger populations mean resources must be stretched further. Poverty supports continued high fertility, which in turn maintains poverty. To break out of this vicious cycle (or positive feedback loop) requires a strong government-run family planning program.

Government action in energy and agriculture is also desirable. The energy problem is not as simple as classical liberals suggest, because no easy alternatives exist in the transition away from fossil fuels. If we move toward reliance on either nuclear energy or coal, we must have strong governmental regulation to minimize environmental problems. In agriculture, it is true that the world could produce much more food than it does. But the LDCs cannot produce more without increased (outside) investment in the agricultural system.

The internationalist thus recognizes some structural problems in the path of LDCs and sees a moral imperative for and positive value in help from developed countries. Specifically, more aid, investment (although regulated), and preferential trade treatment should be given the LDCs. Specific programs have been proposed and constitute the so-called New International Economic Order (NIEO) demanded by LDCs in the United Nations and other forums.

There is also a more radical political economy paradigm. Radicals perceive the international structures as much more stable and binding than do internationalists. These structures grew up during the colonial era, when the colonial powers physically occupied and looted most of the rest of the world. Gradually, that blatant form of imperialism gave way to more subtle forms. But the dominance by developed countries over the international economy is perhaps no less strong today than it was during colonial times. Not only do the industrial nations control trade in the more highly processed and expensive goods, leaving LDCs with low profit margins on often finite raw materials, but they also control the international economic institutions—the International Monetary Fund (IMF), The World Bank (IBRD), and the General Agreement on Tariffs and Trade (GATT). They thus can and do set exchange rates, create new international money, and regulate trade in their own interests. The actual use of force is always a possibility and frequently a reality.

The world can be divided into center nations and periphery nations. The center countries are rich, not simply because of their own efforts or superior technology, but because they constantly extract wealth from the periphery, or the poor states. The days of trading beads for slaves may be over. So, too, the exchange of whiskey and guns for land. That exchange not only took a nonrenewable product in exchange for renewable ones, leaving the Indians with little to trade in the future, but disrupted their culture and society in the bargain. The current trading of television sets, jets, and tanks for oil and copper does have basic similarities. And the "law of the first price" still has force. That is, prices for many materials from LDCs were often set initially in bargaining with commercially ignorant local leaders, impressed by or fearful of the weapons possessed by the traders. As long as abundant supplies of the materials exist, no modern trader has incentive to offer higher prices. Without higher prices, Third World countries cannot obtain the level of economic well-being necessary to refuse those prices that are offered to them.

Even at the governmental level, LDCs are no match for multinational corporations, which act in concert with their home countries, the developed states. Preferential trading arrangements to provide access to developed country markets are largely very limited and ineffectual. Most LDCs trade heavily with, and are therefore heavily dependent on, one or two developed countries, while developed countries have no such dependence on LDCs.

Foreign assistance is seldom given primarily for development support and is seen explictly by most donors as a mechanism of political influence.

In the main, radicals agree with classical liberals that population problems are tied to development. They clearly differ on the prospects for development, however. Energy is a problem only because of the extremely wasteful usage patterns in Western developed countries (Herrera et al. 1976). The United States, for example, has 6 percent of the world's population and consumes 30 percent of global energy; the United States imports nearly 50 percent of its oil. Japan and Western Europe are even more dependent on oil imports. Clearly, if those societies were structured differently (e.g., less dependent on automobiles), the world would have no energy problem, and the LDCs would not have the added burden of high oil import bills. Similarly in agriculture, the meat consumption of the rich requires vast amounts of grain as animal feed and directly competes with the diets of the poor.

Radicals thus prescribe one of two dramatic changes in the international system. Some radical writers feel that the LDCs should withdraw from the system and pursue autarkic development paths. Other critics argue that only a change in the system itself, that is, revolutionary change in the developed world, will help.

A Summary of Political Economy World Views

Table 3.2 summarizes the three political economy perspectives (see Blake and Walters [1976] for a similar summary). Parallel to our summary of political ecology views, the figure differentiates them in three categories: descriptive statements, typical forecasts, and prescriptions.

Descriptively, some of the key differences center on perceptions of the economic deal-making process and the related issue of terms of trade. This can be shown clearly in the writing of three contemporary political economy theorists. The classical liberal position is well stated by Milton Friedman:

> In its simplest form a [free private enterprise exchange economy] consists of a number of independent households. . . . Since the household always has the alternative of producing directly for itself, it need not enter into any exchange unless it benefits from it. Hence, no exchange will take place unless both parties do benefit from it. . . . So long as effective freedom of exchange is maintained the central feature of the market organization of economic activity is that it prevents one person from interfering with another in respect of most of his activities. The consumer is protected from coercion by the seller because of the presence of other sellers with whom he can deal. The seller is protected from coercion by the consumer because of other consumers to whom he can sell. (Friedman 1962, 13–14)

Friedman is saying very explicitly here that as long as exchanges are freely entered into, both parties will benefit from them. Most classical liberals would go one step further and say that within the developed market economies and between them and the developing market economies the vast majority of all exchanges are, in fact, freely entered into and both parties do benefit. This is true of exchanges between white and black, old and young, rich and poor.

TABLE 3.2. *Political Economy Paradigms*

	Important Descriptive Statements	Typical Forecasts	Prescriptions
Liberals	Free markets are mutually beneficial. Economic growth occurs in stages.	The North-South gap will narrow significantly, over the next few decades. The population problem will solve itself. Price mechanisms will solve energy and food problems.	Globally, government intervention in domestic and international economies should be minimized
Internationalists	Free markets are unequally beneficial. Growth stages can be accelerated with help.	The North-South gap will close only slowly. Population might overwhelm resources in some countries and create a poverty cycle. Agriculture and energy problems are long-term and might worsen.	Western nations should assist LDCs with foreign aid and trade concessions.
Radicals	"Free" markets are controlled by the rich. Developed countries hold LDCs in perpetual poverty.	The North-South gap will not close. (Therefore) the population issue cannot be resolved. (And therefore) agriculture and energy will remain problems, especially for LDCs.	LDCs must either break away from the international system, or change via revolution must occur in the developed countries.

Those whom we have called internationalists would argue that this may not be true at all, and if it is, the benefits of the exchange can be very unequally divided. Internationalists argue that there are power relationships that provide the context of economic exchange and that these greatly distort the division of benefits. In some cases the threat of physical force lies just below the surface of a contract. In other cases the dire economic straits of one party may deny that individual or organization the opportunity to seek alternative participants who might provide better terms and may compel acceptance of an offer. For example, a wage of one dollar per day may provide a critical benefit to a worker—the ability to survive. A classical liberal might point out that even if the employer is able to convert that labor to a ten dollar per day benefit for himself, the benefit obtained by the laborer is still positive. More radical observers might counter, however, that the economic power of the employers may well have structured the overall economy so that many individuals face such choices (e.g., by forcing farmers off the land and into urban slums), thus creating and maintaining their own bargaining leverage.

Thus, the internationalist (or the modern liberal, who makes the same argument domestically) points to the terms of trade between individuals, organizations, or nations, to the relative benefits from exchanges. John Kenneth Galbraith argues that very unequal terms of trade exist within the United States:

> Perhaps the oldest and certainly the wisest strategy for the exercise of power is to deny that it is possessed. . . . Socially objectionable exercise of power by organizations in their own interest is thus exorcised or largely exorcised from formal economic thought. Should there be, in fact, such exercise of power, it will be seen how convenient is this contrary belief—and how worthwhile its cultivation.
>
> Cultivation of useful belief is particularly important because of the way power is exercised in the modern economic system. It consists, as noted, in inducing the individual to abandon the goals he would normally pursue and accept those of another person or organization. There are several ways of accomplishing this. The threat of physical suffering—prison, the lash, an electrical impulse through the testicles—is an ancient tradition. So is economic deprivation—hunger or the disesteem of poverty if one does not work for the wages and therewith accept the goals of an employer. But persuasion—the altering of the individual's belief so that he comes to agree that the goals of another person or organization are superior to his own—is of increasing importance. (Galbraith 1973, 6)

Galbraith points to a division of the U.S. economy into one sector controlled by large, powerful corporations and labor unions (the "planning" economy) and another sector dominated by small businesses and nonunion labor (the truer "market" economy). The domestic terms of trade are

controlled by the planning economy. Galbraith sees international economics as an extension of this division into planning and market economies:

> This defines the nature of imperialism in the Third World. It is an
> extension of the relationship between the planning and the market systems
> in the advanced country. As with the market system in the developed
> country, abundant supply, slight or no control over prices, a labor supply
> that lends itself to exploitation, all mean intrinsically adverse terms of
> trade. The result is that same tendency to income inequality between
> developed and underdeveloped countries as exists within the industrial
> country between the planning and the market systems. (Galbraith 1973,
> 125)

Other writers have described the same pattern of relationships in terms of
center (wealthy and strong) countries and periphery (poor and dependent)
countries (see Galtung [1971]). They, too, perceive a further division into
domestic centers and peripheries within each country. One extension of the
argument is that centers in the periphery countries (i.e., wealthy families,
corrupt and authoritarian governments) collaborate with centers in the
center countries to exploit the peripheries in the periphery (the mass of the
world's poor).

And yet, the internationalist will go only so far with such arguments,
recognizing that on the whole the market system can be made to work. It
requires some concerted effort to pressure the more powerful to provide a
more equal share of the benefits—the poor must use the strength of numbers and unity to counter other power (OPEC or other raw materials cartels
can be given as examples, as can labor unions or government social benefits domestically). It also requires the recognition by the rich and powerful
of market distortions created by their wealth and power and the realization
that for moral reasons, and even for the long-term political and economic
survival of the rich, assistance to the poor and weak is needed.

Adherents to the Third World view on this political economy dimension, the radicals, might well call that fuzzy-headed thinking. On what
basis, they would ask, could we expect the rich, who are rich exactly
because of the unequal benefits they obtain in exchanges with the poor,
voluntarily and knowingly to forego such benefits, thereby destroying the
system that works in their behalf? On the contrary, they will use their
economic power to reinforce their position and they will use their control
over the governments of the rich countries to assure their status internationally. Even appearances to the contrary, such as some foreign aid, really
mask mechanisms by which the rich and powerful consolidate their control. Immanuel Wallerstein states the position strongly:

> We live in a capitalist world economy. . . . Capitalism as a system of
> production for sale in a market for profit and appropriation of this profit

on the basis of individual or collective ownership has only existed in, and can be said to require, a world system in which the political units are not co-extensive with the boundaries of the market economy. This has permitted sellers to profit from strengths in the market whenever they exist but enables them simultaneously to seek, whenever needed, the intrusion of political entities to distort the market in their favor. Far from being a system of free competition of all sellers, it is a system in which competition becomes relatively free only when the economic advantage of upper strata is so clear-cut that the unconstrained operation of the market serves effectively to reinforce the existing system of stratification. (Wallerstein 1981, 267–68)

Forecasts follow clearly from these various perceptions of the way in which the world works. Classical liberals argue that the gap in wealth between the rich countries (located primarily in the Northern Hemisphere) and the poor (primarily in the Southern Hemisphere), will close (Kahn, Brown, and Martel 1976). Often they posit that it will close quite rapidly (perhaps even during the next century) because of the powerful market forces operating on behalf of the poor.

Classical liberals see the population issue as essentially an economic one. Economically rational individuals (and classical liberal economists who lean heavily upon the assumption of rational individual behavior) will make decisions with respect to having or not having children on the basis of the relative costs and benefits of an additional child. As we shall see in the next chapter, growing affluence of parents generally raises the cost of children (e.g., education) and lowers their benefits (e.g., child labor). Thus, classical liberals forecast that the population problem will disappear with growing affluence.

With respect to energy and food availability, or the availability of other primary commodities, the classical liberal's faith in the market mechanism is such that he forecasts that as long as prices are not controlled artificially, they will find a level at which demand and supply will equilibrate. Moreover, most classical liberals share the belief of the modernists that that level may not exceed current prices.

Internationalists argue that the North-South gap has not narrowed in the last twenty years, and will do so only slowly over the next twenty. In fact, some countries, commonly referred to as the "Fourth World," have little hope of economic growth. They may well be trapped in a poverty cycle in which population growth matches economic growth. Thus, no per capita economic progress is made and no incentives to smaller families develop.

The internationalist generally has less faith in the market than the classical liberal with respect to issues like food and energy availability. In the face of continued rapid population growth he thinks that these problems may intensify.

The radical states flatly that the North-South gap will not close. Some countries may individually move into the developed camp, but others may well fall out of it. The fundamental structure is so necessary to the rich that it will persist. Additional radical forecasts are derived largely from this one. In the face of continuing poverty, population growth cannot be stopped. And in the face of continuing poverty and growing population, food and raw material availability will be ongoing global problems, especially for the LDCs.

With values (often thinly veiled in the descriptive positions themselves) the descriptive positions give rise to prescriptions. The classical liberal does not fail to recognize the great inequalities that characterize global or domestic economies, nor is he unsympathetic with the plight of the poor (radicals would contest this self-characterization). But the classical liberal argues that ill-conceived governmental efforts to intervene in the market on behalf of the poor will only lessen the overall efficiency of that market and slow economic growth. It is only that growth, in rich and poor countries alike, which has contributed to the steadily improved condition of the poor. Reckless redistribution of income and wealth globally would stop (or at least greatly slow) growth and leave everyone at unacceptably low levels of well-being.

All three of the political economy world views share a perception that the non-Communist world is largely a classical liberal world (although decreasingly so) and classical liberals endorse a continuation of the status quo. In fact, reductions in the current level of interference in the market (such as government price setting domestically and foreign aid) would improve the market's efficiency. To some it may seem particularly harsh to attack foreign aid, but the classical liberal argues that such aid tends to distort the economies of recipients in very harmful ways—for example, food assistance holds down local prices and denies farmers the incentives to produce more locally.

Internationalists share the classical liberal's value on economic efficiency and growth but also value equity highly. They often argue that the trade-off between the values is not so straightforward as the classical liberals believe. Providing better food, health care, housing, and education to the poor in a Third World country may well increase efficiency and productivity by boosting the workers' capabilities. Thus, internationalists have increasingly supported strategies for providing "basic human needs" in LDCs as contributions to both equity and efficiency. Similarly, internationalists deny that the adverse effects of foreign assistance outweigh its benefits to the recipients (except where it is administered poorly) and support increased assistance. In particular, it is seen as critical to the Fourth World countries if they are to be pushed out of the poverty cycle.

Radicals reject the notions that either the unfettered market or the beneficence of the rich will help the poor. That, in effect, leaves only two options. Some radicals argue that the LDCs must break their ties with and dependence on the industrialized nations and pursue autarkic development strategies (as did China prior to the mid-1970s) or pursue strategies tied to the socialist world. Other radicals argue that the developed market economies will never permit such strategies to work—they will either force those who try them to return to the capitalist system (as in the case of Chile) or harass them so constantly (as in the case of Nicaragua) that separate growth becomes extremely difficult. Thus, the second option is revolution in the developed market countries and creation of a global socialist system.

PUTTING THE TWO DIMENSIONS TOGETHER

Putting people and their thought into "boxes" is always dangerous. There are far too many gradations of perspective and too many dimensions of classification for such exercises to succeed fully. Nevertheless, if we are to compare and contrast and organize our understanding of what we and others say, we must classify people.

The political ecology and political economy dimensions of world views or paradigms offer potent categories for understanding the arguments of those who make forecasts about the global development system. There are some relationships between the dimensions. For instance, there is a tendency for both the modernists and the classical liberals to forecast adequate availability of energy and other primary materials. Yet the bases for the forecasts are quite different. There is also a tendency for neotraditionalists to reject the classical liberal positions and argue that reformist or radical policies are needed. Yet many modernists reject those positions as well.

Table 3.3 shows the wide range of possible combinations of positions on the two dimensions (see also Miles [1978]). Many of the best-known forecasts and futures studies of the 1970s—the basis of the citations in Chapter 1 and analysis in Chapter 2—are located on the figure. Some of these forecasts are particularly easy to place, largely because their authors think in terms of these or very similar dimensions and contrast their ideas explicitly with other world views. For example, Julian Simon's recent book (1981) exemplifies almost perfectly the classical liberal-modernist view—more purely even than the work of Herman Kahn (1976, 1979). Similarly, the Bariloche world model project (Herrera et al. 1976) classifies itself as radical-modernist. The *Global 2000* study is a fairly clear example of the internationalist-neotraditionalist perspective, while Heilbroner's work (1975) falls neatly into the radical-neotraditionalist quadrant.

TABLE 3.3.   *Paradigm Dimensions in World Models and Futures Studies*

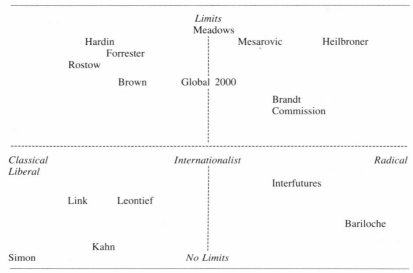

Other studies are much more difficult to classify, and the authors might well dispute the characterizations made here. In some cases this is because the thinking of the forecaster appears to be almost completely dominated by one world view dimension. For instance, *Limits to Growth* (Meadows et al. 1972) is clearly at the neotraditionalist extreme on the political ecology dimension. But it devotes very little attention to the issues of the political economy dimension. Although the authors prescribe a cessation of economic growth and attention to redistribution issues, both of which would seem to require dramatic governmental action and thus may seem radical, the study actually does not prescribe any specific policies or changes in political structures to take the world from growth to stability. The Mesarovic-Pestel report is also dominated by the political ecology dimension, but is somewhat more policy-oriented and its recommendations are fairly clearly internationalist. In contrast, the Brandt Commission report (Brandt 1980) focuses upon political economy issues, taking a strongly internationalist (or weakly radical) approach. Very little attention is given to political ecology issues.

There is still another factor that makes difficult the classification of some studies on the world view matrix of table 3.3. There are, of course, more than two dimensions in thinking about the future, even though we have chosen here the political ecology and political economy dimensions as most often and most clearly structuring thought. In particular, however, there is a difficulty with respect to classifying neotraditionalists by a political economy perspective that does not have a parallel at the modernist end of the political ecology dimension. Part of the problem, as suggested earlier, is that many neotraditionalists seem to have given little real thought to the nature of desirable political institutions and their relationship to the economy. Yet there is more. Many neotraditionalists reject all three of the political economy perspectives outlined here. They perhaps most ardently reject the classical liberal view, seeing it as a "do nothing" and "growth above all" approach in the face of massive challenges to human systems. The policies of internationalists, or reformers (foreign aid, technical assistance, commodity price stabilization schemes), are also often seen as inadequate. Yet the collectivism and authoritarianism which they perceive as implicit in the traditional radical view also repel many neotraditionalists. Many neotraditionalists thus fall back on a different form of individualism, namely, changes in values away from materialism and growth toward values higher in Maslow's hierarchy. In particular, the values of self-esteem and self-actualization seem consistent with sustainable individual lifestyles and a sustainable society.

To a considerable degree this takes such individuals almost unknowingly back to a classical liberal position. In fact, as we have seen in the thinking of individuals like J. S. Mill, there is nothing in the thought of many classical liberals that denies an eventual steady-state economy and an emphasis on values other than accumulation. In fact, Mill and others have looked forward to such a state. Forrester is a good example of a neotraditionalist who becomes a classical liberal in this broader sense. He explicitly rejects many policies, such as efforts to increase food supply and birth control in the absence of industrial production controls, because he sees them as self- defeating in the long run. Large-scale value changes appear to be the answer. Lester Brown is even more explicit in his perception of virtues in the market—for example, he extols the role of higher energy prices in reducing demand and changing values with respect to consumption and growth.

Yet it would be inaccurate to stamp such positions as fundamentally classical liberal. Generally, neotraditionalists feel that the change in value systems will facilitate the noncoercive (or at least democratically acceptable) introduction of new policies with respect to family planning, resource conservation, and pollution reduction—policies that clearly involve much more political oversight of the economy than desired by classical liberals.

Many neotraditionalists are also ambivalent because they recognize some validity in the criticisms of the modernists that much of the world has yet to attain conditions which are sustainable, and thus cannot afford the luxury of slowing economic growth. Thus, with respect to North-South relations neotraditionalists often are generally internationalist in orientation, while searching for other approaches for the domestic economies of the more economically developed world.

Garrett Hardin, although as clearly a neotraditionalist as the Meadows group, is also hard to classify in traditional political economy terms, but for different reasons. He explicitly rejects proposals of the New International Economic Order on the grounds that they represent the Marxist principle that "need makes right" (Hardin 1982, 31). He argues that such international behavior merely increases the number of global poor and intensifies their pressure upon scarce resources. But his support of collective coercion to reduce pressures on global commons (areas, such as the oceans or space, that are used by many and owned by none) distances him from classical liberal views. Thus, it is difficult to place him on the traditional political economy scale.

In general, many neotraditionalists are uncomfortable with existing political economy categories. It might be desirable to begin thinking in terms of a third dimension of world view for those who are very close to the neotraditionalist end of the political ecology dimension. It would distinguish those who favor voluntary individual and sometimes collective action based on value change but who reject a classical liberal orientation from those who favor coercive collective action but reject the radical orientation. The dimension, which may be evolving, has not been explicitly included here because it seems poorly articulated and often Utopian in current futurist thinking.

The classification of world views in table 3.3 must be considered a rough one.

Being able to characterize a major forecast according to its world view provides much insight. For instance, it helps clarify the internal consistencies between different forecasts or prescriptions. It also organizes for us the relationships among description, prediction, and prescription.

For many individuals it may also help clarify their own thinking about the future. Those whom we called "believers" in Chapter 1 are those who have strong roots in particular world views and can use them to shape their own thought. It is doubtful that this summary of alternative world views has shaken any believers from their own positions, but it may have helped them understand a little better the cogency of other viewpoints. And those whom we labeled earlier as "confused" may begin to see a basis for organizing their thought.

World views do not operate alone in determining beliefs about the future. Forecasters rely upon various theories or models that organize concepts and information, or evidence. Some of these theories and models and some of the evidence used are determined by one's world view (and help determine it). In other cases the relationship between theories and models and world views is less clear. In any case, we need to turn our attention from the most general level to more specific ones. In the next several chapters I look in turn at major elements of the global development system: population, economics, raw materials (especially energy), agriculture, the environment, and technology.

4. Population

It is natural to begin with an examination of population. The growth of global population drives most of the other systems in which we are interested. It provides the demand for food, energy, fresh air, and other goods and services. It provides the supply of labor for the economic system and of pollution for the environment. And, forecasts of population size until at least the early part of the next century, both globally and by region, are among the least controversial of all forecasts related to global development. Thus, they provide a relatively noncontroversial base for later chapters.

Forecasts of population are less controversial than other forecasts because of the quality of the data and because of the nature of population growth dynamics. Population data are, on the whole, better than economic or energy or environmental data. Although the number of people in China may vary 10 to 20 percent from one estimate to another, and although estimates in a few small countries, like Saudi Arabia, may vary nearly 100 percent, we are generally confident in our current estimates of population. People are much easier to count than barrels of oil yet to be recovered or levels of DDT in ocean fish. Moreover, population figures can be compared over countries, unlike units of GNP (which because of different currencies and even accounting systems are often difficult to compare directly) or tons of grain production (which vary by quality).

Another reason near-term population forecasts are generally not controversial is that population dynamics change slowly. Almost all of the women who will bear children for the next fifteen years are now alive. Unless fertility patterns change dramatically, the number of children they will have is relatively predictable. And both fertility and mortality rates tend to change fairly slowly. Thus, as we shall see below, forecasts of global population by the turn of the century vary by only about 10 percent from one another.

52

Of course, forecasts of population in the more distant future, say the next one hundred to two hundred years, may differ by a factor of four or more. But such variance is dependent much more on how the forecaster believes population interacts with other global development systems than on population dynamics themselves.

BACKGROUND: HISTORY AND FORECASTS

Forecasters take seriously the old saying that "the past is prologue": by far the most important method of forecasting is extrapolation of the past into the future. We saw in the last chapter how world views that strongly shape images of the future are firmly grounded in long-standing philosophic traditions that frame interpretations of the past and perceptions of the present. Thus, this chapter, like the next several chapters, will look simultaneously at some historical aspects of the issue at hand and at forecasts, many of which are simple extrapolations of the past.

Rates and Totals

Historically, populations of the globe and of various regions have fluctuated markedly but have exhibited a pattern of long-term growth. By 8000 B.C., mankind populated the entire globe and numbered about 5 million (Ehrlich and Ehrlich 1972, 12). The domestication of animals and development of agriculture (the Neolithic revolution) began about that time and supported an acceleration of the slow global population growth rate. By the beginning of the first millennium it had reached about 250 million and attained a level of 500 million by about A.D. 1600. Surges and declines of population are concealed by this slow overall growth rate of less than .05 percent per year. For example, bubonic plague (Black Death) killed perhaps 25 percent of the European population between 1348 and 1350. One study reports 1,828 famines in China in the 2,019 years before 1911, some killing millions. In the Thirty Years' War (1618–48), up to one-third of the inhabitants of Germany and Bohemia died.

Global population growth had begun to accelerate by the eighteenth century, and acceleration since then has been quite steady (table 4.1). Figure 4.1 portrays global population growth from 1400 to 1975. Colonizations beginning about 1600, and the industrial and transportation revolutions of the eighteenth and nineteenth centuries, accelerated the overall growth rate. The medical and agricultural revolutions of the nineteenth and twentieth centuries dramatically reduced death rates and supported much more rapid growth rates. By the early 1960s, annual global population growth had climbed to nearly 2 percent.

It should be understood that the rapid acceleration or explosion in the growth rate is attributable to decreasing death rates, *not* to increasing birth

TABLE 4.1. *Historical World Population Growth Rates*

Period	Annual Percentage Growth
1750–1800	0.4
1800–1850	0.5
1850–1900	0.5
1900–1920	0.6
1920–1930	1.0
1930–1940	1.1
1940–1950	1.0
1950–1960	1.9
1960–1970	2.0
1970–1980	1.8
1980–1981	1.7

Sources: 1750–1900 values from John D. Durand, ''The Modern Expansion of World Population,'' *Proceedings of the American Philosophical Society,* 111 (1967): 137; 1900–1950 values from United Nations, *Demographic Yearbook 1960* (New York: UN, 1961); 1950–81 values from United Nations, *Demographic Yearbook 1981* (New York: UN, 1983).

rates. Population growth rates are frequently discussed in terms of crude birth rate and crude death rate. The total birth rate, or *crude birth rate,* is defined as the number of live births each year per thousand population. The *crude death rate* is the number of deaths per thousand. In the Paleolithic era (more than ten thousand years ago), crude birth and death rates both ranged from fifty up to eighty per thousand (United Nations 1973, 12). Life expectancies at birth were from eleven or twelve up to twenty years. For most of the Neolithic Age (the last ten thousand years), birth and death rates generally ranged from forty to fifty, with life expectancies just over twenty. Crude birth and death rates must be about equal in a population which is growing very slowly.

The revolutions noted above succeeded in reducing death rates to as low as ten per thousand; life expectancies now reach seventy. Global birth rates have also begun to drop, although more slowly. In 1980, the crude birth rate was twenty-eight per thousand and the crude death rate was eleven per thousand. The difference, seventeen per thousand, is 1.7 percent, the global population increase rate in that year.

The global population of 4.7 billion in 1983 would double to 9.4 billion in about 2022 if the growth rate remained at 1.7 percent. The growth rate is now dropping slowly, from about 2 percent in 1964–65 to 1.75 percent in 1982–83, according to the U.S. Census Bureau. Not only First World but also Third World population growth rates appear to be slowing, having dropped from a peak of about 2.3 percent in 1960–65 (United Nations 1980, 1).

Although presumably some old civilizations had their demographers

FIGURE 4.1. *World Population Growth, 1400–1975*

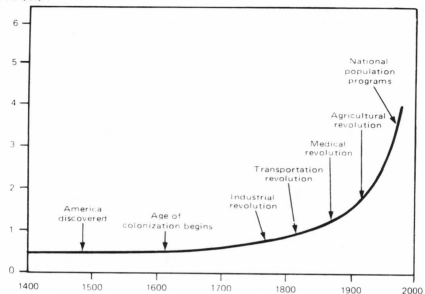

Billions of people

Source: Population Reference Bureau, *World Population Growth and Response* (Washington, D.C.: Population Reference Bureau, 1976), 4. Reprinted with permission.

and their predictions, and although warnings against excess population like that of Malthus can be found throughout history, among the earliest contemporary numerical forecasts were made by Americans and go back at least to Watson in 1815 (Cole et al. 1973, 162). The Americans had the advantage of a regular ten-year census and high rates of territorial expansion and migration, making the extrapolations possible and the issue interesting. Watson, looking ahead eighty-five years, overestimated the U.S. population in 1900 by only 32 percent. Tucker in 1843 missed by only 3 percent.

Demographers of the developed world in the 1930s did not do so well. In the face of steadily declining fertility rates in the first third of the century, they were nearly unanimous in forecasting zero or negative growth for developed country populations in the near future (Pohlman 1973, vii). At the very least their timing was off, as the post–World War II baby boom dramatically increased fertility.

Early global population forecasts were not terribly pessimistic. In 1951 a group of experts reported to the UN secretary-general that "if vigorous effort is put into developing the under-developed countries, we see no reason why their national incomes should not rise at rates higher than the rates at which their populations are currently increasing or may be expected to increase (Cole et al. 1973, 173). In fact, with very few exceptions (notably, the Sahel in the 1970s), they have been right.

As noted earlier, forecasts for global population between now and the end of the century vary little and predict world population to rise to about 6 billion, up from 4.7 billion in 1983. U.S. Census Bureau estimates range from 5.9 to 6.8 billion (CEQ 1981, 20–21), while those of the Community and Family Study Center (CFSC) range from 5.75 to 6 billion (CEQ 1981, 28–29). That seeming agreement conceals much. The medium series of the Census Bureau forecasts a global population growth rate of 1.7 percent in the year 2000, while the CFSC forecast is 1.34 percent. Such differences

FIGURE 4.2. *World Population: Three Futures*

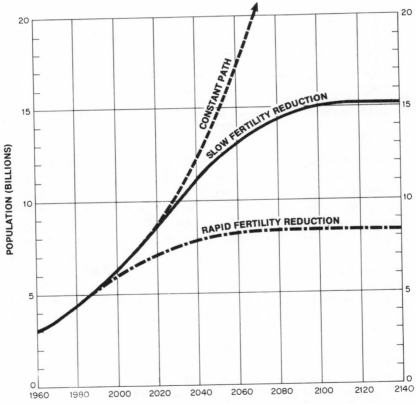

Source: Arthur Haupt and Thomas T. Kane, *Population Handbook* (Washington, D.C.: Population Reference Bureau, 1978), 48. Reprinted with permission.

FIGURE 4.3.   *World Population Growth over the Past Million Years*

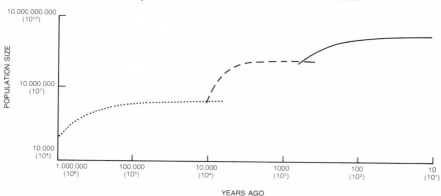

can lead to dramatic longer-term discrepancies in forecasts. At the extremes, post-2000 forecasts diverge sharply, so that by the year 2100 differences of 5 to 10 billion people are quite possible (figure 4.2).

Note that the rapid fertility reduction scenario of figure 4.2 corresponds to a reduction of fertility to the replacement level (each woman on average having one daughter) by 2000, while the slow fertility reduction achieves global replacement fertility by 2040. The former is almost certainly unattainable. The delay of forty years obviously has tremendous significance in terms of ultimate population levels, but is a scenario much closer to the central tendency of population forecasters.

In reality, for reasons I shall discuss below, all forecasters are projecting a gradual transition towards a stable or near stable global population—the debates are over how fast and how high. This makes somewhat propagandistic, as Simon has pointed out (1981), the heavy use by neotraditionalists of the steeply increasing super-exponential (increasing percentage growth rate) curve of population (figure 4.1) as an implication of future trends. Simon and other modernists would prefer to look at the long-term history of global population growth on a ''log-log'' scale, which portrays that growth as three surges, corresponding to the cultural, agricultural, and industrial-medical revolutions (see figure 4.3). This graph makes the current rapid growth look less threatening, because it has happened before and because it appears that stability at a new plateau has solid precedent. We must still address the question, which Simon does not, as to what historically led to the new stability. Was it a reduction in fertility to levels consistent with lower mortality in the growth stages, or was it a resurgence in mortality rates as food provision or other limits were reached by the expanding population?

Distribution

Relatively few critics argue that the United States is now overpopulated, although some neotraditionalists do believe that the current level cannot be sustained. Our destruction of the soil and use of finite resources, they suggest, is reducing the "carrying capacity" of the country's environment (Webb and Jacobsen 1982). Yet the "population problem" is perceived primarily as one of the Third World. Since the beginning of the industrial era's global population surge, there has been remarkably similar growth in Asia, Africa, and Europe (table 4.2). European population nearly quadrupled in the two-hundred years from 1750 to 1983, while Asian, African, and Soviet populations increased by factors of five. It has been, of course, the American population that increased the most rapidly, from a base of only 18 million in 1750 to 649 in 1983, an increase of 3,600 percent.

Thus, the problem, at least to date, has not been an extraordinarily large relative increase in Third World population. Two issues worry the neotraditionalists. The first is the certainty that Third World population growth rates in the next twenty to fifty years will far outstrip those of the developed countries. Thus, by the time some sort of global population stability

TABLE 4.2.   *Regional Population, 1750–2000*

Region	Population (in millions)				
	1750	1850	1950	1983	2000
Asia (except USSR)	498	801	1,381	2,730	3,564
People's Rep. of China	200	430	560	1,023	1,244
India and Pakistan	190	233	434	826	1,108
Japan	30	31	83	119	130
Indonesia	12	23	77	156	199
Remainder of Asia (except USSR)	67	87	227	606	883
Africa	106	111	222	513	851
North Africa	10	15	53	120	188
Remainder of Africa	96	96	169	393	663
Europe (except USSR)	125	208	392	484	511
USSR	42	76	180	272	309
America	18	64	328	649	866
North America	2	26	166	259	302
Latin America	16	38	162	360	603
Oceania	2	2	13	24	29
World total	791	1,262	2,515	4,677	6,130

Sources: 1750–1950 values from John D. Durand, "The Modern Expansion of World Population," *Proceedings of the American Philosophical Society,* 111 (1967): 137; 1983–2000 values from *1983 World Population Data Sheet of the Population Reference Bureau, Inc.* (Washington, D.C.: Population Reference Bureau, 1983).

FIGURE 4.4.   *World Population Growth, 1970–2020*

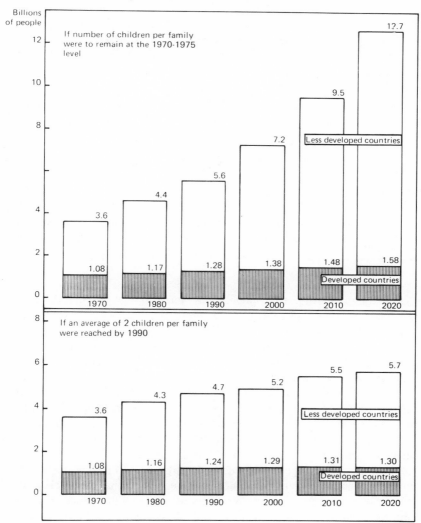

Source: Population Reference Bureau, *World Population Growth and Response* (Washington, D.C.: Population Reference Bureau, 1976), 7. Reprinted with permission.

is attained, populations in the Third World regions will have increased several times over their 1750 base. In fact, already by the year 2000, Asian and African populations will be seven to eight times the 1750 levels, while European population will be four times the 125 million of 1750 (table 4.2). Figure 4.4 expands the comparison of developed and less developed country populations another twenty years. In addition to indicating much higher

TABLE 4.3. *Current Population Densities and Growth Rates*

Region	Population (in millions)	Crop Land (in millions of hectares)	Population/ Land Ratio (population per hectare)	Population Growth Rate (in percentages)
North America	259	114.5	2.26	0.7
Western Europe	424	79.7	5.32	0.5
Other Developed/ West[a]	245	41.7	5.88	1.2
Eastern Europe	114	40.0	2.85	0.7
USSR	272	149.3	1.82	0.8
Latin America	363	92.2	3.94	2.6
Africa	374	110.0	3.40	3.0
OPEC	362	14.0	25.86	2.7
South Asia	1,153	234.0	4.93	2.1
People's Republic of China	1,111	178.3	6.23	1.2

Sources: Food Agriculture Organization, *FAO Production Yearbook* (Rome: FAO, 1978), and Population Reference Bureau, *1983 World Population Data Sheet* (Washington, D.C.: Population Reference Bureau, 1983).
[a]Consists primarily of Japan, Australia, New Zealand, South Africa, and Israel.

future additions to the LDC populations, that figure shows that different assumptions about future fertility rates are of much greater significance for the LDCs.

Second, a number of indicators suggest that Third World regions already are at least as relatively populated as First World regions. One such indicator is population per hectare of cultivated land. In table 4.3, we see both the relative growth rates and population densities of world regions. A modernist would surely point out that none of this truly indicates existing or probable future overpopulation in the Third World—that would require an assessment of the ability of Third World regions physically to sustain their populations, an issue to which I shall return.

Another key distributional issue is the urban-rural division of population. Populations globally have become increasingly urban (see table 4.4). Migration to the cities in First World countries has put pressure on urban absorptive capacities. In the Third World it has overwhelmed these capacities and given rise to vast shantytowns surrounding cities on every continent. Urban employment growth, although often rapid, has had no chance of keeping up with the migrants.

The impact of this urbanization on the Third World has been powerful (table 4.5). In 1960, the world's largest urban agglomeration was the New York and northeast New Jersey region, with a population of 15.4 million. In that year eight of the ten largest urban areas were in First World countries—only Shanghai and Buenos Aires represented the Third World. Fair-

TABLE 4.4. *Urbanization of World Population, 1960–1980*

Nation Status	Percentage of Population in Urban Areas		Annual Growth Rate in Urban Population	1980 Urban Population (in millions)
	1960	1980	1960–1980	
Low Income	13	17	4.1	367
Middle Income	33	45	4.0	513
Industrial	68	78	1.4	557

Source: World Bank, *World Development Report 1982* (Washington, D.C.: World Bank, 1982), table 20.

ly straight extrapolation suggests that in 2000 Mexico City will be the world's largest urban area, with over 30 million people. In that year, eight of the ten largest cities will be in Asia or South America.

Linkages to Other Issues

Some futurists have expressed concern with the implications of population density in and of itself. At the ridiculous extreme, simple extrapolations of exponential growth have suggested an image of a world with standing room only. Tests with animals clearly show deviant behavior (such as the abandonment of the young) with increased population density—some have implied that increased crime rates, divorce rates, child

TABLE 4.5. *World's Largest Urban Areas, 1960–2000*

1960		1980		2000	
SMSA	Population	SMSA	Population	SMSA	Population
1. New York-NE New Jersey	15.4	New York-NE New Jersey	20.2	Mexico City	31.6
2. London	10.7	Tokyo-Yokohama	20.0	Sao Paulo	25.8
3. Tokyo-Yokohama	10.7	Mexico City	15.0	Shanghai	23.7
4. Rhein-Ruhr	8.7	Shanghai	14.3	Tokyo-Yokohama	23.7
5. Shanghai	7.7	Sao Paulo	13.5	New York-NE New Jersey	22.4
6. Paris	7.2	Los Angeles-Long Beach	11.6	Beijing	20.9
7. Los Angeles-Long Beach	7.1	Beijing	11.4	Rio de Janeiro	19.0
8. Buenos Aires	6.9	Rio de Janeiro	10.7	Bombay	16.8
9. Chicago-NW Indiana	6.5	Buenos Aires	10.1	Calcutta	16.4
10. Moscow	6.3	London	10.0	Jakarta	15.7

Source: United Nations, *World Population Trends and Policies 1981* Monitoring Report, Vol. 1 (New York: United Nations, 1982), 157–58.

abuse, and a host of other social maladies among humans can already be traced to the phenomenon. Little serious research has focused on the relationship between population density and social behavior among humans.

More reasonably, one can ask what the key linkages between population and other aspects of the global development system have been and are likely to be. Specifically, we would like to know the positive and negative implications of faster versus slower population growth rates and of more versus fewer human beings.

One can reasonably ask, but the answer does not come easily. Let us first try a mental exercise. We should be able to make two lists: one of clearly detrimental consequences of population growth and one of purely positive consequences. We can look to the neotraditionalists for the negative list. Population growth places pressure upon a wide range of physical and biological support systems. It means that finite and limited natural resources will be consumed at higher rates. It means that ecosystems, like forests, grasslands, and the oceans, will be exploited at higher levels and may suffer long-term, possibly irreversible, damage. It means that given levels of food and manufactured goods production will need to satisfy more people.

The modernist gives us the positive list. The modernist focuses not on the demands associated with higher populations but on the contribution population makes to supplies. More people mean more laborers and thus greater production of food or manufactures. Greater population densities can make it easier to provide services such as access to scarce medical specialists or access to efficient public transportation. More people, at least up to some uncertain level, may mean more musicians, poets, engineers, and scientists, with a related increase in the numbers and variety of artistic creations and technological innovations (see Simon 1981).

The division into a focus by neotraditionalists on demand side implications and by modernists on the supply side is useful, but not strictly accurate. People can, for example, also be looked at as suppliers of pollutants.

But now let us look at these lists from the standpoint of the opposite paradigm. The modernist does not deny that people consume natural resources and that more people consume more of them. But he or she would point out that people also supply them, in that people discover deposits and extract them. The modernist would argue that when global populations were very small so were global resource reserves (known and usable deposits), and that the two have generally grown together. He or she would also point out that the impact of human beings on the environment is not strictly one-sided. Human beings have reclaimed swamps (even ocean bottom) and irrigated deserts.

Few neotraditionalists would accept the modernist list without argument. They would certainly question the assumption that more workers can produce more food and manufactures in an indefinite cycle of growth. They would point out that production requires not just people but land and/or machinery. When there already is inadequate land for the farming population, adding more people will not help. Nor will it help when the growth of industry is already inadequate to supply employment to the existing labor force. And they would question whether there is any evidence that the proportion of creative genius, artistic or scientific, is constant with increasing population. Indeed, they would argue, if increased population were to reduce the average standard of living, so that less leisure time were available, it would almost certainly imply a decrease in that proportion.

FORECASTING: THEORIES AND MODELS

The simplest, and by no means the worst, approach to forecasting population levels is the simple growth model. That model computes population of a time point (t) as population at a prior point ($t-1$) times one plus a growth rate (r):

$$\text{Pop}_t = \text{Pop}_{t-1}(1 + r).$$

This can be generalized to compute from an initial point in time to any subsequent point:

$$\text{Pop}_t = \text{Pop}_{t=0}(1 + r)^t.$$

The model will be completely accurate, of course, only if the growth rate is constant over time. One could extend this model by projecting changes in the population growth rate based on historic trends or because of factors expected to influence that rate in the future. This is exactly what at least one of the most accurate early American population forecasters did, most others relying on constant rates.

Cohort Component Analysis

Prior to the end of the last century, some advances in technique were already being made which have since evolved into the most common approach to population forecasting. That approach is cohort component analysis.

Cohort component analysis represents the population of a region (country, city, or whatever) by age category, or cohort, and by sex. In figure 4.5 we see two such cohort distributions, one for Mexico and one for the United States. Those two are representative of the general shapes of such distributions for less and more economically developed countries, respectively. Generally, the rapidly growing populations characteristic of the

FIGURE 4.5. *Age/Sex Distributions of a Developed and a Developing Country*

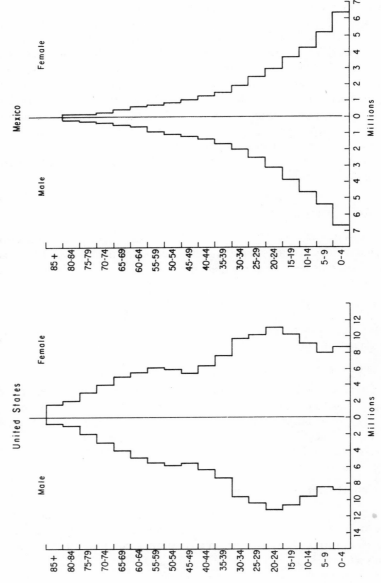

Source: United Nations, *Demographic Yearbook* (New York: UN, 1981).

Third World countries are concentrated heavily in the lower age cohorts, giving the distribution a pyramidal shape. As a region moves towards zero population growth its distribution becomes more "rocket-shaped."

In order to have a complete model for projecting population one must also have two other distributions, one for fertility and one for mortality (figures 4.6 and 4.7). The fertility distributions are, of course, zero at the extreme ends and bulge in the childbearing years. The mortality distributions tend to have small—and sometimes not so small—bulges representing infant mortality. Mortality rates are near zero in later childhood and early adulthood, but then increase steadily with age.

Given these three distributions, forecasting population is very easy. One multiplies the mortality distribution rate by the number of people in respective age cohorts to compute deaths by cohort. One multiplies the fertility

FIGURE 4.6. *Fertility Rates for Mexico and the United States*

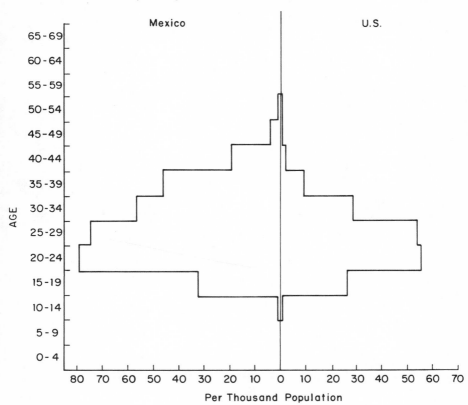

Source: United Nations, *Demographic Yearbook* (New York: UN, 1981).

FIGURE 4.7. *Mortality Rates for Mexico and the United States*

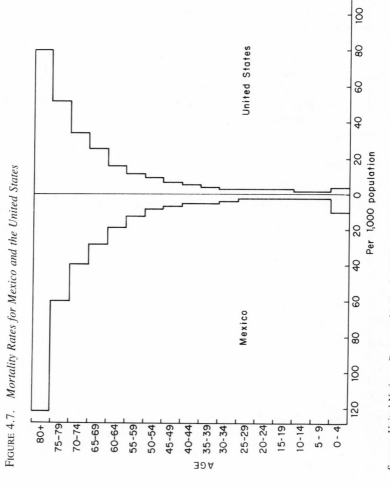

Source: United Nations, *Demographic Yearbook* (New York: UN, 1981).

rates by the number in the cohorts to obtain births. All survivors move up one cohort in five years (or one-fifth move up each year) and births are added at the bottom.

This general approach is used by most population forecasting organizations including the United Nations and the U.S. Bureau of the Census. As described here it is simple and noncontroversial—little more than an accounting scheme. It also helps us understand the concept of population *momentum*. Because the individuals in the lower cohorts will pass upward through the childbearing cohorts, unless there are exceptionally great changes in mortality or fertility distributions, population levels in the next twenty years are fairly easy to predict and difficult to affect.

The cohort component approach also clarifies why reaching equilibrium fertility rates (two surviving children per woman) does not mean zero population growth. If large numbers of individuals are concentrated in lower age cohorts (look again at the Mexican distribution in figure 4.6), even low fertility rates will result in high total birth levels for many years and a greater number of births than deaths. Similarly, and somewhat surprisingly at first, a drop in an LDC of mortality rates per cohort to levels of a more developed country will result in crude death rates per thousand *lower* than in MDCs because of the proportionately lower number of individuals in older LDC cohorts.

The difficulties with the cohort component analysis approach are of two kinds. The first is migration among regions. Such migration is very difficult to predict and often reflects political decisions and events. Migrants will also almost always differ in age and sex distribution from both their home and target populations. Fortunately for demographers, contemporary international migrations are nowhere near the size of the migrations to the Western Hemisphere in the 1800s and early 1900s; except for refugee populations they are quite limited. Many global forecasters are, in fact, concerned only with regional (e.g., continental) population totals, and interregional migration has dwindled even more than intercountry migration.

The second difficulty is much more basic: it is still necessary to project changes in the fertility and mortality distributions to capture realistically population dynamics. There are several possible approaches to this. One is a simple extrapolation of historic changes in the distributions. The United Nations uses a different approach. They posit probable distributions at a future date on the basis of trend extrapolation and judgment (considering, for example, intensity of family planning programs), and then interpolate between the current and future distributions.

Still another possible approach is to relate explicitly to changes in fertility and mortality those factors that have been found to influence them and then to forecast those explanatory variables. In actuality, most attention is directed toward explaining fertility. Death rates have dropped nearly everywhere in the world and demographers expect relatively little further decline. It is the future course of fertility over which debate primarily rages.

Fertility and Mortality Changes

Analyses of changes in fertility and mortality have identified many factors that help explain them: income, health care, education (especially of women), literacy rates, the availability of information concerning contraception. Although much research has been done to investigate the impact of such factors upon fertility or mortality, there remains a surprising amount of controversy with respect to the magnitude of their impact. For instance, a recent World Bank study questions the long-emphasized link between higher education levels and lower fertility, except for education on contraception.

Some significant methodological difficulties have made definitive statements about such relationships very difficult to make. These are worth a little attention because they affect research on all the issues addressed in this volume. First, the quality of our data on fertility and mortality rates is relatively poor. Such data are expensive to gather and the Third World countries, in which we have the greatest interest, can least afford to mount the efforts necessary to obtain the information regularly. Also, fertility and mortality patterns change slowly and normally quite steadily and in one direction, as do some of the related variables, like education levels. If fertility is steadily and slowly dropping, while both income and literacy rates are steadily but slowly increasing, how can we say whether income or literacy (education) is more important in affecting fertility?

Examining the issues across countries (cross-sectionally) eliminates some of these problems—in particular it provides us much variability in the levels of fertility, mortality, and related factors, thus making it easier statistically to examine the relationships between them. But across countries many other factors, such as cultural patterns and religious beliefs, also vary dramatically, raising the possibility that factors other than those we are examining may be more basic explanations of changes in fertility or mortality. Also cross-sectional (across country) analyses intensify some data problems, inasmuch as countries may gather or report data very differently. Thus, those directing many studies of fertility decide not to undertake analyses either for one country over time or for a large set of countries at one point in time, opting instead for intensive surveys in local areas. That allows many methodological problems to be overcome and quite strong statements to be made about the factors underlying fertility and mortality patterns. But most such studies are for one time point and this again makes statements about change in the patterns difficult to make. And many are sufficiently affected by local factors (cultural, religious, legal) that generalization may be shaky.

The Impact of Income

In spite of research difficulties, there is general agreement on the importance of many factors. Perhaps most importantly, the key role of higher income levels in reducing both fertility and mortality is little disputed. In fact, increases in income are so highly correlated with improvements in educational levels, the status of women (especially their entry into the workforce), and health care, that income changes, for which data are easier to obtain, are often used as a surrogate indicator for all of these other factors.

The importance of income as an explanatory variable is especially attractive to the economic perspective and emphasis on individual rationality of the classical liberal: it is always satisfying to have an explanation of a relationship, rather than just a statistical identification of one. In the case of fertility, one can make a cost-benefit argument. At low levels of income, especially in rural areas, additional children may be associated with few costs and relatively great benefits. When the mother is already without outside income opportunities and tied to the home with other children, the opportunity cost of childbearing and childraising is low. Low levels of expenditure on clothing, shelter, education, health care, and even food are probable. Meanwhile, the child will be employed on the farm or earning outside income at a very young age. It has been estimated that a male child in Bangladesh provides labor or income by age six, that his cumulative production exceeds cumulative consumption by age fifteen, and that his cumulative production exceeds his own and one sister's cumulative consumption by age twenty-two (Murdoch 1980, 26). And the sister will work as well. For a couple with no prospects of a private pension or government support in their old age, children also provide needed security.

With increases in individual and national income levels the cost-benefit calculation can change dramatically. Often other sources of income for women do exist. Educational costs may skyrocket. Child labor laws and different expectations for children reduce income flows from the child and social security systems reduce or eliminate the need for support of the aged within the family.

Statistical evidence corroborates this line of argument. In figure 4.8 we see the relationship between the birth rate and the average per capita income five years later (assuming that it takes some time before income levels are reflected in attitudes about children). There is clearly a tendency for increased income to be related to lower birth rates. There are also, however, large deviations from the line drawn to represent that tendency. The deviations, or residuals, can in turn be explained, however, by the

FIGURE 4.8. *The Relationship between Income and Birthrate for Selected Countries*

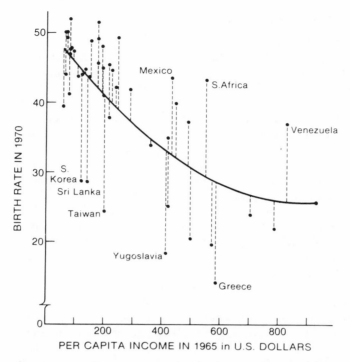

Source: William W. Murdoch, *The Poverty of Nations* (Baltimore: Johns Hopkins University Press, 1980), 61. Reprinted with permission.

degree of income inequality in the countries. Figure 4.9 shows the relationship between the deviations and a standard measure of income inequality, the Gini coefficient. Low Ginis, indicating quite equal divisions within countries of income, are strongly related to birth rates below those "expected" for a given average income level (that is, below the line in figure 4.8), while high Ginis (great inequality) are associated with higher than expected birth rates. These findings are consistent with the individual behavior explanation given above, since unequal income distributions mean that many individuals fall below the average income levels and are not subject to the same incentives for fertility reduction facing those at higher levels of income.

Interestingly, the individual rationality argument and use of cross-sectional data took a surprising twist in the neotraditionalist *Limits to Growth* study. In the computer model underpinning that book a linkage was introduced between income level and desired family size. Figure 4.10 shows cross-sectional data contributing to the linkage in that model. On the basis of individual rationality one could argue that after a certain point, further income increases no longer raise the costs of individual children (the cost of even a private college education has a limit), so that the cost of children as a percentage of income again begins to fall. At that point desired family size might increase. Thus, the *Limits to Growth* model assumes that when income is high enough and growing fast enough, families might seek three children. Above $800 per capita industrial output, and with 3 percent per capita growth, a typical family would want 2.4 children. In contrast, most population forecasters now expect family size in wealthy countries to drop to about 2.1 children.

This relationship linking income and desired family size in the *Limits to Growth* model is very important to its dynamic behavior. At income levels below the turning point in figure 4.10, lower incomes increase fertility,

FIGURE 4.9. *The Relationship between Income Inequality and Birthrate for Selected Countries*

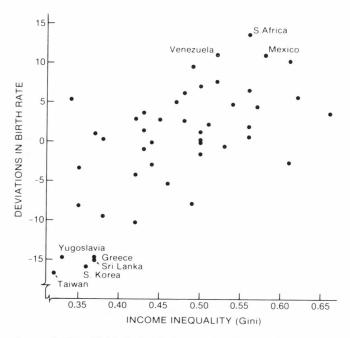

Source: William W. Murdoch, *The Poverty of Nations* (Baltimore: Johns Hopkins University Press, 1980), 62. Reprinted with permission.

Note: Larger Gini coefficients indicate greater inequality.

FIGURE 4.10.   *GNP per Capita and Desired Family Size (Families Wanting Four or More Children)*

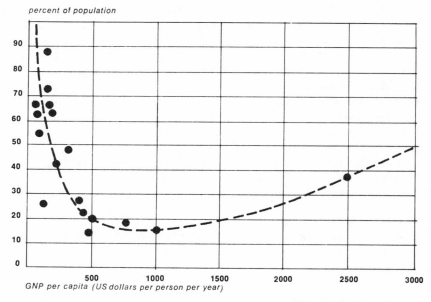

Source: Donella H. Meadows, Dennis L. Meadows, Jørgen Randers, William W. Behrens III, *The Limits to Growth: A Report for the Club of Rome's Project on the Predicament of Mankind.* A Potomac Associates book published by Universe Books, N.Y., 1972. Graphics by Potomac Associates, page 114. Reprinted with permission.

which might well lead to still lower incomes and higher fertility—a vicious cycle (positive feedback loop) pushing the world system toward collapse. Incomes above the turning point can, however, also increase fertility and population, thus contributing to problems like food scarcity.

The most important debates about the determinants of fertility, however, center on the impact of family planning programs. The emphasis on income as a determinant of fertility on the part of some futurists, especially classical liberals and radicals, takes them to the point where they argue that birth control programs are really ineffective. Income must continue to grow, according to the classical liberals—or be dramatically redistributed, according to the radicals—to reduce fertility. Family planning programs and propaganda for smaller families will only be effective if the economic incentives for small families are in place. This position became the slogan of many Third World leaders at the 1974 World Population Conference in Bucharest—''take care of the people and the population will take care of itself.'' At best, some liberals argue, family planning programs will work only if the economic incentives are already in place; at worst, such programs may unreasonably encourage individuals to act against their own economic interests and strong beliefs (Simon 1981).

Evidence on the effects of fertility reduction programs is difficult to evaluate. Such programs are relatively recent, and actual expenditure levels have been quite low. Most studies (although conceivably biased by their association with those who have a vested interest in the programs) suggest that family planning programs do have an impact, either because a considerable number of people have reached the point where they have the incentives but not the knowledge or the means to reduce family size (Brown 1981), or because they are swayed by the propaganda. An analysis by Bogue (1980) of changes in fertility from 1968 to 1975 in eighty-nine LDCs found that family planning effort not only highly correlates with fertility reduction but also has an effect independent of income. Six socioeconomic variables (including income and percentage of females enrolled in school, but excluding income distribution) explain 29 percent of the variation in fertility change. Adding family planning effort to the equation explains an additional 18 percent. In other words, the seven variables together statistically explain nearly half of the differences among LDCs in the rate of fertility decline.

The Demographic Transition

The most widely accepted understanding of how mortality and fertility rates change is summarized in the so-called theory of demographic transition. In preindustrial societies both crude birth rates and death rates were very high—about 40 per 1,000 of population. When the two rates are equal, net population growth is zero. If the rates were both 40 in a stable population, the average life expectancy at birth would be 1,000/40 or twenty-five years (because of high mortality rates at all ages, but especially for infants and children).

In the currently more developed countries, death rates dropped slowly from these levels throughout the eighteenth and nineteenth centuries, with accelerated decline in the last one hundred years (see figure 4.11). Declines in birth rates began later, in the last half of the nineteenth century, but have been more rapid. The gap between the two has never exceeded (on the average for developed countries) about 10 per 1,000, equivalent to population growth rates of 1 percent. Life expectancy at birth is now about seventy years. Since 1,000/70 is about fourteen, if the trend in developed countries toward equal birth and death rates and zero population growth continues, the two rates will stabilize at about 14 per 1,000.

In the LDCs, the equivalent decline in death rates did not begin until the last half of the nineteenth century and accelerated markedly after World War II. The birth rate has been also dropping for about fifty years, but much more slowly. The gap between the two rates has steadily widened

FIGURE 4.11.   *The Demographic Transition*

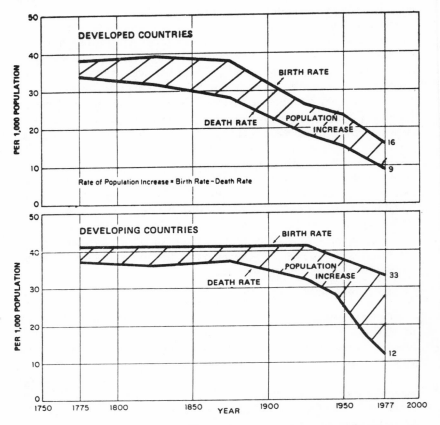

Source: Nancy Birdsall, *Population and Poverty in the Developing World.* World Bank Staff
Working Paper No. 404. (Washington, D.C.: World Bank, 1980), 4. Reprinted with
permission.

and now exceeds 20 per 1,000 or 2 percent net population growth. The
death rate could conceivably drop as low as 7–8 per 1,000 (because the
population distribution of LDCs is skewed to young ages, as discussed
earlier), but is obviously nearing a minimum given current global maximum life spans. Implicit in the population forecasts shown earlier was the
nearly universal assumption that birth rates will continue to decline and
that LDCs will follow the more developed countries toward population
equilibrium. We saw, of course, that there is great debate over the speed of
the demographic transition for LDCs. There is evidence, in countries like
Taiwan and South Korea, that the demographic transition can occur with

remarkable speed. For instance, births per 1,000 in those two countries exceeded 40 in 1960 but dropped to 25 or fewer by 1975 (Murdoch 1980, 72).

The so-called theory of demographic transition obviously is not really a theory, because it begs the most important question: what are the major driving forces of the transition from a high mortality and fertility equilibrium to a low mortality and fertility equilibrium?

The LDCs are a vastly heterogeneous group, and a representation of a demographic transition for the entire group can be quite misleading. Some countries still have high death rates: in at least twenty-two countries death rates still exceed 20 per 1,000 (Hansen 1982, 160–64). In others, birth rates remain at or near preindustrial levels; in at least eleven countries they exceed an incredible 50 per 1,000. In many others, however, the demographic transition is very advanced.

Neotraditionalists, in particular, draw attention to this diversity, while radicals are apt to point to those countries with little or no reduction in birth rates. Proponents of both world views identify these issues to suggest that there may be a set of countries which will not in the foreseeable future complete any demographic transition. These countries—of which Bangladesh and India may be the best examples, but which include many other Asian and African states—may be trapped in a cycle of poverty. Low incomes encourage high fertility rates, which maintain downward pressure on incomes.

On one level this may seem to contradict the earlier arguments of economic rationality. Neotraditionalists, however, argue that it does not, if we distinguish individual from collective behavior. It may be individually rational to have an additional child, because that child will provide more benefit than cost to the family. But in a societal setting of scarce food, high unemployment, and little or no economic growth, the impact of nearly everyone making such a decision will result in further social pressures on the food supply, more unemployment, and additional difficulties in creating such prerequisites for economic growth as capital savings and a healthy and educated population.

This distinction between what is good for the individual and what is good for the society has been captured clearly and dramatically in the concept of the "tragedy of the commons" (Hardin 1980). That tragedy is generally illustrated by the example of farmers sharing grazing rights on a common grassland. Each farmer can benefit individually by adding one animal to his herd because his benefits exceed his costs (including a small average reduction at some point in the quality of the pasture). But if each farmer follows this logic individually, they will collectively destroy the pasture, a result none wants. This conflict between collective and individual rationality has been developed theoretically by Mancur Olson.

(1965) and applied by neotraditionalists to a wide range of historical and contemporary commons.

Radicals give a slightly different twist to the cycle of poverty thesis by arguing that the developed countries profit from the poverty of the LDCs (e.g., low prices on goods imported from LDCs) and at least unconsciously maintain it (Murdoch 1980). By controlling the terms of trade in their own interests, the wealthy prevent the poor countries from accumulating the capital they need. By distorting the economies of the poor countries toward certain production processes (e.g., mechanized farms) and export commodities (e.g., raw materials or plantation crops) that have relatively low labor requirements, we have created a surplus of labor which keeps labor prices down and maintains poverty and high fertility.

The issues of this chapter cannot really be divorced from the issues of the next several chapters. Elements of perspectives concerning the future, like the world views in which they are grounded, are mutually reinforcing. Although forecasts through the year 2000 vary little, we have seen that population forecasts in the longer term vary from those predicting collapse of population because of food scarcities and environmental degradation to those predicting an eventually stable global population at high levels, brought about by reduced fertility levels tied to high incomes. Which type of forecast one accepts thus depends on what one believes about economic growth, the capacity of the environment to absorb pollution and to provide resources, and our future technology of food production. We shall see, of course, that one's forecasts in these areas are in turn dependent on beliefs about population.

The notion of "stability regions," something that has appeared implicitly now and then in this chapter, should be made explicit. There is, in reality, much consensus that continued growth in population, as in other aspects of the global development system, is an unstable and transitory condition. In terms of population, high fertility and mortality rates, coupled with other aspects of preindustrial society, yielded a comparatively stable state that persisted for millennia. The demographic transition may be taking us toward a new "stability region" with low fertility and mortality rates. Some observers say it is inevitable that this new stability region will also be accompanied by high income levels, clean environments, and other desirable features of postindustrial society. Other observers believe that some areas of the world are trapped in the earlier stability region, while still other critics claim the world as a whole may be in danger of falling back to it. Turning to other issues may help us evaluate the claims.

5. Economics

In the previous chapter it was emphasized that barring a catastrophe such as nuclear war or pestilence, forecasts of global population vary little through the end of the century. Dynamics of population growth tend to change slowly. As I turn my attention to long-term global economic development, I am struck by the far greater variation in regional and global economic forecasts. The complexity and variation of economic prognostications was well illustrated by a *New Yorker* cartoon showing a perplexed man watching the evening news. The reporter provided the financial summary:

> On Wall Street today, news of lower interest rates sent the stock market up, but then the expectation that these rates would be inflationary sent the market down, until the realization that lower rates might stimulate the sluggish economy pushed the market up, before it ultimately went down on fears that an overheated economy would lead to a reimposition of higher interest rates.

Besides demonstrating the uncertainty of economic forecasts, the cartoon illustrates the preoccupation forecasts normally have with the short-term. Attempts to say anything about the state of an economy ten or twenty years hence are quite recent. Yet the global economic difficulties of the 1970s awoke in both forecasters and their clients the desire to look at a longer time horizon, however difficult it may be to do so. The relatively smooth global growth pattern of the post–World War II era was broken. World GNP grew at a 5.7 percent average annual rate in the 1960s. Between 1970 and 1973 it accelerated to 6.0 percent. But between 1973 and 1978, after the first oil shock, it fell to 3.3 percent. In the 1980–82 period, it fell to under 2.0 percent. Growth in the industrial countries, which exceeded 5 percent in the 1960s, fell to about 1 percent in the 1980–82 period.

Neotraditionalists have interpreted the period as an augury of a new era, in which global economic growth will be indefinitely constrained. Modern-

77

ists more often portray it as a temporary downturn or deep recession, like many earlier recessions. Neotraditionalists retort that not all downturns prove short-lived, and that even if we have not yet reached a period of indefinite scarcity, global economic troubles may persist. Given the debate over whether recent events illustrate an indefinite change in global growth patterns or a ''normal'' cyclical downturn, I must devote some attention to what is known about economic cycles.

INTRODUCTION: ECONOMIC CYCLES

Much of the uncertainty in economic forecasts stems from the problem of physical capital, that is, the machinery and buildings used in the production of goods and services. The major factor plaguing short-term forecasts (and one which is also important in longer-term forecasts) is that capital is seldom used to full production capacity and the rate of capacity utilization may change dramatically and quickly. Recessions or depressions are periods of underutilization of capital, and, of course, periods during which other production factors, such as labor, are not used fully.

Our theories of recession and depression are inadequately well-developed to provide much assistance in forecasting longer-term economic downturns or recoveries. Even shorter-term economic forecasts, largely extrapolative like most other forecasts, are notoriously poor in predicting the ''turns,'' that is, the beginnings of an economic downturn or of a recovery.

Many economists have tried to chart economic variation in order to identify cycles. Juglar might well have been the first to do so by spotting, in 1856, an average seven-year cycle in France, the United Kingdom, and the United States (Maddison 1982, 64–65). He interpreted these cycles as a function of financial activity (central bank action, interest rates).

The best-known cycle is the four-year business cycle, which the National Bureau of Economic Research (NBER) has identified (irregularly) from 1857 through 1978. It has slightly longer periods for France, Germany and the United Kingdom than in the United States. It is most often explained by an overaccumulation of inventories leading to a period of stock liquidation and low demand throughout the economy. Others have pointed to the coincidence of the business cycle with the election cycle and efforts by politicians to ''prop up'' the economy prior to an election; this is especially noteworthy in the United States, with its four-year presidential election cycle.

Longer cycles are generally explained in terms of factors that shape the rate and type of capital formation. These rates can vary dramatically. For instance, some economists have pointed to an eight-year cycle in the size of cattle herds (herd size being a form of agricultural capital). More important to the larger economy, there may be an eighteen- to twenty-year "construction cycle," driven by major changes in the rates of residential and commercial construction. Nobel Prize-winning economist Simon Kuznets has identified the Kuznets cycle of eighteen to twenty-five years, related to changes in population and immigration.

The best-known of the longer cycles is the Kondratieff cycle, or long wave, of about fifty years. Recently it has received much attention because Kondratieff anticipated the onset of a global depression, identifying 1920 as the beginning of the downturn (Beenstock 1983, 137). According to the calculations of his followers, we should now be into another down phase, and they historically last about twenty-five years.

Explanations for the phases of the Kondratieff cycle vary considerably. Kondratieff himself really did not try to explain the waves, only to chart them. There have been four major bases of explanation proposed (Bruckmann 1983, 6–9). Joseph Schumpeter attributed the cycles to irregular clusterings of innovation, of which four—the steam engine, the railroad, chemicals and electricity, and the automobile—can be identified. After the domestic and international life cycle of an innovation plays out (that is, market saturation is achieved), investment rates and growth drop. The subsequent depression encourages renewed innovation, which is necessary to overcome economic crisis.

A closely related theory emphasizes capital. Jay Forrester, who has spent much time in the last several years constructing a socioeconomic model of the United States replicating various cycles, explains the down phase as a result of large-scale excess capacity in some declining sectors, resulting in a drop in overall investment and construction opportunities. Gradually an economy depreciates its capital and a rebuilding begins, led by new technologies, such as petroleum, automobiles, and private housing in the United States after the Depression (Forrester 1978, 9–11). It has been suggested that currently many developed countries have such long-term overcapacity in basic industries, such as steel and automobiles. New technologies, like electronics and biogenetics, already exist, and are far enough advanced to cut costs and employment in old industries, but not far enough advanced to create whole new life styles and industries to support them and thus to absorb the surplus capital and labor of the old industries. According to the Forrester group, the downturn into which we are moving now will also lower return on capital so that increased incentives will exist for innovations and the pace of technological change will accelerate. Thus, the two explanations, innovation and capital, are closely related.

Still another slight variation, an emphasis on labor, has been espoused by Christopher Freeman. The growth of a dominant technology and capital investment has a central role in Freeman's model: he argues that during the downturn, capital intensity actually grows. Labor displacement characterizes the downturn, as often does material-saving technical change. Nevertheless, Freeman argues that society must encourage the most rapid diffusion of new technologies—in this current case especially microelectronics—in order to speed the adjustment process and encourage new employment (*Forbes*, June 20, 1983, 75).

W. W. Rostow, who also has devoted much attention to the long wave phenomenon, attributes the waves to alternating scarcity and glut in basic commodities, such as food and energy. He argues that we have moved into a period of relative scarcity, characterized by higher prices. His explanation appears consistent with long periods of energy system transition, addressed in the following chapter. Unlike Forrester he foresees a period of expanded investment as we seek to overcome the scarcity.

Long waves, and especially their down phases, are also consistent with the Marxian notion of periodic crises of capitalism. Marxian economist Ernest Mandel attributes the down swings to falling rates of profit in the capitalist world. Capitalism has survived three prior downswings only with the help of external events (e.g., the California gold strikes of 1848, the carving up of the Third World by Europe after 1896). This time he does not feel capitalism will survive (*Forbes*, Nov. 9, 1981, 174).

Many economists are highly sceptical of using such controversial and rather poorly explained cycles as a basis for forecasting. MIT trade theorist Charles Kindleberger has said that "Kondratieff is like astrology." (*Forbes*, Nov. 9, 1981, 166). It has been pointed out that there are simply too few historical examples of the longest cycles to permit statistical analysis and that the periods of all the cycles vary considerably.

The point that is important to us here is that the controversy over the existence and nature of the cycles is great and that it has important implications for forecasting. The prolonged global economic downturn of the 1970s and early 1980s has revived interest in the long waves. Many modernists have come to accept long waves as a basis on which to reject any notion that ultimate limits have caused current economic problems—the global economy will recover again, just as it has in the past. Many neo-traditionalists similarly embrace them as at least a short-run bumping up against limits—we may recover this time, but at some point we will not.

BACKGROUND: HISTORY AND FORECASTS

Turning from cycles to longer-term trends, I shall examine three aspects of historical and forecasted economic growth: rates and totals, distribution, and linkages to other aspects of the global development system.

Rates and Totals

Obviously, economic "progress" did not begin with the industrial revolution. Economic historians disagree on dates and names, but most divide

European economic history of the last fifteen hundred years into periods, or epochs. Maddison (1982) identifies four such eras: agrarianism, from 500 to 1500; advancing agrarianism from 1500 to 1700; merchant capitalism, from 1700 to 1820; and capitalism, from 1820 on. He points out that our differing political ecology world views have adherents among historians. Ladurie emphasizes stability in the French economy between 1300 and 1700, and Abel argues that real living standards in Germany and England fell from the first half of the fourteenth to the first half of the eighteenth century. Both describe basically Malthusian limits to growth at work. Maddison concludes that "the basically agrarian civilization of Europe in 1500–1700 was an advancing one in which technical progress and a modicum of capital formation played some role" (1982: 10–11). The data we have from the period may well be inadequate for a definitive characterization.

The industrial revolution, in which modern industry and its product began increasingly to replace hand production, did not begin from a zero base. Prior to the beginning of that revolution, usually dated from the 1700s and placed in England global industrial production (if not necessarily more general economic well-being) was growing at more modest rates. The real significance of the revolution lay in the acceleration of growth, first in Great Britain, and then throughout the world.

Table 5.1 shows that acceleration. The average growth rate for most of the eighteenth century was 1.5 percent. Thereafter, growth rates never fell below 2 percent, even in the Great Depression decade, the 1930s, until

TABLE 5.1. *World Industrial Production, 1705–1982*

Period	Annual Percentage Growth	Period	Index Value (1913 = 100)
1705–1785	1.5	1701–1710	0.55
1785–1830	2.6	1781–1790	1.81
1830–1840	2.9	1802–1812	3.18
1840–1860	3.5	1820	4.16
1860–1870	2.9	1840	7.40
1870–1900	3.7	1860	14.70
1900–1913	4.2	1880	26.90
1913–1929	2.7	1900	58.70
1929–1938	2.0	1913	100.00
1938–1948	4.1	1929	153.30
1948–1973	5.8	1938	182.70
1973–1978	2.9	1948	274.00
1978–1982	1.5	1973	1,116.00
		1978	1,289.00
		1982	1,387.31

Sources: W. W. Rostow, *The World Economy: History and Prospect* (Austin: University of Texas Press, 1978), pp. 49, 662; United Nations, *Statistical Yearbook* (New York: UN, 1980); United Nations, *Monthly Bulletin on Statistics* 37 (July 1983): xii.

1978. There are two other factors worth noting. First is the truly dramatic cumulative impact of this three-century period of growth—a twenty-five-hundredfold increase in industrial output. This can be compared with a five-fold increase in population in the same period. Second, the growth rate has been quite unstable. It reached peaks (from which it subsequently retreated) of 3.5 percent in 1840–60, of 4.2 percent in 1900–1913, and 5.6 percent in 1948–71. These are the apparent "long waves" of economic growth, or Kondratieff cycles, discussed above.

From the point of view of most readers, one of the most interesting phenomena in the history of economic growth is the decade of the 1970s. The popular perception is that the decade was a "lost decade" during which, because of the two oil shocks and stagflation, economic growth was all but halted. In reality, it was a decade of considerable growth, slow only by recent historical standards.

Three sets of forecasts have been made by international organizations of global growth through the end of the century (table 5.2). Economic forecasts can be difficult to compare because, although generally made in real, or uninflated, dollars, the base year of the forecast and the year of the dollar base varies among forecasts. In addition, even initial conditions are difficult to establish; the floating currencies of the last few years have meant that when the Gross Domestic Product (GDP) of a country is converted to dollars its value can easily appear to increase or decrease by 10, 20, or even 50 percent, simply because of changes in the exchange rate. To avoid some of these problems, the forecasts in table 5.2 have been computed in terms of indexed growth from a common base year.

Although the theory and methodology underlying economic forecasts will be discussed below, it should be noted here that the forecasts of table 5.2 are largely extrapolative in nature. Although each comes from a fairly

TABLE 5.2. *Forecasts of Global Gross Domestic Product (in Trillions of Dollars)*

Source	Base Year	Base Year GDP	Forecast for 2000 (in trillion dollars)			Year 2000 as Multiple of 1975		
			High	Medium	Low	High	Medium	Low
Global 2000 (World Bank)	1975	6.0	17.4	14.7	12.4	2.9	2.5	2.1
Interfutures (OECD)	1975	3.8	13.0	11.1	9.0	3.4	2.9	2.4
Future of World Economy (UN)	1970	3.2	—	13.3	—	—	2.7	—

Sources: Council on Environmental Quality, *The Global 2000 Report to the President* (Washington, D.C.: Government Printing Office, 1981); Organization of Economic Cooperation and Development, *Interfutures* (Paris: OECD, 1979); Wassily Leontief et al., *The Future of the World Economy* (New York: Oxford University Press, 1977).

complex computer model of economic growth that can produce growth rate forecasts somewhat higher or lower than those of recent history, the forecasts are strongly influenced by that recent history. In this sense they present analogies to our population forecasts through the end of the century, in which only slow changes in current growth rates were expected. Also, such forecasting methods concentrate explicitly on the long-run trend, ignoring cyclical behavior for the most part.

Note that the forecasts for the year 2000 vary considerably more than did the population forecasts shown in Chapter 4. Few numerical forecasts exist of global GDP beyond 2000. Those few vary dramatically. For instance, most scenarios of the *Limits to Growth* report indicate a collapse of the world industrial production by the year 2100 to levels below those of the 1970s; in no case do their forecasts show sustainable production levels much above those of the 1970s. In contrast, Herman Kahn suggests a gross world product by 2176 of three hundred trillion dollars, give or take a factor of five (Kahn, Brown, and Martel 1976, 7). That would be a global economy about fifty times as large as that of the 1970s. Clearly, such forecasts have moved beyond extrapolation to a point at which world view assumptions become dominant.

Distribution

In turning to a more detailed examination of how economic benefits have been, are, or may in the future be divided, let us separate the issue into two parts: intercountry and intracountry.

Intercountry. Long-term historical examination of the division of world industrial production is very interesting. Europe was obviously the region that first experienced the industrial revolution. In 1820 it is estimated that 96 percent of global industrial production was located on that continent, a full 24 percent in Great Britain alone (Rostow 1978, 52). It should be noted that extensive Third World handicraft industries, many of which were being destroyed at this time by an influx of European goods and European political and economic control, did exist in this period and are not included in the industrial production figures. By 1963 the European figure was 53 percent (5 percent in the United Kingdom), North America accounted for 34 percent, and the other 13 percent was spread around the globe. These historical figures imply that the economic gap between the North and South, which has received so much attention over the last twenty years, has in fact, been slowly closing almost since it originated at the end of the eighteenth century.

One must be very careful, however, with such economic data. Even the concepts by which we organize our thinking about the economy and our data (GDP, investment, and private consumption) are of quite recent origin. Most were developed during the Great Depression period. Simon Kuznets and Colin Clark did preliminary conceptual work in the 1930s; President Roosevelt called for collecting such data in 1945 (Bell 1982, 24). Humanity has counted itself for a much longer time than it has counted its economy. Application of these concepts to global data-gathering efforts is even more recent. Data bases for the Third World countries have been slowly growing in the post–World War II period, and provide only twenty to thirty years of data in most cases.

The relative paucity of high-quality historic economic data constitutes one reason that the political economy perspectives can all draw on historical "data" to support their interpretations. For instance, there are markedly different interpretations of the impact Britain had economically on India (Thorner 1955; Lamb 1955). One view is that Britain mercilessly exploited India and that per capita incomes were lower in 1900 than in 1850. It is pointed out that in 1798/99 the East India Company sold over £3 million of Indian piece goods in Britain, but by 1832 India had become a net importer of textiles and its own industry was in shambles. Among market penetration techniques used by Britain was a set of inland transit duties to which Indian textiles were subject but British products were not.

The extreme opposite view is of Britain as modernizer. It portrays an India before the arrival of the British as impoverished and rent by conflict. The British established order and security, built railways and irrigation systems, and began a modernization process. In between the two views is an argument that the British furthered a lopsided development: ports and railways facilitated the export of raw material and the distribution of British manufactures (and British military control), while much of the Indian economy remained archaic.

Clearly these positions, all accompanied by "evidence," correspond to political economy world views. After a fairly extensive review of conflicting historiography, Macpherson concludes:

> In sum, one cannot give, for the British era, definitive answers to the significant questions, such as the long-run trend of real *per capita* output, the relation between farm output and population growth, the extent of the decay, if any, of the "native arts and crafts," the savings-investment and capital-output ratios, and aggregate time-series of employment, money and real wages. (Macpherson 1972, 133)

One undisputed issue is that the population of India grew considerably in the period.

Figure 5.1 shows the North-South gap for most of the recent period for which we have GNP data. These data reveal that the North-South gap, at least in per capita GNP terms, has not been closing in recent history. In absolute terms this gap has been increasing, from over three thousand

Figure 5.1. *GNP per Capita in Developing and Developed Countries*

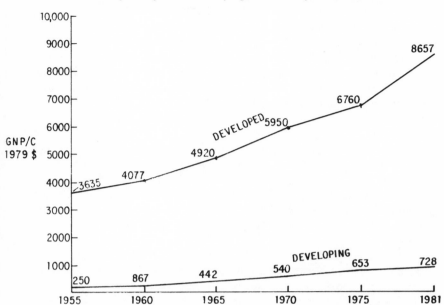

Sources: Ruth L. Sivard, *World Military and Social Expenditures* (Leesburg, Va.: World Priorities, 1982), pp. 27–29; World Bank, *World Development Report* (Washington, D.C.: World Bank, 1982), pp. 110–11.

dollars per capita annually in 1955 to almost eight thousand dollars per capita annually in 1981. In ratio terms, the gap has remained quite stable at between 10–14 to 1.

These figures exaggerate the magnitude of the North-South gap. First, GNP captures only the commercial portion of the economy, omitting entirely the noncommercial economy, especially subsistence farming, which accounts for a larger portion of the economy in LDCs than in MDCs. Second, exchange rates often misrepresent the real purchasing power of income. Real purchasing power can be as much as three times its dollar exchange rate (Kravis, Heston, and Summers 1978, 1). In general, this is a systematic bias that understates the real purchasing power of incomes in LDCs. At the extreme, such factors mean that a typical basket of goods purchased by the poor in Western Europe for one dollar would cost twenty cents in Asia (ILO 1977, 21).

It is also often argued that GNP is not a very good measure of economic well-being. In particular, with affluence income is increasingly spent on luxuries and even on goods and services whose purchase is dictated by employment, not consumer-directed consumption (e.g., commuting expenses, work clothes). Thus, some kind of physical quality of life index has frequently been put forward as an alternative indicator of well-being. Components of such an index are normally measures such as life expectancy, educational access and/or literacy, shelter size per person, and calorie or protein intake. We can examine the North-South gap in terms of such basic human needs. Table 5.3 shows the change from 1960 to 1976 in two such measures for four groupings of countries, and the ratio between the two developed groups and the two developing groups. Clearly, such measures show a closing of the North-South gap—indeed, quite a rapid closing.

None of this suggests that income levels themselves are unimportant. It is, however, difficult to know which measures are most appropriate. Often, in such a case, the measure chosen will be that which reinforces a particular world view. Radicals and internationalists are thus most likely to point to income measures. This is ironic, because it is these same world views that place more emphasis prescriptively on satisfying basic human needs.

Forecasts of the North-South gap on the basis of physical quality of life are rare; most forecasts are economic. Some see a continuation of the present gap or even an increase. In this class is the second report to the Club of Rome, which suggests that without considerable aid increases the economic gap between developed countries and Latin America will increase from five to one up to eight to one by 2025 (Mesarovic and Pestel 1974, 59). More commonly forecasts anticipate a slowly decreasing gap. Table 5.4 shows the initial gaps and computed gaps from the three forecasting groups introduced earlier. Table 5.5 shows the percentages of the world economy falling into regional groupings as computed initially and in the year 2000, according to the same three studies.

TABLE 5.3. *North-South Gap in Literacy and Life Expectancy*

	Adult Literacy Rate (percentage of adult population)		Life Expectancy	
	1960	1977	1960	1977
Low-income countries	28	54	42	57
Middle-income countries	53	65	53	60
Industrial market economies	97	99	70	74
Non-market industrial economies	97	100	68	71
Ratio of rate in industrial economies to rate in all other countries	2.40	1.67	1.45	1.24

Source: World Bank, *World Development Report 1982* (Washington, D.C.: World Bank, 1982), 110–11.

TABLE 5.4.   *Estimates and Forecasts of Ratio of North to South per Capita GDP*

| Source | 1970–75 | Forecasts for the Year 2000 | | |
		High	Medium	Low
Global 2000	11.3	11.8	12.3	12.1
Interfutures	10.5	9.3	8.2	7.4
Future of World Economy	12.2	—	7.5	—

Sources: Council on Environmental Quality, *The Global 2000 Report to the President* (Washington, D.C.: Government Printing Office, 1981); Organization of Economic Cooperation and Development, *Interfutures* (Paris: OECD, 1979); Wassily Leontief et al., *The Future of the World Economy* (New York: Oxford University Press, 1977).

Intracountry.   The issue of income distribution and potential changes in the distribution within countries has long been at or near the center of most domestic political controversies. In periods of considerable growth in average income the redistribution issue receives less attention because incomes of the poor also grow, at least in the absence of highly unfavorable redistributions of income toward the wealthy. (The issue also disappears in societies that have experienced no growth over long periods of time and in which social structures have evolved justifying and enforcing distribution patterns.)

Growth in average incomes as well as those of the poor has characterized most of the world for the post–World War II period; the more

TABLE 5.5.   *Historical and Projected Shares of Global GDP*

Source	1970–75 (in percentages)	2000 (in percentages)
Global 2000		
Developed Market	63	61
Developed Centrally Planned	17	14
Developing Market	15	20
Developing Centrally Planned	5	5
Interfutures		
Developed Market	62	50
Developed Centrally Planned	16	18
Developing Market	15	24
Developing Centrally Planned	6	8
Future of the World Economy		
Developed Market	63	44
Developed Centrally Planned	19	20
Developing Market	13	29
Developing Centrally Planned	4	6

Sources: Council on Environmental Quality, *The Global 2000 Report to the President* (Washington, D.C.: Government Printing Office, 1981); Organization of Economic Cooperation and Development, *Interfutures* (Paris: OECD, 1979); Wassily Leontief et al., *The Future of the World Economy* (New York: Oxford University Press, 1977).

developed countries have witnessed such a pattern for a considerably longer period. If, however, the forecasts of slower average economic growth in the future are correct—and even a neoclassical-modernist like Herman Kahn foresees an eventual stabilization in economic output—then the redistribution issue can be expected to reemerge. If growth falters while much of the Third World remains in absolute poverty (inadequate food and shelter, illiteracy), then the issue can be expected to reemerge with a vengeance, both domestically and internationally.

I shall address this issue at greater length in the theory/models section. There is relatively little we can say about trends in intracountry economic distribution, because patterns change slowly and because data are exceptionally poor. For many countries, and for most in the Third World, we have only one or two measurements of income distribution, not the multiple and consistent measurements we would need across time to describe trends (see, for example, Adelman and Morris [1973]; Paukert [1973]; Jain [1975]; Ahluwalia [1976]; Cromwell [1977]).

Overall, the pattern of income distribution in the more developed countries has been moving in the last fifty years toward greater equality. Although this appears to some degree in basic earned income, greater equality is evident in income figures which include governmental transfer payments, that is, supplements to the income of the poor (for the United States, see U.S. Department of Commerce 1977). This phenomenon can be traced to the growing social welfare role of governments throughout the developed world, a trend which may also be peaking.

In LDCs the trend has generally been in the opposite direction, at least for the last twenty years, a period over which we have some data. According to one study, in 1960 the poorest 40 percent of the population in LDCs received an average of 11.9 percent of the income in their countries. By 1975 this had fallen to 9.8 percent, and that study projects the figure to fall to about 6 percent by 2000 (Ahluwalia, Carter, and Chenery 1979, 27). This should not be interpreted to mean that the poor in these countries are becoming absolutely poorer. Average incomes in the LDCs have grown rapidly enough that even with a lowered share in the total, the poorest 40 percent have often had stable or steadily increasing incomes.

Linkages to Other Issues

The issue of income distribution within countries and attempts to interpret the meager data we have on changes over time have been highly charged ones emotionally for scholars because of the direct linkage to political economy issues. It is important to distinguish between factors that influence economic growth and distributional patterns ("backward" linkages) and aspects of the global development system that are affected by economics ("forward" linkages). Although this chapter focuses on the "backward" linkages, leaving "forward" linkages for other chapters, I want here at least to list some of the key issues with respect to economic impacts on other aspects of the global development system. Here too, we can create two lists, however controversial, of impacts. The "positive" list can be culled from the thinking primarily of modernists and the "negative" list from neotraditionalists.

Modernists would point to growth in life expectancies, relative abundance of food supply, economic ability to address environmental issues and allocate resources to them, and even the growth of our ability to find and extract raw materials as historical concomitants of economic growth, and probable future benefits as well. Growth has also often defused the potentially extremely divisive distributional issue, as noted earlier.

Neotraditionalists would put forward a similar list of issues adversely affected by continued economic growth. They would note pressure on limited, nonrenewable resources and upon ecosystems, damage to which could in fact halt or reverse growth and actually threaten human existence. Economic cycles may have their own environmental costs. For instance, the depression in global agriculture of the 1920s and 1930s, brought on in part by large production surpluses, led farmers to try to plant their way to higher incomes and helped create the Dust Bowl problems of the 1930s. Farmers have subjected some high plains prairie soils to the plow in the last several years for similar reasons and loss of land to wind has increased considerably (*Forbes,* Aug. 30, 1982, 109–14). We can see in both perspectives the internally reinforcing statements of causality (some would say circular argumentation) which I outlined before and which tend to push forecasters to the extremes of two "stability regions"—the everything-will-be-good Utopia and the everything-will-be-bad doomsday.

Going beyond this brief recapitulation of world view thinking, some interesting issues have been raised with respect to the impact of continued economic growth on larger social systems. Contrast, for instance, the notions of Schumacher (1973) and Toffler (1980). Schumacher's popular argument in *Small Is Beautiful* represents the older theme that modern industrial production processes have alienated human beings from their work. Because of the division of production into highly routinized, simple, and repetitive tasks on assembly lines, and the reliance on strictly hierarchical structures to direct that work (also in nonfactory environments), people now work to live instead of living to work. Schumacher reminds us, in writing of Buddhist and Christian economics, of the important role that labor can and should serve in our daily lives and our spiritual or intellectual self-fulfillment. His forecast is essentially for continued alienation from labor unless our values reshape production patterns.

In contrast, Toffler sees in *The Third Wave* a reemergence in modern postindustrial societies of linkages between production and consumption

which he argues were lost in the industrial era (second wave). Toffler
foresees with continued economic growth the emergence of a "prosumer"
(one who produces for his own consumption). The prosumer economy can
be seen in the growth of do-it-yourself home and auto repair, the spread of
small machinery (robots) into the home workshop and kitchen, and the
increasing share of leisure (often prosuming activities) relative to paid
labor. Toffler even relates the trend to the reports of declining rates in
productivity gains. His argument is that productivity measures only traditional paid labor, where production is not for one's own use, and does not
capture the tremendous growth in production on one's own time for one's
own consumption. Toffler portrays prosumer activities as much more fulfilling and meaningful than the production work of the second wave.

Another important issue with respect to the relationship between economic growth and social organization has been raised by Hirsch (1976). In
the introduction to *Social Limits to Growth* Hirsch poses three questions
that frame his inquiry:

> 1. Why has economic advance become and remained so compelling a
> goal to all of us as individuals, even though it yields disappointing fruits
> when most, if not all of us, achieve it?
> 2. Why has modern society become so concerned with distribution—
> with division of the pie—when it is clear that the great majority of
> people can raise their living standards only through production of a larger
> pie?
> 3. Why has the twentieth century seen a universal predominant trend
> toward collective provision and state regulation in economic areas at a
> time when individual freedom of action is especially extolled and is given
> unprecedented rein in noneconomic areas such as aesthetic and sexual
> standards? (Hirsch 1976, 1)

Hirsch argues that the three questions are interrelated. Among the most
important elements of his attempt to answer them is a division in the nature
of goods into "material" and "positional." Extending Hirsch's argument,
one could define material goods as those that help satisfy needs at the lower
end of Maslow's need hierarchy (food, shelter, clothing), whereas positional goods address higher-level needs, especially self-esteem (a larger
house than others have, lakefront property, a Rembrandt painting, an
oriental carpet). Many goods are valued at least in part because they can
never be possessed by everyone. Hence, economic growth does not bring
satisfaction—those at higher levels will always set standards of consumption unattainable by others, no matter how much their absolute incomes
increase. Similarly, the highest educational degrees or corporate titles
become status symbols that are inherently scarce—if more people obtain
any one college degree, a more advanced one replaces it in defining quali-
fications needed; if more corporate vice-presidential positions are created,

they become less important in the hierarchy and begin to be differentiated as assistant, associate, and senior.

The issues raised by Hirsch in a fresh and evocative manner are not new. It takes little imagination to see the linkages to major world views, especially the neotraditionalist emphasis on value change. For instance, individuals who value ''self-actualization'' or the development of their own potential (as opposed to defining one's worth in relation to others) need not continue the fruitless struggle for positional goods.

FORECASTING: THEORIES AND MODELS

Economic forecasting need not be numerical. R. Buckminster Fuller is making a forecast which pretty clearly identifies his world view when he says that ''cosmic evolution is also irrevocably intent upon making omni-integrated humanity omnisuccessful, able to live sustainingly at an unprecedentedly higher standard of living for all Earthians than has ever been experienced by any'' (Fuller 1981, xvii). Nor are the qualitative arguments that underlie such a prognostication necessarily any less sound than the equations underlying a numerical forecast. Too often, however, nonquantitative forecasts are simply assertions of belief, conditioned by world views and unsupported by serious thought.

Simple Growth Models

I focus here initially upon the more quantitative approaches. Simplest among these are extrapolation and curve fitting. Extrapolation is the extension into the future of the past and in economics is likely to be exponential rather than linear. Parallel to the simple growth model of the last chapter for population, we can formulate one for gross domestic product (Y), based on a given, historically based, growth rate (YR):

$$Y_t = Y_{t=0}(1 + YR)^t.$$

Extrapolative techniques in economics have an inherent modernist bias, since they explicitly assume that no changes will occur which will affect the growth rate. Interestingly, this is in sharp contrast to extrapolation in population, which tends to reinforce neotraditionalist arguments (e.g., as used by Malthus; see also figure 4.1). The modernist bias of the techniques in economic forecasting can be illustrated by the Leontief study for the United Nations (1977). Leontief began with targets for economic growth in both LDCs and MDCs which would help narrow the gap between North and South. Using those targets he extrapolated growth and computed the requirements for it. Although he concluded that the computed requirements were not difficult to obtain, many other observers would disagree. For instance, he computed that global oil consumption would increase to 5.2

FIGURE 5.2.   *Gross World Product per Capita, 1776–2176*

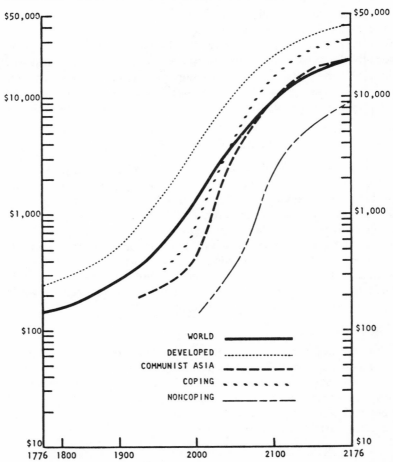

Source: Herman Kahn, William Brown, and Leon Martel, *The Next 200 Years* (New York: William Morrow, 1976), 56. Copyright © 1976 by Hudson Institute. By permission of William Morrow and Company.

times the 1970 level by 2000—much more than energy experts generally say is possible.

Curve-fitting techniques aim to find standard patterns in past behavior of an indicator (e.g., GDP) and then use those patterns to project the future. The Kondratieff long wave is one such pattern, and those using it now generally do so, as Forrester has, to reinforce the neotraditionalist argument that economic decline or collapse is quite possible. Another standard pattern is the logistic curve, or S shaped curve. This was applied to future economic growth by both Mesarovic and Pestel (1974) and Kahn, Brown, and Martel (1976) to suggest the natural leveling off of economic growth over time (figure 5.2).

Production Function Models

More frequently forecasts are produced by equations that relate one or more factors to economic production growth. The simplest of these production functions is that of Harrod-Domar. Gross Domestic Product (Y) is simply the capital stock (K) divided by a capital-to-output ratio (Q):

$$Y = K/Q.$$

This equation says that it takes a certain number of dollars of capital (machinery, factories, or office buildings) to produce one dollar of output per year. The number of dollars of capital required is the capital-to-output ratio. Given that ratio and the amount of capital available, we can compute the output level.

This production function can be developed into a dynamic model of economic growth fairly easily. Specifically, a certain fraction (k) of GDP (Y) is set aside for investment (I) in new capital:

$$I = kY.$$

The rest of GDP goes toward private consumption or is spent by the government. When investment is added to capital and depreciation (D) is subtracted, we obtain an estimate of capital in the next time period ($t + 1$):

$$K_{t+1} = K + I - D.$$

This equation provides the basis for calculating GDP (Y) in the next time period and keeping the model going across time.

We can also compute GDP per capita (YPC) if we know population (POP):

$$YPC = Y/\text{POP}.$$

This model and variations of it are widely used in economic forecasting and planning around the world. Among the refinements possible is to distinguish between domestically generated investment (savings) and that which comes from abroad (e.g., from multinational corporations). Total domestic and foreign investment availability is a major constraint on growth. Even when total investment levels are adequate, the exports and other sources of foreign exchange earnings for a country may be too low to pay for imports of the inputs, technology, or investment goods (e.g., machinery) needed to run the economy at levels that it otherwise could attain. These two possible constraints on growth, investment levels and foreign exchange, have given rise to a whole category of models called "two-gap" models (see, for example, Chenery [1971]). Internationalists rely heavily on them in their arguments in support of more foreign aid and technical assistance, trade preferences, and other elements of a new international economic order.

The *Limits to Growth* model used a variation of the Harrod-Domar model. It has been widely criticized for doing so by modernists, both classical liberal (e.g., Simon [1981]) and radical (e.g., Herrera et al. [1976]). The thrust of their criticism has been that the model ignores the contribution of labor to production. Notice that if we increase population in the above equations it will have no effect on GDP (Y), but will reduce GDP per capita (*YPC*) proportionately. This is, of course, consistent with the neotraditionalist view that we must concentrate on stopping population growth.

Nevertheless, there is much evidence that growth in labor supply, and especially, improvements in its quality, do contribute to advances in output (Denison 1974). This evidence has been codified in an alternative production function developed by Cobb and Douglas in 1928. The Cobb-Douglas function includes employed labor (L) as a factor of production along with capital (K),

$$Y = aK^{\alpha}L^{\beta}$$

where a is a scaling factor and α and β are parameters. Placed into the dynamic growth model provided above, this equation can lead to an increase in GDP per capita (*YPC*) when population and thus labor are increased. Not surprisingly, the equation has found favor with modernists. Neotraditionalists can still defend their nonuse of it, however, by pointing out that especially in the Third World, where unemployment and significant underemployment of the potential labor force has been estimated at 40 percent (ILO 1977, 18), increments in population do not correspond directly to increases in employed labor force, as is often assumed in the modernist models.

Capital and labor are not the only factors of production which can be put into production functions and economic forecasting models. Among those which have received the most attention are energy (E) and other raw materials (M). A class of models called KLEM models with all four inputs—capital, labor, energy, and raw materials—has been developed, but used only for national studies (Hudson and Jorgenson 1974). The *Limits to Growth* model, and that of the second report to the Club of Rome both used other equations to introduce the impact of growing scarcity or shortage of energy and raw materials on economic production. No such equations were present in either the UN or Bariloche models, both of which are modernist in orientation.

The suggestion here that Cobb-Douglas (capital and labor) models support modernists forecasting economic growth and that Harrod-Domar (capital only) models support neotraditionalists should be tempered. Although such an inference is true for LDCs with rapid population growth, it is not true for MDCs with slowing rates of population growth. In fact, the use of Cobb-Douglas for MDCs most often leads to forecasts of slowing growth, as the countries reach population and labor force stability.

The fact remains, however, that detailed analyses have shown that even growth in capital and labor together only explain roughly half of economic growth in industrial countries. The other half must be attributed to growth in the quality of both workers (education) and capital (technology). These factors explicitly enter practically none of the forecasting models.

The Role of Technology

A major reason why technology is absent from most quantitative models is that no index of technology exists. Various techniques for representing technology in the measurement of capital or labor have been developed but none has been used in global forecasts. Modernists, such as Herman Kahn or Buckminster Fuller, would argue that this is a critical omission and constitutes a major reason for their rejecting the quantitative forecasting methodologies. How can one introduce materials or energy as potential constraints and then leave out technology which can help us overcome such constraints? The neotraditionalist authors of the *Limits to Growth* say they deal with this by multiplying estimates of resource availability by a factor of five in some scenarios or by assuming more efficient pollution control in others. The modernist authors of the Bariloche Foundation report go considerably further. They introduce a continuing growth in economic output of about 1 percent per year, independently of the growth in capital or labor—growth which they attribute to anticipated technological advance. The technology issue is a difficult one and I devote a later chapter to it.

Global Debt and Economic Forecasts

It should be obvious by now that world view often shapes the choice of production function used. This has also been true with respect to treatment of another key factor influencing debates over economic futures, LDC debt levels. Many observers have expressed great concern over the buildup of LDC debt, especially since oil prices increased in the 1970s. Overall for non-oil exporting LDCs, that debt has grown from $97 billion in 1973 to $664 billion in 1983 (IMF 1983). Until recently, the growth of debt continued to accelerate. In 1973 the balance of trade deficit (a major debt contributor) in non-oil developing countries was $11 billion. In 1981 it reached $108 billion and in 1983 it was still $68 billion. If we were to use the two-gap model favored by the internationalists and discussed above, such a debt level would imply increasing probabilities of slowed LDC

growth as needed imports become unaffordable. Such debt-based constraint on growth was introduced in the neotraditionalist Mesarovic-Pestel
model but not in most scenarios of the modernist Leontief model.

The debt issue is exceedingly complex, particularly because of the fact
that economic models are not up to the task of forecasting structural
changes in trade patterns between countries. This has been an important
critique by radicals of all such models, because the radicals argue that the

FIGURE 5.3.   *Terms of Trade, 1954–1975*

Note: The World Bank primary commodity terms of trade index is based on unit values of
developing countries' exports of 34 primary commodities, excluding petroleum. The index is
weighted by 1967–69 values of these exports and is deflated by the World Bank's index of
prices of manufactured goods in world trade. In 1967–69, the total export value of these 34
commodities from developing countries represented approximately 60% of their total exports,
excluding petroleum.

developed countries control prices of traded goods to their benefit. Thus, the terms of trade for LDCs are moving against them, something not captured by these economic models.

That is an argument which is difficult to assess; however, the data in figure 5.3 support it. Over the 1954–75 period the terms of trade for non-oil LDCs deteriorated quite steadily, interrupted only in the early 1970s, when raw materials prices temporarily surged. These data have two weaknesses, however. First, the choice of 1954 as the initial year is questionable because at the end of the Korean War global raw materials prices were at unusually high levels. Second, figure 5.3 excludes petroleum. Petroleum prices are much higher now than in 1970, and at least until 1973 we considered OPEC countries to be in the LDC category. An alternative image of terms of trade is shown in figure 5.4. With a different base year and the inclusion of petroleum it appears that in the late 1970s the terms of trade shifted quite significantly in favor of the LDCs. Those of us who do not want to spend our lives creating such indices are dependent on those who do, and it clearly is not an easy task. Nor is it free of world view bias.

Distribution

The terms of trade frame the methodological debate on intercountry inequality. There is a related research-based debate over the claims made in slightly different forms by both classical liberals and radicals against internationalists—that foreign assistance is at best neutral and probably harmful to recipients—and the claim of radicals against classical liberals and internationalists—that trade relations with MDCs often retard LDC growth. The results of the empirical research are as yet neither conclusive nor convincing (see, for example, Dolan and Tomlin [1980]).

With respect to domestic distributional issues, the thinking of classical liberal and internationalist economists has been heavily influenced for about twenty years by the notion of the Kuznets curve (Kuznets 1963). The Kuznets argument is that in the early stages of development only a few sectors and a few individuals are brought into the modern economy and receive the economic benefits of it. Thus, their incomes outstrip those of their fellows and overall income inequality increases. After a time, however, growth spreads through the economy and eventually nearly everyone benefits from modernization. Thus, income distribution begins to become more equal, albeit slowly. This U-shaped pattern has been corroborated by many studies, including a recent one by the World Bank (*World Development Report 1980*).

It has, however, been suggested that this pattern is an artifact of the cross-sectional (many countries, one point in time) approach to analyzing it. It is impossible to look at one developing country over a wide range of incomes (longitudinally) because we have few measurements of income

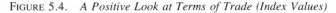

FIGURE 5.4.   *A Positive Look at Terms of Trade (Index Values)*

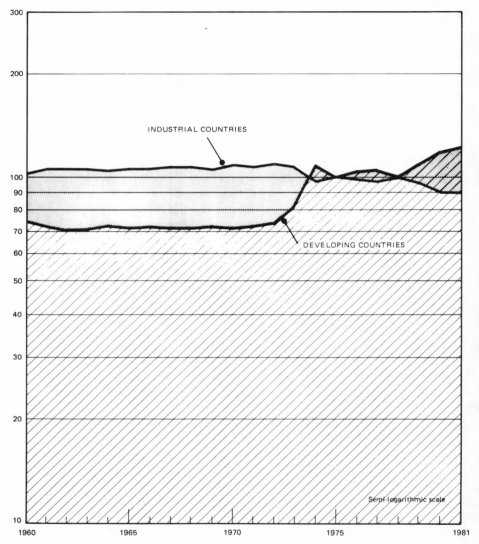

Source: World Bank, *Commodity Trade and Price Trends* (Washington, D.C.: World Bank, 1981), 9. Reprinted with permission.

distribution for single countries. One study, however, looked at seven countries with incomes below three hundred dollars per capita and which thus should be experiencing increasing inequality with growth according to the Kuznets curve (Loehr and Powelson 1981, 134–35). There were two separate measurements of inequality for each of these countries, and the authors found that in only one country was inequality actually increasing.

This study would also seem to contradict the radical argument that the Third World is locked into a pattern of intercountry inferiority and high intracountry inequality. Again, however, reader beware: data are poor, and conclusions based on them are tentative.

Structural Change

Discussion of economic development forecasting would not be complete without a consideration of structural change. It is fairly widely accepted that at least two important structural changes are occurring in the global economy: a shift of the economies in the economically most advanced countries toward services (and reductions in primary and manufactured good shares) and an emergence of considerable industrial capacity in a set of countries known as the Newly Industrialized Countries (NICs). It is reasonable to posit a relationship between the two trends.

The increased dominance of the service sector within what may now erroneously be called industrial countries (the United States, Western Europe, Japan, and a few others) has been noted for many years. Daniel Bell (1973) drew attention to it in terms of the emergence of postindustrial society. Alvin Toffler (1980) labeled it *The Third Wave*, in contrast to the first (agricultural) and second (industrial) revolutions. It has been estimated that the United States has had a chiefly services economy since 1950, and that in 1982 services generated 67 percent of the GDP (*Forbes,* April 11, 1983, 143). In spite of political rhetoric, this has not meant deindustrialization, any more than industrialization led to the dismantling of agricultural capacity. It has meant relatively slower growth in industrial production and will lead to some declines in industrial capacity for import-vulnerable industries.

Most scholars (e.g., Kahn, Brown, and Martel [1976]; Naisbitt [1982]) have focused on the importance of information handling within the modern services sector. According to one calculation, nearly half of the U.S. work force now falls into the information sector (Hamrin 1980, 19). Perhaps the most imaginative and insightful look at the information sector was that by Peter Drucker (1969). Drucker makes an analogy between the information industry and the electrical industry. The first practical electrical generator was invented in 1856. It was refined significantly, and practically all contemporary electric-apparatus companies were formed by 1879. In that year, Thomas Edison designed the electric light bulb and made possible the modern electric industry. Analogously, the computer has been available since the late 1940s and refined significantly, while major computer manufacturers have grown. Drucker said in 1969, however, that the key information systems necessary for delivering knowledge cheaply and universally to users did not yet exist. Perhaps just in the last decade, with the explosion and rapid change in personal computers, communications systems, and data banks, have we really begun to develop an information industry. Drucker feels that the information revolution yet to come will be as major a discontinuity as the industrial revolution.

The second and related major structural change is that the NICs, and to a lesser degree other LDCs, have experienced relative growth in their manufacturing sectors. Moreover, LDCs have expanded their share of global manufacturing value added from about 10 percent in the early 1960s to over 14 percent by the end of the 1970s. In the same period, the LDC share of world trade in manufactures rose from 4 percent to 9 percent (Beenstock 1983, 111). Interestingly, this increased global role of the LDCs in manufacturing is especially noticeable since the mid-1960s.

There is no room for doubt about the interrelationship of the two structural trends. North American steel capacity declined from 156 million metric tons in 1974 to 152 million metric tons in 1980; forecasts for 1990 are near 140 million tons (*Forbes,* Nov. 7, 1983, 99). At the same time, capacity in major NICs went from 33 to 60 million tons and will possibly rise to 112 million tons by 1990. And Americans should not believe that somehow they have borne the brunt of the adjustment process. In West Germany, employment in the steel industry dropped from 352,000 in 1970 to 237,000 in 1983 (*Berliner Morgenpost,* Dec. 4, 1983, 39).

Interpretations of these developments obviously vary with political economy perspective. Classical liberals tend to see a natural progression in the development. Beenstock points out that in the last half of the nineteenth century, Great Britain, then the dominant economic power, experienced declining rates of profit, slower growth in domestic investment (and greater outflows of investment), and slower growth rates, as industrial capacity rose in other Western European economies and the United States. Profits as a share of GDP in OECD countries have fallen since 1955, but at faster rates since 1967. Although some might attribute that fall in profits to the beginning of the downturn of the Kondratieff cycle, Beenstock rejects the cycle theory. He argues that economic dynamism has shifted again, at the expense of the MDCs. In fact, problems of richer countries in the 1970s are only partly attributable to energy problems, and primarily a result of the major economic structural transition that picked up speed in the late 1960s.

Radicals more often portray the same phenomenon as not a challenge by LDCs of MDCs in industry, but as a relative abandonment by MDCs of heavy industry (with its pollution and intensity of energy and materials) as they move toward more dynamic and eventually more profitable service and information sectors. It is not altogether clear whether this is to the benefit of some LDCs. The extensive automation and robotization of manufacturing may make it a sector with low employment prospects, thereby failing to meet the employment needs of the LDCs. Thus, large amounts of capital may be being used for the employment and profit benefit of a very small elite in several LDCs, reinforcing the structural problems which have long been associated with the dependence of those countries on the MDCs. Moreover, the debt levels of LDCs—to a considerable degree accumulated in the process of industrializing (and highly concentrated in the NICs)— may lead to a real loss of economic momentum in those countries, as MDCs place pressure for stabilization of or repayment of the debt.

Modernists, like Drucker or Toffler, look at the structural changes from the viewpoint of the First World countries, at the leading edge of technological change. Implications for Third World countries are much less often considered, and generally argued to be beneficial. Neotraditionalists devote surprisingly little attention at all to the structural patterns.

Forecasted economic futures vary from affluence for the entire world, to continued poverty in the LDCs, to collapse of the global economy. Whether one interprets the global economic downturn in the 1970s as a temporary result of energy shocks and some structural changes, as a long-term decline within the Kondratieff cycle, or as an indicator of our hitting ultimate limits, depends a great deal on one's world view.

World views generally shape the theories or models one selects for forecasting. This came through strongly in our review of production functions and decisions by various scholars to include or exclude labor, energy, materials, and technology. It appears in approaches on distributional issues and in perspectives on global debt. World views even stamp the "data" (e.g., terms of trade or North-South gap indicator) one relies upon.

6. Energy

In essence this is a chapter on raw materials, not simply energy. Procedures for forecasting demand and supply of energy and metals, for example, are largely identical. More importantly energy has often been called the "master resource." That is, given adequate and inexpensive energy it is always possible to assure supplies of other resources—at the extreme, all minerals exist in very diluted form in seawater, and could be extracted given sufficient energy. Conversely, given inadequate or very expensive energy, current methods of raw material extraction may become uneconomical, effectively rendering other materials unavailable. Forecasts of non-energy raw material supply and demand may be even more complicated than forecasts for energy because of the multitude of different materials and because of the complex substitutions possible among them. For all these reasons, I focus here on energy as a surrogate for raw materials generally.

Although most of the issues addressed in this volume have attracted not only expert but also general public attention for some time, it is interesting to note that energy has not historically received the same attention. Prior to 1970 one could read regularly about the population boom and global food problems, or about the North-South gap, or about environmental issues—but not about energy availability. Now, many feel that energy availability constitutes the central issue and the volume of studies and pronouncements has become almost tiring. The perception of energy's importance is the culmination of attitudinal change throughout the 1970s, which seemed slow at the time, but in retrospect looks quite rapid. The first "oil shock" occurred in 1973–74, when the limited embargo by Arab oil producers following the October 1973, Arab-Israeli War was accompanied by gasoline shortages and dramatically higher oil prices. The "energy crisis" was generally seen, however, as transitory and a result of OPEC and oil company market manipulation. At the governmental level (national and international) much debate centered on establishing a floor price for oil at $7.00 per barrel (it had quadrupled to $11.50) so that energy producers would increase supplies and undercut OPEC without fear that their investments would be lost in a dramatic price collapse.

Real prices did erode somewhat in the mid 1970s, although they hardly collapsed. In December 1978, the second "oil shock" began when Iranian oil exports stopped for almost seventy days as a result of the revolution against the Shah. They resumed at lower levels than before. During 1979–80 oil prices again more than doubled, to above $30 per barrel. Public opinion polls traced a very slow change in public attitudes. By the beginning of the 1980s widespread belief in oil company manipulation had begun to coexist with belief in a long-term fundamental energy problem or crisis.

BACKGROUND: HISTORY AND FORECASTS

I look here at the background of the energy issue from three perspectives: totals and rates of growth in global demand and supply; distributional aspects; and linkages to other issues.

Rates and Totals

Global energy demand has grown dramatically in the last fifty years, at rates generally exceeding even those of economic growth. Table 6.1 re-

TABLE 6.1. *Global Energy Demand, 1925–1981*

Year	Energy Consumption (in 10^{15} Btus)	Annual Growth Rate (in percentages)
1925	48.8	—
1950	85.8	2.3
1955	110.4	5.1
1960	137.9	4.5
1965	179.9	5.5
1970	211.8	3.3
1973	244.4	4.9
1974	245.5	0.4
1975	244.7	−0.3
1976	260.6	6.5
1977	268.4	3.0
1978	275.0	2.4
1979	281.4	2.3
1980	281.5	0.0
1981	279.1	−0.9

Sources: 1925–65 values from Joel Darmstadter et al., *Energy in the World Economy* (Baltimore: Johns Hopkins Press, 1971), 10; 1970–81 values from United Nations, *Yearbook of World Energy Statistics* (New York: UN, 1979 and 1981), 3.

veals the pattern preceding the "energy crisis" of the 1970s. It also shows the drops in energy demand growth following the two oil shocks. From 1973 through 1981 global energy demand grew at only 1.6 percent per year, compared to earlier rates near 5 percent.

Forecasts of energy supply and demand have had an amazingly poor historical record. Reasons for this—among them the necessity of reliance on inherently unreliable geological estimates and the important role of political decisions—will become clearer as I discuss theories and models. Examples of incorrect forecasts are easy to find: in 1891 the U.S. Geological Survey declared that there was little or no chance of finding oil in Kansas or Texas; in 1939 the Interior Department announced that U.S. oil supplies would only last thirteen years (Kahn, Brown, and Martel 1976, 94–95).

As poor as such forecasts were they hardly compare with those made in the late 1960s or early 1970s. In most cases the problem was, as usual, heavy reliance upon extrapolations. For instance, in the 1950s and early 1960s the future of nuclear power looked so bright that it was being said that electricity would become too cheap to meter—people would simply be charged a fixed monthly rate. The Atomic Energy Agency projected installed nuclear capacity in the United States alone of two thousand gigawatts (thousand megawatts) by the year 2000. One seldom now sees estimates over three hundred to four hundred gigawatts. Not only was nuclear production growing rapidly before 1970, real oil prices were moving down steadily. This prompted Adelman, a widely respected expert on the world oil market, to write in 1972 that

> the high reference prices and continued heavy investment in oil and gas exploration and development, and in nuclear power, mean an ever greater potential supply pressing against limited outlets. The only means of lasting oil price stability is by international agreement, whereby the inevitable long decline in prices might be spread out over a generation. Of course, even the agreement must gradually buckle and fail as companies and governments evade it, find loopholes, chisel and cheat. (Adelman 1972, 262)

Perceptions of the inability of OPEC to maintain the major increases in oil prices which followed Adelman's forecast were widespread, especially among classical liberals, who viewed OPEC as a transient aberration in the world market. Typical is the forecast of Kahn, Brown, and Martel in 1976: "It doesn't seem likely that oil prices will stay very high for more than 5 or 10 years, and possibly much less. They might easily return to something like $3–7 in the Persian Gulf long before the new coal infrastructure has been amortized [fifteen to twenty years]" (Kahn, Brown, and Martel 1976, 60). Naturally the jury on this forecast is not quite in, but the forecast appears increasingly far off the mark.

In the mid-1970s a different type of forecast became common. Many studies began to accept not only the probability of continued high or even increasing oil prices, but of growing global shortages before the end of the century. Such forecasts did not come from classical liberals—who argued that, except for short-term supply interruptions, like the 1973–74 and 1979–80 oil shocks, the notion of shortages makes no sense—but rather from neotraditionalists and governmental study groups.

Among the studies foreseeing probable shortages or considerably higher prices was that of the Workshop on Alternative Energy Strategies (WAES), under the direction of Carroll Wilson, a former head of the Atomic Energy Commission and a member of the Club of Rome (Wilson 1977). The Workshop foresaw a significant tightening of the world energy market in the late 1980s. Perhaps the most famous shortage forecast came from the CIA, which based its projection in part on the likelihood of the USSR becoming a net oil importer by 1985 (CIA 1977). The CIA argued that by 1985 projected global supply of energy would fall noticeably below projected demand. By 1981 the Department of Energy projected world oil prices in the year 2000 at between $50 and $95 per barrel in real 1981 dollars, compared to $37 in 1981 (U.S. DOE 1981, 1–3).

By the early 1980s, it was possible for Griffin and Teece to conclude that ''the new orthodoxy of the early 1980s is that [oil] prices will continue to rise at a rate 3 to 4 percent faster than the rate of inflation, once the temporary glut evaporates. This view has become embedded in government policy and in the planning assumptions of the major petroleum companies'' (1982, 2). In other words, whereas extrapolation of the experience of the 1950s and 1960s had led to widespread expectations of continually decreasing prices, extrapolation of the 1970s eventually led to similarly widely held expectations of increasing prices.

Among the many factors complicating forecasts in the 1970s and early 1980s (such as political and geological uncertainty) has been our ignorance of how energy consumers and producers would respond to higher energy prices. Because energy prices for the twenty years prior to 1970 had been fairly stable, with a slight downward trend, there was no empirical basis for estimating the impact on consumers or producers of the much increased oil prices after 1973. Some initial studies after the first oil shock argued that the United States could be exporting oil by 1985 as a result of the higher oil prices, and the national goal of Project Independence (zero imports by 1984) reflected such belief. Some oil companies promised that if ''unleashed'' from oil prices controlled below the world market level, they could make the United States independent of foreign oil within a very short time.

Whereas over the last decade the ability of higher prices to produce greater energy supplies has increasingly been downplayed, the impact of prices on demand has come gradually to be seen as much greater than once thought. This phenomenon appears clearly in the annual periodic projections released by Exxon. In 1973 the forecast of (non-Communist) global energy demand made by Exxon for 1985 was slightly over 160 million barrels per day of oil equivalent (Exxon 1977, 9). By 1977, the company did not believe global demand would reach that level before 1990 (the 1985 demand projection was about one hundred thirty million barrels). The company's 1980 forecast for demand in the year 2000 was under 160 million barrels per day (Exxon 1980, 9), lower than their earlier forecast for 1985. The company's 1980 projections for the contributions of various energy types to this demand can be seen in table 6.2. The Council on Environmental Quality has even more recently suggested that the United States could maintain historical economic growth rates with no growth in energy demand through 2000.

In light of past experience, an intelligent consumer of energy forecasts will be forgiven a skeptical approach to all forecasts. More recent forecasts and projections do, however, reflect an increasing understanding of the overall energy system. And although I have cited a number of poor and incorrect forecasts in this and other chapters, some forecasts have proved considerably more accurate. For instance, in the late 1950s, M. King Hubbert predicted that growth in U.S. oil production would cease about 1970 and begin a long, slow decline (Wildavsky and Tenenbaum 1981, 233). Events bore out that prediction almost exactly; U.S. oil production started to decrease in 1970 and has not surpassed the level of that year, in spite of high prices. Hubbert based his forecast on a method using an estimate of total resources ultimately recoverable and a bell-shaped production life-cycle curve. I shall return to the approach later.

TABLE 6.2. *World Energy Supply by Energy Type*

Energy Type	Percentage Contributions to Global Supply			
	1965	1980	1990	2000
Oil	42	47	38	31
Coal	37	26	27	28
Gas	15	19	20	19
Hydroelectric and solar	6	6	7	8
Nuclear	0	2	6	10
Synthetics and very heavy oil	0	0	2	4

Source: Exxon Corporation, *World Energy Outlook* (New York: Exxon Corporation, 1980), 10. Reprinted with permission.
Note: These are the most recent published projections by Exxon, although the rapidity of change in the energy situation subjects them to the same uncertainties as earlier ones.

TABLE 6.3. *Percentage Distribution of Global Energy Consumption, 1950–1981*

Region	1950	1960	1970	1980	1981
North America	50.0	38.9	37.2	30.6	30.5
Western Europe	22.2	19.7	20.1	18.2	17.8
Eastern Europe/USSR	17.5	22.1	22.4	24.6	24.8
Latin America	2.5	3.1	3.7	5.0	5.0
Africa	1.5	1.6	1.5	2.0	2.4
Japan	1.8	2.4	5.0	5.0	5.0
Centrally planned Asia[a]	1.3	8.2	5.3	7.5	7.4
Developing Asia[b]	1.7	2.2	2.6	3.9	3.8
Middle East	0.3	0.7	1.1	1.8	1.7
Oceania	1.0	1.0	1.1	1.2	1.2

Source: United Nations, *Yearbook of World Energy Statistics* (New York: UN, 1980 and 1981).
[a]Centrally planned Asia includes the PRC, Vietnam, Laos, Mongolia.
[b]Developing Asia includes rest of Asia.

Distribution

One fundamentally important characteristic of the modern world energy system is the geographic separation of consumer and producer regions and thus the large energy trading volumes. In table 6.3 we see the distribution of global energy consumption over the last thirty years and in table 6.4 that pattern is projected through the end of the century. Among the other aspects of interest in these two tables is the steadily increasing portion of global energy consumption in the Third World both historically and in the projection. One estimate puts growth of developed country energy demand between now and the end of the century at 50 percent, compared to 200 to 250 percent growth in the LDCs (Sewell et al. 1980, 48). The implications of this, should energy prices remain high or climb higher, are obvious: the Third World will be especially hard hit.

TABLE 6.4. *Forecast of Percentage Distribution of Global Energy Consumption, 1990–2000*

	1965	1980	1990	2000
United States	34	28	23	20
Canada	3	3	3	3
Europe	22	20	18	17
Japan	4	5	5	5
Centrally planned economies	26	30	30	31
Other[a]	11	14	21	24

Source: Exxon Corporation, *World Energy Outlook* (New York: Exxon Corp., 1980), 9. Reprinted with permission.
[a]"Other" consists primarily, but not exclusively, of LDCs.

Production during the oil and gas era has increasingly been in geographical areas other than those of consumption. By 1965 the United States imported 9 percent of its energy consumption, Europe 47 percent and Japan 66 percent. By 1980 the percentages had increased to 22 percent, 52 percent, and 88 percent, respectively. One forecast for the end of the century is for import levels of 11 percent, 43 percent, and 74 percent, respectively, in the three areas (Exxon 1980). OPEC's oil production in 1979 of 32 million barrels per day, most of which is exported, met nearly one-fourth of total global energy demand. Total world trade in energy in 1980 was about one-third of total global production.

Linkages to Other Issues

I want to look briefly here at the forward linkages of energy in the global development system, that is, at the impacts energy has on other elements of it. Other chapters deal with many of these in more depth. I shall return in the next section to backward linkages, or those factors which affect energy demand and supply patterns. Energy is intimately related to many other global issues. In particular, three issue areas should be identified: the economy, the environment, and social/political structures.

Economic Impact.   The reduced growth rate in global energy supplies since 1973 has contributed to the reduction in economic growth discussed in the previous chapter. Whereas world economic growth was 5.7 percent in the 1960s, it fell to under 2 percent in the 1980–82 global recession. Most forecasters now foresee continued slow economic growth throughout the 1980s, at least in part because of lower growth in energy supplies (higher oil prices are essentially equivalent to lower energy supply growth because users can buy less).

This tendency toward forecasting lower economic growth somewhat confuses analysis of the severity of the global energy problem. If we avoid significantly higher energy prices and periodic physical shortages only because of reduced economic growth and therefore reduced energy demand growth, the energy problem should not be judged to have been solved. Unfortunately, most forecasters do not address this issue directly, and knowing how much of even currently slower growth to attribute to energy prices and supply is an unsolved issue. For example, Exxon expects average economic growth in industrial countries of less than 3 percent per year from 1980 to 2000, compared with nearly 5 percent between 1965 and 1973. They attribute this slackening jointly to "slower growth of the labor force, reduced future productivity gains, and rising energy costs," but make no effort even to rank order the factors by importance (Exxon 1980, 5). As we saw in the last chapter, global economic forecasting models (and almost all national models) fail to include energy as a factor of production in such a way that we can seriously evaluate the impact of its price or availability. Thus, forecasters make generally subjective estimates of its impact.

Growth is by no means the only economic issue tied to energy. The rise in energy prices has accompanied and partially explained the global inflation of the 1970s. That inflation has roots stretching back at least to the 1960s, when the United States simultaneously pursued the Great Society and the war in Vietnam. The greater amount of money pursuing goods and services in the United States pushed up prices. Much of this money moved abroad as the United States ran inflated balance of payments deficits (and even by 1972 trade deficits), so that we exported inflation. The unusually rapid global economic growth of the 1960s put pressure on raw materials supplies, also fueling inflation. The agricultural failures of the USSR, South Asia, and North Africa in 1972–74 had a further impact on prices (for a good discussion of the factors underlying global inflation in the early 1970s, see Fried [1976]). Although global inflation cannot be blamed exclusively on energy, it is a major factor. Because energy—like food, for which prices also rose in mid-1970s—is a necessity, this inflation particularly hurts the poor of the world.

Unemployment has resulted from both relative energy scarcity and higher prices and from governmental efforts to control inflation by accepting (on behalf of a portion of their populations) higher unemployment levels. Unfortunately, the trade-off between the two evils did not work in the 1970s the way it had earlier, and the result was stagflation: unemployment *and* inflation. There is speculation that in the longer run higher energy prices might reduce unemployment as industries substitute human labor for energy. At this point, however, it is an open question as to whether energy and labor are substitutes or complements (see, for example, Pindyck [1977], and Fuss [1977]).

Much of the concern about economic consequences associated with higher energy prices and the energy transition centers on international issues. Many countries have had to borrow to pay the increased price of oil. After the 1973–74 price increases, Great Britain and Italy were placed in especially precarious positions. The 1979–80 price increases helped push even West Germany and Japan into trade deficits, more unemployment, and slower growth. Throughout the entire period, debt of LDCs has mushroomed, as documented in Chapter 5. In fact, the LDCs initially paid a lower growth penalty for high energy prices than did the OECD countries, simply because they borrowed heavily to avoid an economic downturn. There is considerable fear that private banks cannot justifiably loan more in the mid and late 1980s, although LDC problems are eliciting some loans in efforts to protect the earlier ones. As banks hesitate to provide additional funds, growth in many LDCs has slowed significantly and loan defaults have become an increasingly likely possibility.

Recycling efforts have involved taking money that the OPEC countries deposited abroad and lending it to oil importers, who return the money to OPEC. On each cycle, the total debt (or investments of OPEC) continues to grow. Additional money has also been created by several oil importers, like the United States, to assist in payment. Money in the private Eurocurrency markets was less than $200 billion in 1972 but was over $1,500 billion by 1981 (Morgan Guaranty Trust 1981, 13). OPEC financial assets grew from $7 billion in 1973 to $343 billion by 1980, and may reach $1 trillion by 1985 (*Business Week,* Oct. 6, 1980, 69). The rapid surge in gold prices more than tripled the values of gold held by government (and others) in the last half of 1979. Altogether, these changes meant that a tremendous amount of international money and debt existed in 1982 that did not exist in 1972. But the economic downturn in 1980–82 slowed money supply growth and at least temporarily dampened inflation. Gold prices were cut by more than half. The international monetary system is now very different from what it was before 1972 and is still in flux.

The implications of these developments are many. Uncertainty and major change makes long-term planning very difficult and rational behavior less likely. Major international monetary panic remains a possibility.

Environmental Impact. The severity and immediacy of the economic problems have directed the attention of many observers away from the environmental issues associated with energy and the transition from oil and natural gas to alternative sources of energy. The weakening of the commitment to a solution to the problem of the environment as a result of energy-based economic difficulties is one of the two major bases for the general perception that energy problems are competitive with environmental ones. The other basis is that many proposed substitutes for oil and gas are seen as less "friendly" to the environment. This is the case especially with coal and nuclear power, the two major contenders in the last ten years. There are also environmental problems with oil shale, geothermal power, and even solar energy.

Nuclear power has nearly been eliminated as the primary future energy source (in the United States) because of environmental (including safety) issues. These issues include the safety of the reactor itself under normal and abnormal conditions, a formerly abstract issue that the accident at Three Mile Island made concrete. They also include the security of plutonium in the nuclear cycle and the threat of its diversion to nuclear weapon construction by terrorists after theft, or by governments that obtain it as a by-product of their own nuclear power plants. These issues in total have made absurd the estimates of the Atomic Energy Commission in the 1960s that the United States would have two thousand gigawatts of nuclear power by the year 2000 (the equivalent of about two thousand average-size nuclear plants). Estimates now seldom exceed three hundred gigawatts.

Coal has also been undermined by environmental issues. Safety and health issues are major (for instance, the high incidence of black lung disease). The U.S. industry has, however, been largely transformed into one based on strip mining, and land reclamation issues have come to dominate among production-related environmental concerns. The coal issues on the consumption side center on air pollution. Coal burning is very dirty relative to oil and natural gas, and technology for control of particulate emissions (e.g., stack gas scrubbers) is very expensive. Sulfur dioxide has proven to be a major problem—in the atmosphere, it combines with water to form sulfuric acid. Acid rain in Sweden has eliminated fish from an estimated two thousand lakes; in upstate New York the fish population has been destroyed in one hundred to two hundred lakes (Congressional Quarterly 1979, 95).

Some potentially critical environmental issues may, of course, be partly resolved by an accelerated transition from oil and natural gas. Smaller and more fuel efficient automobiles are much less polluting than gas guzzlers.

An even more potentially severe environmental threat, however, is now posed by the increase in atmospheric carbon dioxide. Estimates are that the concentration could double before 2050 if we continue our patterns of fossil fuel use. Scientists disagree among themselves, but many experts fear a doubling would cause one- to two-degree centigrade temperature increases through a greenhouse effect, precipitating an ecological catastrophe. Rapid movement from oil and gas, unless coal makes up the difference, could at least slow down the carbon dioxide concentration growth rate.

Social/Political Impact.   Most of the debate surrounding the energy issue is couched in terms of economic and environmental impact of various policies and energy systems. Nuclear energy, for instance, is attacked primarily on environmental grounds. Its costs have soared, partly because of environmental pressures, also making it vulnerable to purely financial considerations.

Underlying the energy debate, however, is another set of issues not even well understood by participants, and badly articulated. These issues affect choices between solar and nuclear power, between a nationalized or privately owned oil industry, between public transit and private automobiles. The root of the issue lies in values concerning how society is best organized. We must remind ourselves of the fundamental impact that the energy system structure has on the social (including political) system.

The importance of man's domestication of fire, that is, the beginnings of an energy system based on combustion of wood, is symbolized in the Greek myth of Prometheus. Prometheus stole fire from the gods and gave it to man, also teaching him various arts and sciences. The abilities to cook, to maintain encampments secure against wild animals, and to develop some metallurgy followed from the new energy system. The growth of man's early civilizations—extraordinary social achievements—is hardly conceivable without fire.

The wide use of coal can hardly be compared to the domestication of fire, but the impact was profound. Alexandre Eiffel would not have been able to construct his tower in Paris in 1889 had it not been for the advances in the iron and steel industry of the ninteenth century, stemming in large part from the relatively concentrated and even heat of coal. That construction project symbolized the advances that made possible our present cities and railroad systems.

The oil and natural gas age can take at least partial credit for several phenomena: the existence of some of the world's largest corporations (in oil and automobiles); the undertaking of perhaps history's largest construction project—(the U.S. interstate highway system); the suburbanization of the United States and, increasingly, of major cities everywhere; and even the great expansion of the U.S. global role (including recent strengthening of commitments to desert real estate around the Persian Gulf). We could also name the green revolution and the major social and political consequences it has had. Or the development of aviation and its impact on global relationships.

We are now in the early and probably critical stages of another energy transition that will have very major consequences for all social systems, including economic and political ones. No collective social choice was exercised in earlier transitions; there were no public institutions which both recognized the occurrence of the transition and possessed the tools to shape it. This time both of these prerequisites of collective social choice are in place and the debate is underway.

Consider some of the social implications of a nuclear-based society. One of the most obvious is a significant governmental role in the system. Government would need to deal directly with safety issues, including provision and transportation of fuel and disposal of wastes. Custody over nuclear weapons-grade material or centuries-long waste disposal control will not be left to private industry. Nuclear power is a highly centralized power source, and nuclear "parks" with massive generating capabilities (subject to government regulation) have been proposed. Nuclear power produces electricity which must be distributed by power lines. The distribution grid is capital-intensive and, because it makes no sense to have more than one grid, it is a natural monopoly. Private utilities in that position are subject to constant governmental scrutiny, including price control.

Consider in contrast an energy system based upon small-scale solar collection systems, primarily rooftop collectors. Whereas the nuclear system would favor centralization of populations (to increase efficiency in distribution systems and to use waste heat from the plants) the solar-based energy system favors decentralization for collection purposes. Moreover, use of solar energy implies continued development of the sunbelt over the snowbelt in the United States. Thus, its implications for land use are very different from those of a nuclear-based energy system. Installation and maintenance of solar energy sources would be capital-intensive, but unlike nuclear systems would not favor capital concentration. Installation and maintenance would require a large labor force, and the degree to which solar systems need to be specialized would support craft rather than assembly line-type labor. The lower-grade energy obtained from solar energy systems (not as concentrated as from nuclear ones) favors smaller-scale and, in today's terms, more primitive industrial processing. Thus, not only would the governmental role in the energy system be much reduced, but large-scale industrial entities would have less influence in the energy system.

Consider a coal-based energy system. Almost certainly such a system would combine reliance on coal-generated electricity with a synthetic fuels industry producing gaseous and liquid fuels. In many respects, the society likely to be based on such a system appears more similar to our current one than do those based on nuclear power or solar energy. Specifically, the industry would be capital and technology intensive and would provide benefits to highly concentrated capital. Government would not need to help provide capital but might in some cases do so in order to reduce the private risk associated with major investments in relatively new energy processes (e.g., coal liquefaction). The system would require the fewest changes in our current energy consumption patterns, including the use of private automobiles and gas-heated private homes. It should not surprise us that many major U.S. corporations see a coal-based system as our best answer and that government is providing significant support.

FORECASTING: THEORIES AND MODELS

The theory of energy systems and their change over time is not at first glance subject to the same kind of major ideological or paradigmatic divisions we saw for economic systems. However, a more detailed examination of how people study energy and forecast energy futures reveals a fairly strong modernist/neotraditionalist division in approaches. There is in recent literature a fairly wide acceptance of basic geological perceptions of the way in which the system operates and these perceptions tend to reinforce the neotraditionalist views.

Geological Perspectives

At the most fundamental level of supply is the geological availability of the fossil fuels, which dominate the energy system. It is important to recognize that not all fossil fuels are equally available and to establish categories of availability. The most common scheme for categorization (figure 6.1) is often referred to as "McKelvey's Box," after the former head of the U.S. Geological Survey who popularized it. By no means can all of the oil, coal, or other natural resources that exist ever be produced. Some will never be found or discovered; still more will be too costly to produce with current or future technology. The portion that has been discovered and that is economical to produce is labeled "known reserves." Known reserves of oil globally are now about 650 billion barrels, with annual discoveries averaging about 15 billion barrels. The higher oil prices of the 1970s increased the amount of oil extractable from known fields, boosting recovery rates up to as much as 60 percent of oil in place (surprisingly this did not give rise to upward revisions of known reserve estimates).

The existence of these different reserve and resource concepts and widely differing assumptions about recoverability help explain the great and confusing range of pronouncements about oil and natural gas "resources." So, too, does the fact that public policy is affected by estimates; the companies who must ultimately provide the data have a strong interest in favorable policy (Wildavsky and Tenenbaum 1981). For many years, however, geologists have tried to estimate the amount of conventional oil we can ultimately expect to discover and recover globally—ultimately recoverable resources. These estimates have ranged from 1 trillion to 4 trillion barrels and generally fall into the range of 1.5 to 2.0 trillion barrels.

Energy Transition

Once an estimate of ultimately recoverable resources exists, we can go one step further and sketch the life cycle of the resource production. Geologist M. King Hubbert developed this technique, and as noted earlier, put forward a remarkably accurate forecast of U.S. oil production based on it. It has come to be known as "Hubbert's curve" or "Hubbert's pimple." Figure 6.2 shows two such curves, for ultimate oil resource estimates of 1.35 and 2.1 trillion barrels. Each curve shows the annual production level, while the total area under the curve is the ultimate resource level. Note that by 1975 well under half of the globe's oil had been produced, regardless of the estimate of ultimate resources accepted. Also note that although the peak levels of annual production are quite different, both

FIGURE 6.1. *Energy Resources Availability (The McKelvey Box)*

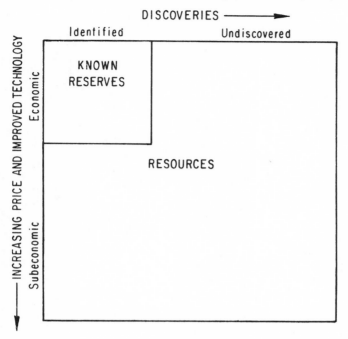

Source: Adapted from Julian Simon, *The Ultimate Resource* (Princeton: Princeton University Press, 1981), 36.

curves peak near the end of the century, and fall to or below the 1975 level by 2030. This then suggests a roughly 60-year transition period away from oil and natural gas (which has a similar life cycle).

The concept of "energy transition" and the belief that we are now undergoing one has become widely accepted. As we saw in the last chapter, at least one explanation of the long, or Kondratieff, waves involves cycles of increasing resource scarcity. Although the existence, much less the nature, of Kondratieff waves is controversial, the existence of energy transitions and their importance is not. And these transitions have had roughly the same period (about sixty years) as the long waves have had.

There have been several historic energy transitions which help put the current one in perspective. In 1850 the United States (and presumably most of the world) derived nearly 90 percent of its energy from wood (Stoker, Seager, and Capaner 1975, 7). Coal use grew steadily and quickly in the last half of the nineteenth century and in 1890 provided 50 percent of national energy needs. Coal's dominance peaked in 1910, about sixty years

FIGURE 6.2. *Oil Production Life Cycle (Hubbert's Curve)*

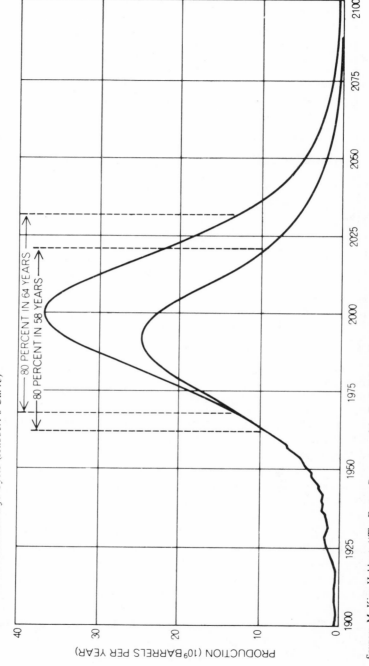

PRODUCTION (10⁹ BARRELS PER YEAR)

80 PERCENT IN 64 YEARS
80 PERCENT IN 58 YEARS

Source: M. King Hubbert, ''The Energy Resources of the Earth,'' *Scientific American* 225 (September 1971): 69. Copyright © 1971 by Scientific American, Inc. All rights reserved. Reprinted with permission.

Note: Higher peak represents total estimate of 2.1 trillion barrels; lower peak is estimate of 1.35 trillion barrels.

after it began its rapid climb, at 70 percent of all energy produced and consumed in the United States. Oil and natural gas contributed an additional 20 percent in 1910. Sixty years later, in 1970, they reached the 70 percent level that coal had attained in 1910. A second 60-year transition had been made.

The transition away from dependence on oil and natural gas will be slow. In 1980 they still provided about 70 percent of the world's energy supply. By 2000 this may be reduced to under 50 percent, although their absolute level of global production and consumption will have risen (IEA 1981, 56). Absolute decreases in conventional oil and natural gas production are likely to begin about the turn of the century, according to most forecasters.

There are two major differences between the current energy system transition and the two previous ones (wood to coal; coal to oil and gas). First, both of the prior transitions were made largely because of the greater attractiveness of the new fuels. Although there were some pressures on wood supply, coal was a superior fuel for steelmaking and for railroad locomotives. Similarly, the energy quality, convenience of use, and cleanliness of oil and gas made them preferable for many users to somewhat less expensive coal. In the current energy transition, no superior energy source is pulling us away from oil and gas—indeed, we have not yet determined what the next best alternative is. This provides support for neotraditionalists who feel that past long economic waves were related to the earlier energy transitions, and that this economic downturn might be much more severe.

Second, the transition is being stretched out somewhat by OPEC. In the early 1970s, Saudi Arabia had plans to more than double its oil production levels rather than nearly stabilize them as subsequently happened. Because so much of the world's oil and gas is concentrated in the OPEC nations, they have been able to raise prices significantly above those that would have occurred in the market were these resources more widely held. The high prices have dampened global oil and gas demand (and thereby, also production) compared to that expected theoretically on the basis of Hubbert's curve, thus shaving the top off the peak of the oil-gas production life cycle. This will ultimately prolong somewhat the availability of oil and gas. Given our uncertainty about substitute fuels, this may prove to be desirable. Figure 6.3 shows a recent reworking of this production life-cycle based on a lower projection of peak production and a longer tail.

OPEC and the Transition

The shape of the transition to come thus depends to a large degree on the coherence and power of OPEC. That coherence and power currently appears very high to many observers. Several factors determine a cartel's

FIGURE 6.3. *Hypothetical Oil Production and Resource Depletion Profile*

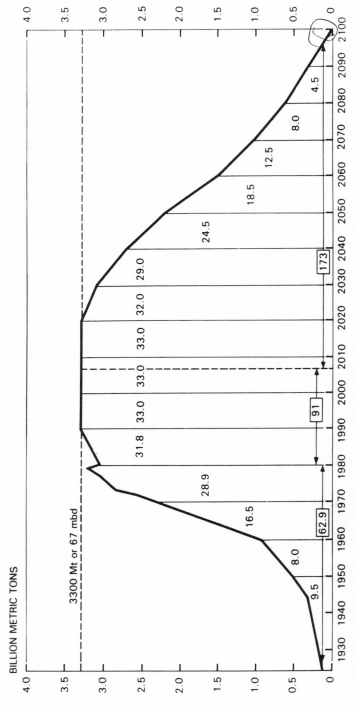

Source: International Energy Agency, *World Energy Outlook* (Paris: OECD, 1982), 215. Reprinted with permission.

success or failure. One is the physical and economic capability to constrain production. The physical capability requires control by the cartel over a significant portion of the resource, a control which OPEC has. It produces over one-half of global oil and controls perhaps two-thirds of known oil reserves. The economic capability often hinges upon having some resources to fall back upon during a period of reduced income following a production cutback. Several OPEC members gained this capability during the 1960s. The early success of OPEC, moreover, so strengthened the economic position of many members that even significant drops in sales now pose no threat. Indeed, the opposite problem appeared possible after the 1979–80 oil shock: revenues were so great that many members sought further reductions in output, in part to provide some relief from the economic burdens and possible social turmoil accompanying the tremendous income. That now appears ancient history: global demand for OPEC oil has fallen so much that many members again desperately need revenues and even the wealthiest feel some pressure.

A cartel's success or failure also depends upon important market characteristics. In general, *demand elasticity* should be low. That is, consumers should reduce consumption by only a fraction of a percentage for each percentage increase in price. In the case of an oil cartel, this means that overall energy demand should be relatively unresponsive to prices and that oil demand as a portion of energy demand should also be quite unresponsive—consumers should not be easily able to do without energy or to substitute other energy forms for oil. *Supply elasticity* should also be low. That is, noncartel producers, both of oil and of potentially competing energy supplies, should not be able to raise production significantly, thereby undercutting the cartel. In the case of OPEC, these conditions were met throughout the 1970s, when both elasticities appeared low. There is, however, great debate and uncertainty among economists and energy experts about the magnitude of these elasticities in the long-run. Although short-run supply elasticities, or responses to price, may be low, in the longer run new energy systems (synthetic fuels, oil shale, tar sands, even fusion power) may mean much higher elasticities. The same is true on the demand side, as the long process of transforming transportation, housing, and industrial systems works itself out.

Still other factors underlying cartel success or failure lie in the character of cartel members and their pattern of interrelationships. OPEC contains members who always urgently need additional revenues for economic growth (especially Indonesia, Gabon, and Ecuador, but also Nigeria, Algeria, Iran, and Venezuela) as well as members who most often have no immediate need for much of the revenue they obtain (Saudi Arabia, Kuwait, and the U.A.E., and to a lesser degree Libya). The revenue absorbers in the first category cannot afford to cut back production in case external demand falls, whereas the savers in the second category can. The mere existence of the second category is of great value to a cartel (CIPEC, the international copper cartel, has no such members). Relatively greater power is wielded by this category of member and much depends upon their political relationship with other members. All else being equal, no member has any interest in damaging the cartel; but global issues, from the status of Israel to the superpower conflict, can also enter into member decisions.

This description of the geological basis for forecasting energy futures, and of the notion of an energy transition, largely supports neotraditionalist views of a fairly pessimistic energy future. We have now entered into a period of increased scarcity of oil and gas, and a transition away from them has begun. But there is no clear energy system toward which we are moving and most of the options are considered by many experts to be seriously flawed on economic or environmental grounds.

Economic Perspectives

There are, however, some alternative perceptions of the situation. To begin, many modernists seriously question some of the assumptions implicit in the above argument. For instance, some analyses of ultimate energy resource availability are much more optimistic. Although there may only be 1.5 to 2 trillion barrels of ultimately recoverable *conventional* oil, there is a very large, and to date little known, volume of unconventional oil—very heavy oil, tar sands, oil shale. For instance, estimates of heavy oil in Venezuela alone range from 1 to 3 trillion barrels—figures comparable to global estimates of ultimately recoverable conventional oil (*Petroleum Economist*, May 1980). It is thought that 500 billion barrels may be recoverable at current oil prices. In addition, the technology is known to convert coal, of which there are vast quantities, to synthetic petroleum or natural gas. Herman Kahn estimated such fossil fuels (table 6.5). It should be noted that his estimate for potential global oil shale is exceptionally and unreasonably high. If the true figure is even 10 percent of that Kahn cites, however, and if we leave aside other issues such as environmental ones, there appears to be no need for concern about energy futures until at least the middle of the next century. Modernists argue that in addition to abundant fossil fuels, we already have the option of nuclear fission energy, and that technological advance has rapidly moved us toward economically viable solar energy and will soon bring us a nuclear fusion option, thus providing us with what have been called the eternal fuels. Thus, our problem is not one of inadequate options but of difficulty of choice among the options.

Another line of attack on the largely geological perspective of limited fossil fuels comes from the classical liberals, and is very much a methodological one. There is now a long history of incorrect forecasts of future

TABLE 6.5. *Fossil Fuel Resources (in Qs)*[a]

Energy Source	Proven Reserves		Potential Resources	
	U.S.	World	U.S.	World
Oil	0.3	3.7	2.9	14.4
Natural gas	0.3	1.0	2.5	15.8
Coal (incl. lignite)	15.0	95.0	30.0	170.0
Shale oil	12.0	19.0	150.0	2,000.0
Tar sands	—	1.8	—	1.8
Total	27.6	120.0	185.0	2,200.0
Years of world consumption at current projections	48	102	120	500

Source: Herman Kahn, William Brown, and Leon Martel, *The Next 200 Years* (New York: William Morrow, 1976), 63. Copyright © 1976 by Hudson Institute. By permission of William Morrow & Company.
[a]$Q = 10^{15}$ BTU.

energy scarcity based on attempts to evaluate geological resource bases, technological development potential, demand growth, substitution patterns, and political decisions. Why not, it can be argued, take a much easier approach and simply examine the long-term trend of energy availability and prices? Simon suggests we use two long-term measures of real scarcity—the price of a resource relative to the consumer price index, and the price relative to wages. Relative to the consumer price index, the prices of coal since 1800 and of oil since 1880 have fluctuated but have shown no clear upward trend indicating increasing scarcity, in spite of obvious continuing use of resources. Electricity prices, a better indicator of energy prices for consumers, went down steadily relative to other prices between 1920 and 1980 (Simon 1981, 96–98). Even real gasoline prices in the United States were twenty cents per gallon lower in 1978 than in the mid-1930s—and depressions depress prices (Simon 1981, 356). Relative to wages, declines in the cost of energy have been very dramatic. None of this denies that some known deposits of fossil fuels—and eventually even the total resource base of some fossil fuels—will be largely depleted. It suggests, however, that we should not play down the possibilities of substitution and of technological innovation. Most importantly, "engineering" attempts to forecast energy futures by looking at all the contributing factors on demand and supply sides may be less accurate than simpler extrapolation of long-term trends.

Elaborating on this "economic" approach in contrast to the "engineering" or "geological" ones, classical liberal economists would point out that we may well have misjudged the severity of the current energy situation by confusing the short-term response of the market with the potential long-run response. The relationship between prices and production levels can, as noted earlier, be summarized by means of an elasticity. An elasticity of ''1'' means that a one percent increase in energy prices will elicit a one percent increase in energy supplies. An elasticity of greater than ''1'' implies great responsiveness (high elasticity) of supply to prices, and an elasticity of less than ''1'' implies low responsiveness (relative inelasticity) of supply. Clearly, however, long-run elasticities are higher than short-run elasticities, because it takes time to make investments and to build facilities in response to higher prices. We may well have underestimated long-term supply elasticities. The same is true on the demand side, as indicated by the continued downward revision of demand forecasts as the longer-term response of demand to higher prices becomes clearer.

On the demand side of the global energy system, one of the most important theoretical linkages is between economic growth and energy consumption growth. The nearly one-to-one relationship between economic growth and energy consumption growth has long been recognized. Specifically, on a global average basis, every one percent increase in gross world product was accompanied for many years by a little more than a one percent increase in global energy consumption. Countries in the process of rapid industrialization (e.g., China, Taiwan, South Korea, Brazil) require significantly more than a 1 percent increase in energy availability—in fact as much as 2 percent more energy—to achieve 1 percent economic growth. Rapid industrialization emphasizes transportation systems and energy intensive heavy industry. Economies that are already industrialized (e.g., the United States, Great Britain, France) generally require slightly less energy growth. Specifically, for the 1960s the United States needed about 85 percent additional energy for each 1.0 percent economic growth. For OECD countries as a whole, the figure was 1.13 percent (Levy 1978–79, 289).

The reduced growth rate in global energy supplies since 1973 has had two consequences. First, it has reduced economic growth. Whereas the OECD countries grew at an average annual rate of 4.8 percent between 1951 and 1973, they grew at only 3.8 percent per annum from 1975 to 1979 (Healey 1979–80, 217). Most forecasters foresee even slower economic growth in the 1980s, in large part because of lower growth in energy supplies (higher oil prices result in lower supply growth because users can buy less). Neotraditionalists would point out that to date, slower economic growth has been more important in explaining reduced energy demand growth than has any price-induced conservation. Reduced energy growth has also, however, begun to break the global one-to-one energy to economic linkage. The United States is now using about 0.7 percent of additional energy for every 1.0 percent economic growth. For OECD countries the ratio has dropped to 0.81 percent. The experts really do not know the degree to which the two growth rates can be uncoupled. Some suggest that the rate of energy consumption growth in the United States could approach zero without lowering economic rates. For instance, Exxon has estimated that by the year 2000, the United States will use 33 percent less energy for every dollar of GNP than it did in 1973. By 1980, energy usage per dollar of GNP had already fallen 7 percent (Exxon 1980, 7).

In general these economic analyses, favored by both classical liberals and modernists, prove more optimistic than the geological or engineering ones, favored by neotraditionalists.

Energy is the "master resource." Not only does extraction of all other resources depend on availability and price of energy, economic development has occurred only as energy use has grown. In the early stages of industrialization—a level of economic development just now being attained in many LDCs—energy consumption growth is often twice as fast as economic growth. Thus, the future of economic development, particularly in the LDCs, depends on ever higher energy consumption levels. That fact makes the debate over future energy availability and cost central to the broader debate over the global development system. We have seen that forecasts range from ever greater abundance and lower prices to sharp restrictions in availability and higher prices.

7. Food and Agriculture

No issue is of greater importance and concern in a discussion of global development and global futures than food supply. Although in developed Western economies famines, and even food shortages, appear a thing of the past, it is impossible to ignore the current existence of them elsewhere. Starvation reports from Africa or South Asia are heard fairly regularly.

The food issue caught the attention of the public in Western market economies in the early to mid-1970s because it actually affected them through higher prices, if not through physical shortages. After two decades of considerable food surpluses, that had posed significant storage and disposal problems in the United States and Western Europe during the 1950s and 1960s, the situation changed. Crop failures beginning in 1972 and extending into 1973 and 1974 afflicted the Soviet Union, the portion of Northern Africa immediately below the Sahara (the Sahel), and much of South Asia. The Soviet Union moved quickly and secretly, before others became aware of the extent of their crop problems and import intentions, to secure contracts on grain imports. The United States was the ultimate source of most of the grain to be imported, although some contracts eventually filled with U.S. grain were written in Europe and elsewhere. It even, in effect, subsidized the Soviets by maintaining support payments for farmers facing low prices in a market which only later recognized and responded to the changed demand situation. This "Great Grain Robbery" contributed to dramatic increases in world food prices and exacerbated African and South Asian difficulties in importing needed food. It was also responsible for the imposition of a quota on soybean exports from the United States to Japan, something which severely shook Japanese faith in the reliability of its principal external food supplier (Japan also upset the United States by its hoarding behavior during the period, that is, by increasing its import demand in fear of higher prices and shortages). Global

124

wheat prices have since come back to levels below those prior to 1972–74. And surplus disposal problems have reappeared in the United States and Western Europe, to the extent of posing a major crisis for the European Community in 1983–84. But in 1980 global food reserves, counting the grain production equivalent of idled U.S. cropland, stood at forty days of world consumption—the same as 1974–75 and half the 1965 figure (Hansen et al. 1982, 188).

As important as the issue is, there is a surprising amount of misinformation and even more controversy over the current and recent global food situation. Many observers have come to believe that the world food situation actually has been getting worse—that food availability per capita globally, or at least in LDCs, generally has deteriorated. We shall see that, except for the events described above, this is not the case.

Whether the gains achieved (very unequally around the globe) can be maintained, much less improved upon, is a different and more complicated issue and opinion varies widely. At least since Malthus argued that food production grows arithmetically (linearly) while population grows geometrically (exponentially), the ability of mankind to feed itself in the future has been a matter of major academic and governmental debate (it has always been a matter of public concern).

On the one hand, the very fact that world population has quadrupled in the 180 years since Malthus made his arguments, without experiencing any but scattered regional famines (average diet improved significantly over this period) tends to discredit the argument altogether. On the other hand, a large portion of the additional food production in the last century and a half came from new agricultural land (especially in the United States), and much of the rest came from great increases in productivity based on decreasingly expensive fossil fuels. Moreover, about one-half of the global population still subsists on diets not improved over the time period. Some experts argue that there is still a great deal of unutilized or underutilized land, especially in Latin America and Africa, and that great technological advance can still be expected in agriculture—for instance from genetic engineering. Other experts point to the marginal quality of most land not now under cultivation, the ecological consequences of its use (for instance, the continuing advance of the Sahara in Africa as a result of land overuse), and the increasing expense of energy-based inputs.

Agricultural issues extend beyond the considerations of aggregate global food availability, however. For instance, a key question for LDCs attempting to develop economically has been what balance to strike between agriculture and industry. During the 1950s and 1960s, the conventional wisdom was that the smoothest and fastest route to development was via industry. It had become obvious that the industrialized countries were able greatly to improve their agricultural systems with the mechanization, fertilizers, pesticides, and technological research of their industrial sectors. Moreover, it was clear that in international trade, agricultural exports earned little compared to exports of manufactured goods.

However, during the 1970s it was increasingly recognized that agriculture needed more direct attention in most LDCs. The slow growth of agricultural production had often failed to keep up with demand, leading to high food imports, that constitute a serious drain upon foreign exchange earnings. Furthermore, the relative success with the industrial sector created dual economies—half modern and half traditional, half well-paid and half in poverty. Migration from farms to cities and concomitant social tensions increased accordingly.

For the developed societies, especially the United States, a major agricultural issue has been food aid policy. A presumption existed for many years that foreign assistance to LDCs in the form of food was a highly positive contribution, despite the scandals which often developed around its distribution within the recipient country. More recently, many policymakers and analysts have come to question whether there have not been important negative effects of such food. Two are especially likely. First, food aid has likely depressed food prices in recipient countries and contributed to the long-run underdevelopment of the agricultural sector. Second, a dependence on food aid creates a vulnerability among recipients to cutbacks, either because of decreased availability in donors or because donors wish to exert political leverage with recipients.

BACKGROUND: HISTORY AND FORECASTS

Rates and Totals

In looking historically at global food supplies, it is most important to look at grain production because grain is the staple, the bulk of food supplies. Table 7.1 shows the growth since World War II in global grain production. Since global population growth has never exceeded 2 percent per annum, it is clear that in recent years grain production growth has generally outstripped population growth. This correctly implies a somewhat improved average global diet. The average conceals critical local distinctions that I shall address shortly.

Another aspect of table 7.1 should be highlighted. Note the high growth rates in grain production starting in the late 1940s and continuing into the 1960s. Although initially this reflects the inclusion of the end of World War II within the base period, it clearly also reflects the global "green revolution." The possibility of increasing agricultural yields by application of fertilizer has long been known. But among other problems, the largest was long the tendency of fuller, heavier grain to fall over or "lodge" from the extra weight, either rotting or making harvest less efficient. Research

TABLE 7.1. *World Grain Production, 1945–1981*

Year	World Grain Production (in million metric tons)	Annual Growth Rate (in percentages)
1945	445	—
1950	594	5.9
1955	731	4.3
1960	970	5.8
1965	1,019	1.0
1970	1,213	3.5
1975	1,359	2.3
1980	1,561	2.8
1981	1,664	6.6

Source: Food and Agriculture Organization, *Production Yearbook* (Rome: Food and Agriculture Organization, 1948–81).

programs, the most famous of which was the Rockefeller Foundation project in Mexico under Norman Borlaug, gradually developed strains with shorter or thicker stalks. Use of these became widespread in Mexico by the mid-1950s and quickly spread throughout the world. By 1977 35 percent of the Third World's wheat and rice areas were sown to high-yielding varieties (World Bank 1981c, 21).

Forecasts of global and regional food production and consumption are less common than forecasts of population, economic growth, or energy consumption or production. Among the most highly respected forecasts are those of the U.S. Department of Agriculture (table 7.2). If correct, these forecasts would mean that between now and the end of the century global food production will grow slightly faster than population, although quite a bit slower than the 1945–81 rate.

As has been the case in other issue areas, we can turn to the *Limits to Growth* report and to *The Next 200 Years* for longer-term forecasts that are diametrically opposed. The Meadows team presents alternative scenarios of the global future, but even in the most optimistic of their sustainable

TABLE 7.2. *Projected Food and Grain Production in the Year 2000*

Projection	Food Production Index (1969–70 = 100)	Food Production Annual Growth Rate (in percentages)	Grain Production Index (1969–70 = 100)	Grain Production Annual Growth Rate (in percentages)
Low	191.5	2.19	191.2	2.18
Medium	191.0–194.0	2.21	193.1–198.1	2.26
High	198.0	2.30	201.4	2.36

Source: USDA projections as reported in Council on Environmental Quality, *The Global 2000 Report to the President* (Washington, D.C.: CEQ, 1981), Vol. 2, pp. 81, 92.

FIGURE 7.1. *Kahn's View of Possible Future Food Production*

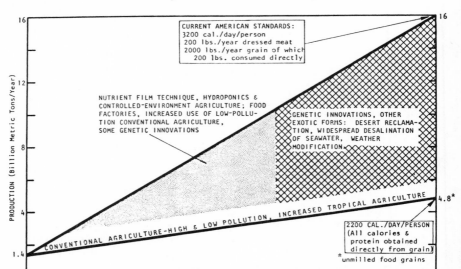

Source: Herman Kahn, William Brown, and Leon Martel, *The Next 200 Years* (New York: William Morrow, 1976), 134. Copyright © 1976 by Hudson Institute. By permission of William Morrow & Company.

world scenarios global food production at the end of the next century (2100) is only about twice current levels. Contrast this with Herman Kahn's projections (figure 7.1). His data show something closer to an eightfold increase by 2100. Interestingly, however, Kahn projects only about a doubling in conventional agricultural production thus clarifying considerably the basis for the differences in the two extreme forecasts—the inclusion in the Kahn forecast of much unconventional agricultural production resulting from technological innovation. The Kahn scenario rests heavily on techniques such as nutrient-film, hydroponics, food factories, and genetic innovation.

Food comes not only from grains, of course. Fish is an important source of protein in many areas of the world, such as Japan. The global ocean fish catch increased steadily until 1970. The failure of the Peruvian anchovy fishery thereafter was the most spectacular indication of a topping out of global ocean fish catch and contributed to the food shortages of 1972–74 (CEQ 1981, 105). That failure was related to a Pacific Ocean weather pattern known as El Niño. Another occurrence of this cyclical pattern in 1982–83 may affect catches in the near future. Total fresh water and ocean fish catch was stable at about 70 million metric tons through the 1970s (table 9.3). There is a great deal of debate over the future. Some experts have argued that exploitation of heretofore unused species, such as Antarctic krill; development of ocean aquaculture; and/or the dramatic expansion of mariculture on the continents can lead to a resumption of increases in the fish catch rate. Others feel that 60 to 70 million metric tons will remain as about the upper limit for sustained annual ocean catch, and that marine pollution could reduce that.

Another and more important source of food globally is livestock. Although most of the global herd is grazed, in the developed countries a significant portion is fed. In 1970 slightly more than one-third of all grain produced globally was used to feed livestock; by 1990 one forecast is for almost half of all grain production to be used for feed or other non-food uses, such as alcohol production (McLaughlin et al. 1979, 188). The heavy use of grain for feed, particularly in the MDCs, has been criticized because it takes about seven to twelve calories of grain to produce one of beef (pork and poultry require less grain). One fact that is not often recognized is that livestock herds provide some insurance against bad years. Their slaughter in a bad year provides calories and protein, and reduces pressure on grain supplies. This is exactly what the USSR did until the early 1970s, when it decided for political reasons not to slaughter livestock and thereby to accept subsequent years of low meat supplies, but rather to import grain. The failure to use this food system "slack" disrupted the global market.

Forecasts of livestock herd size and their potential feed requirements are hard to come by. As indicated above, they depend heavily on political decisions and on the health of the basic grain market. Interestingly, efficiencies of meat production also vary considerably around the world. In 1980 it took 3.85 pounds of feed to produce a live-weight pound of pork (7.1 for beef) in the United States and nearly twice that in the Soviet Union (Wädekin 1982, 885). Thus, major impacts on feed requirements could come from changes in agricultural practice.

I have shown how inadequate forecasts have been historically. Agriculture is no exception. At the turn of the century Sir William Crookes reported in his Presidential Address to the British Association of Science that

> there remains no uncultivated prairie land in the United States suitable for wheat growing. The virgin land has been rapidly absorbed, until at present there is no land left for wheat without reducing the area for maize, hay, and other necessary crops. It is almost certain that within a generation the ever increasing population of the United States will consume all the wheat growing within its borders and will be driven to import and . . . scramble for a lion's share of the wheat crop of the world. (Wortman and Cummings 1978, 86)

Distribution

Global totals may be less useful in understanding what is happening in agriculture than in any issue discussed to this point.

The increases in production historically (table 7.1) have not been evenly spread globally. As we see in figure 7.2, over the 1955 to 1981 period total food production gains in LDCs outstripped gains in developed countries by .5 percent to 1 percent per year on the average. Global per capita gains have been much lower, however, and the LDCs have not done as well as the MDCs. In fact, over a twenty-five-year period per capita LDC food production grew by only about 10 percent. LDC production gains have themselves been even less equally distributed (figure 7.3). Of all major LDC regions only East Asia (including Taiwan and South Korea) has had significant per capita gains. In Africa there have been losses. Those patterns reflect, among many other factors, the differential use of the green revolution grains. Of total wheat and rice area, 41 percent is sown to high-yielding varieties in Asia, 31 percent in Latin America, and only 7 percent in Africa (World Bank 1981c, 21).

Per capita production patterns do not necessarily reflect per capita consumption patterns. Trade is very important for some countries, even though a much lower percentage of global food than of global energy enters world commerce. In 1973–74, five countries exported a third or more of their grain production; for the United States it was almost exactly one-third (Nau 1978, 208). Ten countries depended on food imports for 10 percent or more of cereal consumption. Belgium and Luxembourg topped the list with 90 percent dependence and, surprisingly, the list included only four LDCs: Egypt (28 percent), South Korea (27 percent), Bangladesh (16 percent), and Brazil (10 percent).

Grain trade, however, has been growing very rapidly, more than doubling in volume between 1970 and the early 1980s (table 7.3). Note that from 1934 to 1938, only Western Europe was a significant regional importer; it has recently become less dependent on imports. All LDC regions shifted from balanced, or net exporter, status to net importer status by the late 1970s. The most significant changes in the 1970s were the entry of both Africa and the USSR and Eastern Europe into the global market in major volume, supported by an expansion of U.S. exports. The growing African dependence on food imports is of serious concern because of the poverty of the continent and the scarcity of foreign exchange with which to buy food (although Nigeria, which earns considerable foreign exchange with its oil exports, accounts for much of the grain imports).

Such political decisions constitute only one reason why forecasts of global consumption patterns are risky. In the case of LDCs, fluctuations in domestic capabilities to expand production and to pay for imports make

FIGURE 7.2.   *North and South Food Production Growth*

(1969–1971 = 100)

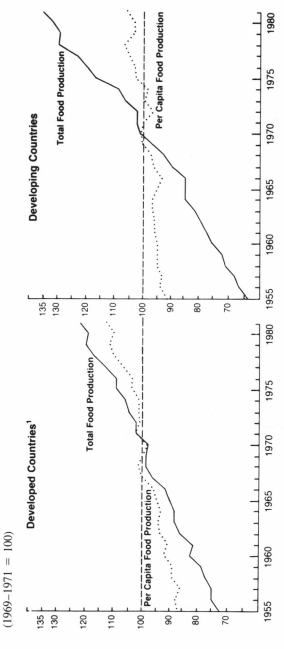

Source: John P. Lewis and Valleriana Kallab, eds. *U.S. Foreign Policy and World Development: Agenda 1983* (New York: Praeger, 1983), 282. Copyright © by the Overseas Development Council. Reprinted with permission of Praeger Publishers.

Note: Data do not include centrally planned economies; inedible fiber products such as cotton, hemp, and wool; or non-caloric products such as tobacco, coffee, tea, and spices.

[1]United States, Canada, Japan, South Africa, Europe, Australia, and New Zealand.

FIGURE 7.3. *Food Production per Capita in LDC Regions*

(1961–1965 = 100)

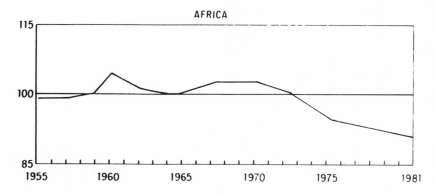

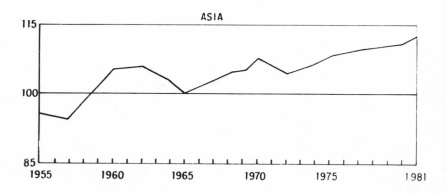

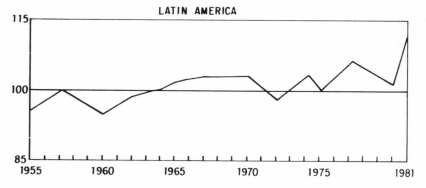

Source: Food and Agriculture Organization, *Production Yearbook,* (Rome: FAO, 1965, 1975, 1981).

TABLE 7.3. *Annual World Grain Trade (in millions of tons)*

Region	1934–38	1948–52	1960	1970	1977–78	1983–84[a]
North America	5[b]	17	42	54	155	126
Latin America	2	0	(1)	4	(3)	(3)
Western Europe	(10)[c]	(14)	(25)	(22)	(22)	(1)
Eastern Europe/USSR	1	—	1	(1)	(27)	(34)
Africa	0	(1)	(5)	(4)	(22)	(41)
Asia	(1)	(5)	(19)	(37)	(38)	(54)
Oceania	3	3	6	8	11	14

Sources: Food and Agricultural Organization, *Trade Yearbook* (Rome, FAO, 1959, 1972); U.S. Dept. of Agriculture, *World Agricultural Situation* (Washington, D.C.: Government Printing Office, 1978); U.S. Dept. of Agriculture, *World Agriculture: Outlook and Situation* (Washington, D.C.: Government Printing Office, March and September, 1983).
[a]Projected.
[b]Figures without parentheses indicate net exports.
[c]Figures within parentheses indicate net imports.

forecasts difficult to generate. Nevertheless, one forecast has been produced, in calorie terms, from U.S. Department of Agriculture models (table 7.4). It suggests that all LDC regions other than Africa are likely to improve average diet levels through the end of the century. Compare the values forecast for the year 2000 with the roughly 2,300 calories per day estimated by the Food and Agriculture Organization (FAO) to be minimum requirements to avoid malnutrition. National figures should be 10 percent to 15 percent above that to ensure adequate calorie intake for the poorest classes. Average caloric availability in the United States was 3,652 calories per day in 1979 (Sivard 1982, 31).

Linkages

In this section I turn to the factors that influence agricultural production and consumption patterns. Here I want to touch on some of the "forward

TABLE 7.4. *Per Capita Daily Caloric Consumption in LDC Regions*

Region	1969–71	1973–74	1985	2000
Latin America	2,525	2,540	2,680	2,920
North Africa/Middle East	2,421	2,482	2,448	2,495
Other African LDCs	2,139	2,071	2,238	1,835
South Asia	2,036	1,954	2,150	2,155
Southeast Asia	2,174	2,270	2,320	2,383
East Asia	2,140	2,205	2,325	2,493
Average (all LDCs)	2,165	2,135	2,300	2,350

Source: Based on CEQ, *The Global 2000 Report to the President* (Washington, D.C.: Council on Environmental Quality, 1981), 95.

linkages,'' that is, the aspects of the global development system influenced by agricultural consumption and production patterns.

Foremost among such linkages is that to nutrition and the incidence of malnutrition or starvation. Figures on the prevalence of either are difficult to establish. No one officially dies of starvation—people die of dysentery, pneumonia, or other conditions associated with a weakened condition resulting from inadequate food—so there are no national or UN statistics on it. Clearly, current life expectancies at birth of only forty-five years in the twenty-five poorest African countries suggest the presence of malnutrition-related death. However, no one takes a census that questions the nutritional status of the respondents. And the difficulties of computing estimates of those malnourished are impressive: How do we establish the calorie intake threshold? How do we compute food availability when, especially in LDCs, much food is consumed by producers (subsistence farming) and never enters the market, upon which production statistics rely? If we know production, how would we adjust for waste and spoilage or for inequities in consumption patterns? Even in the United States, where the data are presumably more accessible, a presidential commission concluded in 1984 that it could not ascertain the extent of hunger in this country.

In spite of the difficulties, estimates have been made. For malnutrition they range as high as 1.3 billion people globally, nearly one-third of the total world population (Hopkins, Paarlberg, and Wallerstein 1980, 13). More common are estimates between 400 million and 500 million people. Most of those estimates (e.g., Wortman and Cummings [1978, 23]) are derived from the Food and Agriculture Organization. Forecasts of global malnutrition, based on numbers like those in table 7.4, most often suggest that the percentage of global population falling into the malnourished category will gradually diminish through 2000, but that the absolute numbers will not, and may slightly increase.

Turning to the effects of agricultural production, the ones that have received most attention and over which there is most controversy are environmental. Although I shall examine these in detail in a later chapter, let me note them now in passing.

The most critical effects are those on land use. Much of the potentially arable land not now under cultivation and not requiring irrigation is currently forest area. On a global basis—and there are local exceptions—significant deforestation has taken place over the last forty years. In 1966 forests covered one-quarter of the world's land surface. In 1978 the figure was one-fifth, and one projection for 2000 is at one-sixth. (CEQ 1981, 117). Much of the reduction can be attributed to agricultural pressures. In addition, desertification (the transformation of productive land to desert) is resulting in several locations from overgrazing of pasture. There is a debate about how much soil is being lost to erosion as a result of poor agricultural practices, and about how reversible the process is, but there is no doubt that soil erosion is occurring. In the United States, a 1975 USDA Soil Conservation Service report indicated national losses of 3 billion tons per year, compared to sustainable losses (offset by soil-building processes) of 1.5 billion tons (cited in Brown 1978, 24).

A second environmental issue related to agriculture is pollution. Already pesticides and fertilizers in runoff are identified as among the most important pollutants globally. Fertilizer consumption is projected to more than double by 2000 (CEQ 1981, 100). Pressure on global water supplies, both in terms of demand for renewable and fossil water and in terms of pollution of it, are becoming increasingly important issues.

Still another "forward linkage" of agriculture is to the social system; in particular the green revolution has had important social effects. The introduction of a high technology package of inputs to agriculture, namely advanced seeds, fertilizers, pesticides, and machinery for planting and harvesting, has disrupted traditional patterns not only of production but of land tenure. Some farmers have inevitably been quicker to grasp the new procedures than others, or for historical reasons had easier access to the credit generally needed to take advantage of them. Those individuals have not only prospered but have often bought out others or displaced traditional tenants. Although the global movement from farms to cities is often conceptualized in "pull" terms (that is, the greater opportunities of the city) there is, in the creation of surplus farm labor, a great "push" factor. In the lowest income countries, the labor force employed in agriculture dropped from 77 percent of the total in 1960 to 71 percent in 1980; the percentage of urban-dwellers went from 13 percent to 17 percent. In industrial market economies the agricultural labor force dropped from 18 percent to 6 percent of the total in the same period (World Bank 1982, 146–49). Because the range of landholding and tenancy relationships varies so greatly globally, it is impossible to generalize on the impact of the green revolution in social patterns. It has, however, been great and disruptive (see, for example, Johnson 1972; Wortman and Cummings 1978).

FORECASTING: THEORIES AND MODELS

There are two major approaches to the forecasting of agricultural supply and demand. The first relies heavily upon a physical interpretation and representation of the agricultural system; the second depends on a more "economic" perspective. The physical approach is more often used for long-term forecasting and I examine it first.

Physical Approaches

On the supply side the physical approach projects crop production as the product of two factors: the amount of land under cultivation and the yields obtained from each unit of land. Beginning with the amount of land, there is now between 1.4 and 1.5 billion hectares of land under cultivation globally (a hectare is a metric unit equivalent to about 2.5 acres). The FAO estimates that there are 3.19 billion hectares of land which could ultimately be brought under cultivation; that estimate has been adopted by a wide range of both neotraditionalists and modernists (e.g., Meadows et al. [1972] and Kahn, Brown, and Martel [1976]). Table 7.5 shows the distribution of land globally, both currently and potentially arable, based on a more recent and considerably higher estimate by the FAO of potentially arable land.

Much more debate, however, centers on how quickly, if at all, areas under production can move toward that upper limit. On the somewhat conservative side is the USDA, which estimates a mere 62 million hectare increase by the year 2000 (CEQ 1981). In comparison, Leontief projects a more than 15 percent increase, or 227 million hectares additional cultivated area by 2000 (Leontief et al. 1977, 4).

The difficulty in making longer-term forecasts of land availability is, of course, that there are competing uses for both the arable land itself (such as forests) and for the resources (such as water) that would be required to bring additional land under cultivation. At one extreme in the long run, Herman Kahn makes calculations of ultimate production potential on the assumption that a full 3.19 billion hectares, most of which is now forest or "marginal" land, could be brought under cultivation. He argues that this is possible because society will be rich enough to afford to invest the resources to cultivate the land (again we see the optimistic and self-reinforcing "stability region"). He does not directly address the competing needs

TABLE 7.5. *Cultivated and Arable Land, by Region*

| | Area (in millions of hectares) | | | Cultivated Land | |
| | | | | As Percentage of Area Potentially Arable | Per Person (in hectares) |
Region	Total	Potentially Arable	Cultivated		
Africa	3,033	965	181	19	0.37
Asia	2,757	1,058	455	43	0.17
Oceania	850	512	46	9	1.90
Europe	487	226	140	62	0.29
North and Central America	1,934	494	234	47	0.93
South America	2,055	702	162	23	0.43
USSR	2,240	604	231	38	0.9
World	13,356	4,561	1,449	32	0.32

Sources: Food and Agricultural Organization, *Production Yearbook* (Rome: FAO, 1981), 45–56; United Nations, *Demographic Yearbook* (New York: UN, 1981).
Note: Potentially arable includes permanent crops, arable land, and permanent pasture.

FIGURE 7.4. *Arable Land Availability, 1650–2100*

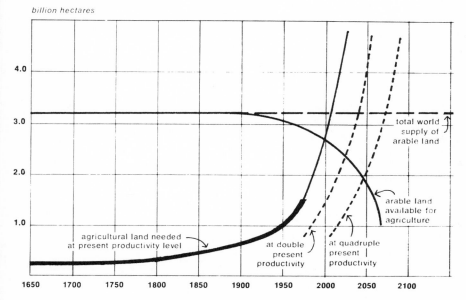

Source: Donella H. Meadows, Dennis L. Meadows, Jørgen Randers, William W. Behrens III, *The Limits to Growth: A Report for the Club of Rome's Project on the Predicament of Mankind* (New York: Universe Books, 1972), 50. Reprinted with permission.

for the land. Simon goes one step further and downplays the global trend of deforestation altogether, pointing to a few counter examples like the United States, South Korea, and China. At the other extreme, the Meadows report argues that as global population continues to grow, less and less of that 3.19 billion hectares will be available for agriculture, because more and more will be used for cities, transportation systems, or other uses associated with growing numbers of people. They make a forecast of the maximum land actually available for agriculture (figure 7.4). Because of population growth and the withdrawal of land from actual or potential agricultural use for other uses, the maximum land for agriculture falls to 2 billion hectares by 2050. On the same graph are calculations of land needed for food production. Note that even with quadrupled productivity, scarcities are forecast by 2050. Unfortunately, their calculation for maximum arable agricultural land is flawed. The authors assume each additional person requires .08 hectares of nonagricultural land, a figure based on research in forty-four western U.S. counties. The western United States is notorious globally for its sprawl, however, thus biasing their calculation (Meadows et al. 1972, 51n).

FIGURE 7.5.   *Typical Fertilizer Response Curve (Corn Yield in Iowa, 1964)*

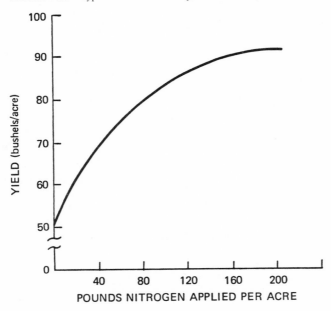

POUNDS NITROGEN APPLIED PER ACRE

Source: U.S. Department of Agriculture, as adapted by Lester R. Brown, *By Bread Alone* (New York: Praeger, 1974), 117.

In determining probable yields per hectare, the most common forecasting approach is to rely on a yield function such as that shown in figure 7.5. That figure shows a relationship between fertilizer (in this case nitrogen) and yield, in bushels per acre. As additional pounds of fertilizer are applied, yield is increased, but every pound produces less additional yield—that is, every pound of fertilizer has decreasing marginal utility. Representations of production like that of figure 7.5 assume, of course, that a balanced package of inputs (e.g., pesticides, water) is applied.

Debate over the availability of one of these, water, will most likely intensify in the next few years. In many areas of the world farmers have tapped large aquifers, often referred to as fossil water because they exist as a result of accumulation processes over hundreds of thousands of years, or of geological processes that placed the water there thousands of years earlier. Many of these are being depleted. For instance, the Ogallala Aquifer, stretching from northern Nebraska to Texas, may run dry within twenty to forty years. Already farmers in east Texas are finding it impossible economically to justify pumping from deeper levels with higher priced energy and are abandoning the effort. In the San Joaquin Valley of California, land has settled as much as thirty feet from groundwater depletion

(*Compressed Air Magazine,* May 1982, 7). In other areas, chemical contamination of such reservoirs is the major problem: gasoline infiltrated the drinking wells of Cherryville, Pennsylvania.

Skeptics point out that less than 1 percent of the nation's groundwater is polluted, that thirty years ago it was being said that the Ogallala would be dry in twenty years, and that techniques such as desalination (three hundred thirty plants already operate in the United States) and aquifer recharging in surplus years (under way in the Los Angeles area) can extend supplies.

The rough theoretical yield curve has its real world counterpart in figure 7.6. There we see increases in Mexican wheat yields over time (and effectively also with increased fertilizer input) as new varieties have been developed. One must be very careful with such curves, however, since significant changes in agricultural practice (e.g., double-cropping) or in seed types may necessitate a shift in the curve itself upward, rather than merely a move along the curve. Historically, this is illustrated by figure 7.7.

In figure 7.7 we can see that Japan has some of the most intensive and technologically advanced agriculture in the world; its long-term historical rice yield curve does not yet show signs of saturation. That curve simultaneously suggests the dramatic progress in yields that could potentially be made, given similarly high levels of farm inputs, in Asian LDCs. Still,

FIGURE 7.6. *Mexican Wheat Yields, 1950–1974*

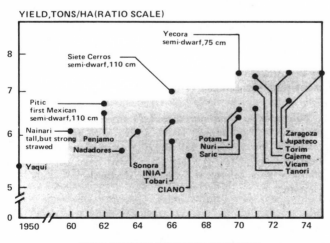

Source: Sterling Wortman and Ralph W. Cummings, Jr., *To Feed This World* (Baltimore: Johns Hopkins University Press, 1978), 161. Reprinted with permission.

FIGURE 7.7. *Current Rice Yields in Selected Asian Countries*

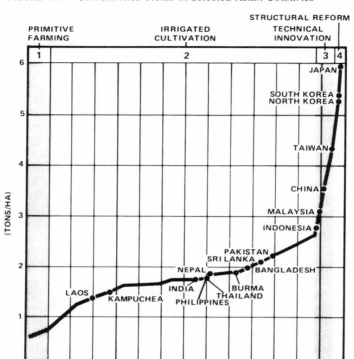

Source: W. David Hopper, "The Development of Agriculture in Developing Countries," *Scientific American* 235 (September, 1976): 200. Copyright © 1976 by Scientific American, Inc. All rights reserved. Reprinted by permission.

Note: Solid line shows historical growth of rice yields in Japan.

some agriculturists argue that there has been recent evidence of a yield plateauing in the United States and elsewhere (Wittwer 1980, 63).

Clearly much of the argument here is technological. Recombinant DNA techniques might produce grain strains which could provide, or "fix," their own nitrogen from the air, greatly reducing fertilizer needs. Currently fertilizer use globally, most of it nitrogen, is projected by the USDA to more than double to about 220 million metric tons by 2000 (CEQ 1981, 100). Hydroponics, the growing of food in tanks of nutrient saturated water, already has some commercial applications (in Florida) and could significantly affect land requirements. Minimal tillage and newer irrigation forms (trickle, spit, or drip) could reduce needed inputs of other types, such as water.

Another important issue is climate. There is fairly general agreement that the global climate of the 1950s and 1960s was very favorable in a historical context because of its relative stability. If it was, in fact, unusually stable, it is highly probable that the future will hold a return to more normal and more disruptive fluctuations in weather patterns. Agriculture, like other elements of the global development system, is subject to cycles. Whether they are related to sunspots, locust hatches, or human investment patterns, those cycles can be very disruptive. Storage of food from the good years as insurance against the bad has been a function of government for millennia. The existence of a global agricultural system has increasingly allowed shortfalls in one area to be met by surpluses elsewhere. It may also be gradually leading to less caution with respect to overall levels of stocks and thus greater vulnerability in case of geographically widespread climate problems.

Much of the discussion surrounding climate, however, focuses on whether or not there is likely to be a general warming or cooling trend around which this increased variability is probable. The major argument supporting global cooling is that there has been a moderate cooling trend since the 1940s (Thompson 1980, 100). Some observers have argued that the increased level of atmospheric dust resulting from human activities could cause this to continue by cutting insolation. More frequently, projections warn of a global warming trend because of the "greenhouse effect." Deforestation and the burning of fossil fuels increase atmospheric carbon dioxide, which allows normal insolation but retards infrared (heat) radiation from returning to space.

There is obviously much uncertainty over this question. That extends to an evaluation of the potential impact of either warming or cooling. Although greater variation is almost universally deleterious for agriculture, either consistent warming or cooling could help some areas, as well as hurting others. Prolonged trends in either direction would obviously be detrimental on a wide scale, because agriculture would need to be abandoned in areas that eventually became too hot or too cold. It has been noted that severe winters in the 1300s and early 1400s in Europe were followed by mild ones from 1450 to the mid-1500s, followed again by severe ones until the late 1600s and that these were periods of economic recession, expansion, and recession, respectively (Wallerstein 1976, 27). Neotraditionalists have made much of the climate issue, while modernists have largely ignored it.

Economic Approaches

The debate between neotraditionalists and modernists over agricultural futures within the context of a "physical" approach to food supply has prompted some critics to question the approach altogether. Already more "economic" techniques dominate on the demand side. For instance, to forecast food demand, a relationship between income level and percentage of income spent on food, called an "Engel curve," is typically used. That curve indicates that expenditures on food normally drop from about 70 percent of income at the lowest income levels to less than 10 percent at the highest. Radicals have noted that this indicates the food problem to be in fact an income problem, since given more income people will buy the food. Similar curves break the total expenditure on food down by categories, revealing mostly unprocessed cereals and starchy roots at low incomes and primarily processed livestock at higher income levels.

Naturally, all of these income/demand relationships are affected by food prices through elasticities of demand, which tend to be remarkably low for food (in contrast to what we increasingly see for energy). A major basis for the traditional and dramatic boom-or-bust cycles in agriculture is the low demand elasticity for food, coupled with high supply elasticities. When shortages appear, demand remains high and prices rise dramatically. It takes a while longer (at least one growing season) for supply to respond, but when it does, the magnitude of the response, especially in the United States, where there has been surplus capacity, often leads to major overproduction and a price bust.

Some critics have suggested putting less effort into the analysis of land, yields, and so forth, and downplaying the importance of the events of 1972–74. Instead, it is argued, we should look at the long-term trends in prices and food availability. We have already seen that the long-term trend in food availability has been positive, even if irregular by region and slow in per capita increase rate. The price of wheat stayed at or below two dollars per bushel and seventy-five dollars per ton throughout the 1950s and 1960s and surged to five dollars per bushel in 1973–74. The price has subsequently come down considerably in real terms. Even at its peak, in 1973–74, however, wheat prices in real terms were below peaks obtained in the early 1900s or early post–World War II period, and the long-term real price trend has been downward (Simon 1981, 74). In 1982, grain dollar prices were lower (in real terms) than at any time since the 1930s (Timmer, Falcon, and Pearson 1983, 4). In table 7.6 we see the price of U.S. wheat (a good indicator of global market prices) in real terms since 1950. In terms of purchasing power, the downward trend in the cost of wheat for most peoples is even more dramatic.

Of course, one should note that such "long-term" arguments, as made by Simon back to 1800, rely upon a starting date effectively as arbitrary as those that emphasize the upward trends of the early 1970s, and which Simon views as short term. Futurist and head of the Worldwatch Institute Lester Brown points out that recent evidence on the collapse of the Yucatan Mayan civilization suggests that overexpansion of agriculture and deterio-

TABLE 7.6.   *U.S. Wheat Prices, 1950–1982 (in dollars per metric ton)*

Year	Current Dollar Price	Constant (1981) Dollar Price
1950	66.9	301.4
1955	61.7	238.2
1960	59.2	207.7
1965	58.1	197.0
1970	57.0	178.7
1971	62.1	179.5
1972	69.1	181.8
1973	136.8	301.3
1974	178.0	316.7
1975	138.4	214.9
1976	122.7	187.3
1977	95.5	134.3
1978	124.9	148.3
1979	156.3	166.1
1980	168.3	162.5
1981	154.6	154.6
1982 (Jan.–June)	141.1	—

Source: World Bank, *Commodity Trade and Price Trends* (Washington, D.C.: World Bank, 1982), 63.

ration of land quality was perhaps the major factor (Brown 1981, 3–5). Thus, arguments with an even longer time horizon reopen the possibility that limits on production expansion are near.

Political Economy Issues

Some of the political economy issues have intruded directly into the debates over agricultural futures (Hopkins and Puchala 1978). The issue of food aid has attracted much attention. Under Public Law 480 (Food for Peace) the United States gave away—or much more often sold on concessional terms—$30.3 billion of generally surplus food from 1954 through 1980. As U.S. surpluses have disappeared, and exports have surged, the program has declined in importance from 27 percent of U.S. exports in 1960 to 3 percent in 1980 (Hansen 1982, 190). In addition, humanitarian programs of short-term famine relief have existed throughout the period. Few policy analysts question the correctness of the humanitarian programs, but both classical liberals and radicals have come to question the broader concessional sales programs. Classical liberals see them as distortions of the market not effectively different from dumping (selling surpluses below cost). Radicals see them as tools by which the dependence of the LDCs on MDCs is maintained and their internal markets distorted. In response to such criticism, internationalists have moved much more toward support for technical assistance and investment assistance in agriculture, as opposed to aid in the form of food.

Another debate has centered on the creation of global food reserves, or stocks. Almost everyone agrees that it would be desirable to have a global food reserve. The debate rages over who should pay for it, who should hold it, and what should be the rules for adding to it or liquidating it. We have made no real global progress on these issues.

Still another argument continues over the desirability of trying to stabilize agricultural prices over time, especially those of the primary agricultural commodities exported by LDCs. Internationalists point to the desirability for both importing and exporting countries of relatively stable prices. For LDCs it would mean that export earnings could be better forecast and assured, and their development efforts could become more regular. Classical liberals often reject such programs and emphasize instead reducing trade barriers, including those set up by LDCs to protect and subsidize food purchases (Johnson 1980). They point especially to the tendency of the LDCs to maintain low food prices domestically, thus both encouraging demand and dampening incentives for farmers, and argue that these prices are a primary basis of the LDC food problems (Johnson 1978, 275). Low food prices reduce farmers' incentives while simultaneously forcing the government to buy food abroad. I shall return in Chapter 10 to the very important role that government action has come to play in agricultural systems.

8. Technology

Few studies of the future specifically address the issue of technological change in more than implicit or passing fashion. This is surprising because technology is so central to the process of global development and to the differences in perception of that process by modernists and neotraditionalists. Even a book like Alvin Toffler's *The Third Wave* (1980), which is almost technologically deterministic in its approach, does not explicitly attempt to sketch the range of possible or probable future technologies and how those could shape broader social change. The approach of most studies is ad hoc, selectively emphasizing one or more possible future technologies and their impact. At the extreme with respect to this type of approach is much of science fiction. Often a single technological development (a medical technique, a weapons system, or a form of space travel) frames a science fiction story, and the author can elaborate with considerable imagination on some of the implications of the development upon social relations.

The reason most authors take indirect or partial approaches to technology is obvious: as difficult as forecasting population growth or energy demand over the next twenty years might be, such forecasts are trivial compared to the difficult task of anticipating technological developments. And as complicated as it may be to evaluate the impact of changes in income on fertility or of energy price on economic growth rates, those are straightforward compared to forecasting the impact of semiconductor technology on employment, or of recombinant DNA on agricultural production. A major difficulty is our inability to measure or quantify technology in any meaningful way: there is no such thing as an index of technology.

In my discussion of technology here, I outline the relationship between technology and other aspects of global development. After presentation of a little background I shall, as in previous chapters, look at forward and backward linkages. Whereas for most issues the emphasis has been on the backward linkages (factors influencing or causing change in the issue area), here the balance is more even; indeed, the impact of technology on other aspects of global development is of greater interest.

BACKGROUND: HISTORY AND FORECASTS

Technology need not be physical or tool-based. One can also refer to a social innovation, for example, a bicameral legislature, the nuclear family, or suburbs, as technology. Here, however, I will focus primarily on physical technology.

Totals and Rates

Human beings are often said to be distinguished from other animals by their tool-making and -using capabilities. That is not strictly true, since even insects have been shown to use tools. Yet primitive man excelled in developing tools as weapons, food gathering and storing implements, clothing construction aids, and shelter construction materials. Control of fire was a major breakthrough. Roughly the last ten thousand years have been characterized by a series of technological developments, often called "revolutions," and the period is frequently divided by these technological stages. Each stage is normally related to cultural, social, and political developments. Among these revolutions and some of their principal technologies are the initial agricultural revolution (simple farming, herding); the urban revolution (the plow, wheeled vehicles); the irrigation revolution (canals, flood gates); the metallurgical revolution (forged iron); the pastoral revolution (windmills); the mercantile revolution (ocean-going sailboats, compass); and the industrial revolution (steel and coke, internal combustion engines) (see DeVore [1980, 52–53]). Many scholars have identified the current period as one of a cybernetic, information, or nuclear revolution, characterized by developments in electronics and nuclear physics.

Although it is difficult to measure technology, one approach to doing so in limited areas of application is the "envelope" curve, shown in figure 8.1. Over time various means of locomotion have gradually increased the speed of human transportation. In their initial forms, the new technologies may be slower than earlier ones, but they develop rapidly until some upper limits are reached and newer technologies supplant them, at least for some purposes. The envelope curve is a curve drawn along the upper side of the individual technology curves (which are "saturating exponentials," like the agricultural yield curve of figure 7.5). The envelope curve of figure 8.1 is clearly an exponential curve that, if extrapolated, would suggest that

FIGURE 8.1. *Trends in Transportation Speed*

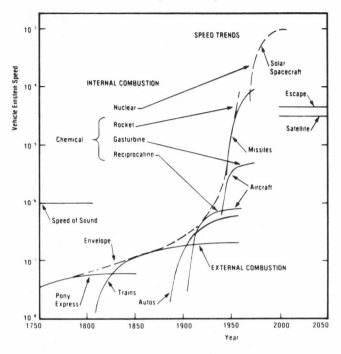

Source: Paul W. DeVore, *Technology: An Introduction* (Worcester, Mass.: Davis Publications, 1980), 11. Reprinted with permission.

mankind could attain the speed of light by the end of the century. Since that speed is believed theoretically to be a hard barrier (except in science fiction), most would argue that the curve will turn and become a logistical, or S-shaped, curve.

In figure 8.2 we see another such series of technological advances, this time for improvements in energy conversion efficiencies. Carnot gave us a formula for the maximum efficiency of any one machine (based on highest and lowest operating temperatures); that and a seemingly hard upper limit of 100 percent conversion of input energy suggests that an S-shaped envelope curve is appropriate here, too.

Although such energy efficiency improvements appear relatively smooth and predictable, sources of primary energy have not been. In 1930 Robert A. Millikan, a Nobel Prize winner and founder of the California Institute of Technology, wrote in response to fears expressed by science writer Frederick Soddy about the potential of nuclear power:

FIGURE 8.2. *Trends in Energy Conversion Efficiency*

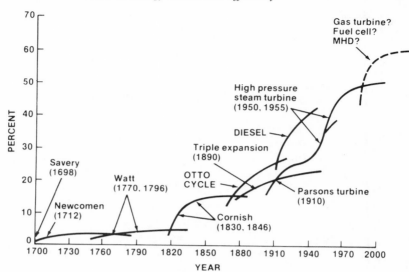

Source: Paul W. DeVore, *Technology: An Introduction* (Worcester, Mass.: Davis Publications, 1980), 173. Reprinted with permission.

Since Mr. Soddy raised the hobgoblin of dangerous quantities of available subatomic energy, [science] has brought to light good evidence that this particular hobgoblin—like most of the hobgoblins that crowd in on the mind of ignorance—was a myth . . . The new evidence born of further scientific study is to the effect that it is highly improbable that there is any appreciable amount of available subatomic energy to tap. (Sinsheimer 1980, 148)

Figures 8.3 and 8.4 reveal still additional technological progressions, although this time in terms of discrete developments rather than distinct technologies. Note that the vertical axis scales on these figures and on figure 8.1 are logarithmic (units increase by factors of ten). If the scales were normal arithmetic, the steepness of the curves' rise would be much greater—it would appear as if after a long period of practically no change there was an explosion of change. The use of a logarithmic scale emphasizes growth rates; if a line is straight (linear) on a logarithmic scale, the process is growing at a constant rate; on an arithmetic scale, the constant growth rate would add a larger amount in each time period because of the higher base, and the growth rate might incorrectly appear to be accelerating.

Futurist John Platt demonstrated another way of indicating the rapidity

FIGURE 8.3. *Trend in Explosive Power*

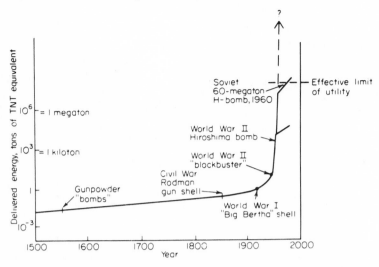

Source: Robert U. Ayres, *Technological Forecasting and Long-range Planning* (New York: McGraw-Hill, 1969), 22. Reprinted with permission.

of technological progress by compiling a list of changes occurring in the last one-hundred years (1969, 1117):

1. Increase in speed of travel by a factor of 100
2. Increase in control over infectious disease by a factor of 100
3. Increase in energy resources by a factor of 1,000
4. Increase in data handling speed by a factor of 10,000
5. Increase in power of weaponry by a factor of 1 million
6. Increase in speed of communications by a factor of 10 million

These changes summarize many of the curves we have seen.

Such curves and lists make it appear perhaps easier to forecast technological developments, at least the practical results of them (computing power, transportation speed, explosive power, energy efficiency) than was suggested earlier. We should not be misled, however. Whether to fit exponential curves or S-shaped ones to past trends—and if S-shaped, when the "turning point" will occur—are problems plaguing all extrapolative forecasts. Simple exponential extrapolation from some past curves would have led to the following conclusions (Ayres 1969, 20):

—vehicles will attain the speed of light by 1982
—immortality will be achieved by 2000

FIGURE 8.4.   *The Evolution of Integrated Circuits*

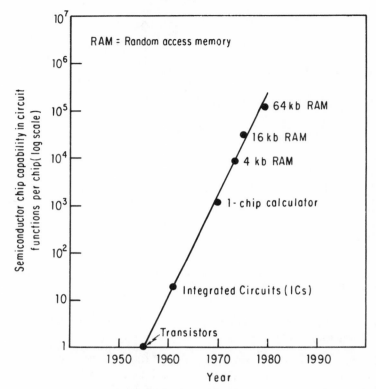

Source: James A. Cunningham, "Using the Learning Curve as a Management Tool." *IEEE Spectrum* 17 (June 1980): 48.

> —a single person will control the energy equivalent of the sun by
>   1981

We have missed on at least two of three.

Then, of course, we have absolutely no basis for extrapolation in some areas. When (if ever) will we achieve gravity control (Arthur Clarke [1962] says by 2050) and how fast will the cost of doing so fall? Or, for that matter, when will we achieve net energy gain in controlled fusion energy and how rapidly will the net energy (energy out/energy in) ratio rise?

It has become a cliché to say that the rate of technological progress overall has been increasing. As "evidence" we are told to look at the number of scientists and engineers now working, or at the number of books produced, or at the innovations around us: computers, space shuttles, artificial hearts, and so on. Professor John McCarthy of Stanford has suggested, however, that such claims may at least be greatly exaggerated. Between 1890 and 1920, he points out, electricity, telephones, automobiles, airplanes, and the radio all came to the popular market. It would be hard to argue that recent changes in energy systems, transportation, or communication will prove more significant. Jerome Wiesner, president of MIT, echoed the same argument by referring to the United States as a "technologically mature" society in which most innovations are leading to replacements of old technologies, rather than creating new industries (Hamrin 1980, 140).

Thus, rate of technological change is both largely unmeasurable and very uncertain.

Distribution

We know, of course, that most technological advance is occurring in MDCs. There are relationships among the number of scientists at work, the levels of spending on research and development (R&D), and the rate of scientific discovery. In 1979 about $150 billion was spent on R&D globally, about 1.5 percent of gross world product (Norman 1979, 5). Some three million scientists and engineers were employed (about .1 percent of global population). The 1978 breakdowns for non-Communist regions are shown in table 8.1. Developed countries have twenty times as many scientists and engineers per capita as developing countries. The North-South imbalance is even more pronounced when one looks at the priorities for R&D: 24 percent of spending goes to the military and 8

TABLE 8.1. *Regional Distribution of World Research and Development Budgets, 1978 (excluding communist countries)*

Region	Total R&D Budget (in billions of dollars)	Share of World Total (in percentages)	Number of Scientists, Engineers in R&D (in thousands)	Share of World Total (in percentages)
Developing countries	5.4	4.4	241	11.3
Africa	0.5	0.4	15	0.7
Asia (without Japan)	2.0	1.6	126	5.9
Latin America	2.3	1.9	70	3.3
Middle East	0.6	0.5	30	1.4
Developed countries	117.7	95.6	1,890	88.7
Western Europe	51.7	41.5	780	36.6
North America	50.2	40.8	661	31.0
Other (including Japan)	16.4	13.3	450	21.1
World Total	123.1	100.0	2,131	100.0

Source: UNESCO, *Statistical Yearbook* (New York: UN, 1982), pp. v–17, v–18.

TABLE 8.2.   *Distribution of World Research and Development Budget,*
by Program

Program	Percentage of Total R&D
Military	24
Basic research	15
Space	8
Energy	8
Health	7
Information processing	5
Transportation	5
Pollution control	5
Agriculture	3
Others	20

Source: Colin Norman, *Knowledge and Power: The Global Research and Development Budget* (Washington, D.C.: Worldwatch, 1979), 6. Reprinted with permission.

percent to space (table 8.2). Although there are civilian spinoffs of spending in these categories, and even Third World benefits (e.g., satellite mapping, communications), the category of most obvious relevance to the Third World, agriculture, receives only 3 percent of global expenditures.

From a radical perspective these imbalances are evidence that control over technology has become a major tool in the continuing dominance by the North over the South (Sagasti 1979). Data over time—which would enable us to examine changes in the pattern of imbalance—are hard to find. Within the developed world itself there has been a shift. In 1965 the United States spent 3 percent of its GDP on R&D and that amounted to 70 percent of total R&D by OECD nations. By 1975 the United States rate had dropped to 2.3 percent (West Germany and Japan reached that level from less than 2 percent earlier) and the United States accounted for less than 60 percent of OECD R&D (Norman 1979, 11–12).

Forward Linkages

It is an understatement to say that the impact of technology on other aspects of the global development system is a matter of controversy. Perhaps more than any other single issue, the impact of technology distinguishes modernists from neotraditionalists. A very positive and optimistic attitude toward the current and future role of technology has dominated literature and public attitudes since at least World War II. Among the best known technological enthusiasts are Buckminster Fuller, Alvin Toffler, C. P. Snow, B. F. Skinner, Marshall McLuhan, Zbigniew Brzezinski, Herman Kahn, and Arthur Clarke (Gendron 1977, 3–5). Positive attitudes have been encouraged by developments in many areas. In medicine, for example, progress has been striking. Besides the overall evidence of globally increasing life expectancies, we have seen the development of the Salk polio vaccine in 1955, the global elimination of small pox by 1977, and steady progress in the cure rate for cancer. In space, we saw the first man-made satellite in October, 1957, and the first man on the moon in 1969 (an almost incredible leap in twelve years).

Technological enthusiasts proclaim the beneficial impact of technology in many areas. The end of scarcity, the relative freedom from labor, and victories over disease are among the more direct benefits. Because of the association between scarcity and social conflict (including war), reduction in such conflict is a possible secondary benefit.

Skepticism or outright opposition to particular technologies and even to technological change broadly has, of course, a long history. Among the best known movements historically were the Luddites. In the late 1700s the apparently apocryphal Captain Ned Ludd destroyed knitting machines in England and between 1811 and 1816 England was swept by revolts involving the smashing of machinery by people called Luddites. The word "sabotage" has its origin in the use by the Dutch of wooden shoes (in French, *sabot*) to stop machinery. Thoreau used the metaphor of the machine against the war in Mexico: "Let your life be a counterfriction to stop the machine." Mario Savio of the University of California at Berkeley echoed that sentiment in 1964 by calling for students to throw their bodies on "the machine" to stop it, referring to the university and the larger "establishment."

In recent years the growth of environmentalist movements and of antinuclear (both weapons and plants) movements has often taken on a distinctly antitechnology cast. Those who attacked the construction sites of nuclear plants in New Hampshire, California, and elsewhere throughout the world could be called neo-Luddite as easily as neotraditionalist.

For the most part, those who have taken up the antitechnology banner have been careful to limit the targets of their attacks. Almost no one can fail to cheer advances in medical technology, and few fail to share a sense of accomplishment with respect to mankind's movement into space, or the first footfall on the moon, July 20, 1969. Yet the range of criticism of technology in modern societies (I shall address developing countries shortly) is broad.

Technology may cost jobs. Automation has been a potential threat for centuries. The modern economy has managed to expand employment with sufficient speed to more than offset reductions in some industries. But the disruption of individual lives goes on, even for those who obtain new employment. The mass global migration from rural agriculture to urban industry and services is the dominant example. The modernist would argue that such disruption is a small price to pay for abundant food coupled with supplies of labor for other economic sectors. The neotraditionalist would argue that in many cases we could have achieved the abundance at a much lower cost.

Technology can also lead to a change in social power and control patterns. I discussed this issue earlier in some depth with respect to the alternative social implications of different energy technologies. One of the key factors underlying the massive outpouring of support for solar technologies has been the gut-level feeling of individuals that they can control and own their own power and thus be independent of the utilities and the government. Modernists may question the relative efficiency and cost of solar energy; the neotraditionalist is willing to pay a price in terms of efficiency to satisfy other values.

Technology can also have military applications that outrage the moral sense of people, not to mention placing them in physical danger. The large-scale mass movements in Europe against nuclear weapons which opened the 1980s and have spread to the United States illustrate this. The sense of outrage may carry over to related technology, that is, nuclear generating plants. The modernist might argue that this is an emotional reaction; the neotraditionalist would reply that technologies, once "unleashed," can develop their own constituencies and push otherwise rational people into courses they would not ordinarily pursue (e.g., the other side has biological weapons, therefore we must develop them and have them available, at least as a bargaining chip).

Within both the classical liberal and more radical literature there has generally been a supportive, modernist approach to technology, although not without exception. Radicals (and often internationalists) strongly believe that the implications of a technology depend on its political and social context. For example, Nestlé's baby formula may be an appropriate technology in MDCs, but advertisement and sale in the LDCs to mothers who often do not need it, cannot easily afford it, and may misuse it constitutes simply another example of the historic pattern of exploitation and disruption of LDCs by MDCs.

Less dramatic than baby formula, but more important in the long run, is the general issue of predominant technology development in the North for its own purposes. This can lead, suggest internationalists and radicals, either to use of that technology to disrupt, dominate, control or exploit the South (e.g., weapons sales) or to transfer to the South technology that may not be appropriate given its own production conditions (especially labor-displacing machinery in a labor-surplus and capital-short environment).

There tends to be a close relationship between the arguments made by the neotraditionalists with respect to technology in more modern, more economically developed societies, and those made by internationalists (and to a lesser degree radicals) with respect to the technological relationship between rich and poor internationally. First, there is a recognition of the critical importance for LDCs of technological advance. Procedures for facilitating, implementing, and making less costly the transfer of technology from North to South—such as simplified licensing procedures and a "code of conduct" for multinational corporations—have become part of the proposed New International Economic Order (Ramesh and Weiss 1979). Second, there is a recognition that technology carries values that will come into conflict with the existing culture. There is real uncertainty as to whether the transfer of technology can be controlled in such a way as to preserve what is valued in existing institutions and social structures, or whether it will inevitably bring with it the values and concomitant social structures of the modernized West (Goulet 1977).

Third, there is a strong fear that technology developed in the North may not be "appropriate" for the South. Although a technology may be deemed inappropriate for many reasons, the most often cited is that MDC technologies tend to be capital intensive and labor-saving, whereas the LDCs tend to have shortages of capital and surpluses of labor. The green revolution agricultural technology is often given as a prime example. That technology requires applications of fertilizers (and normally of other chemicals) and makes reasonable (although not inevitable) the introduction of large farm machinery. That in turn has a tendency to make larger plots more efficient and desirable and to lead to land consolidation and farmer displacement. Thus, the technology tends to be both capital intensive and labor displacing. Similarly, there is a propensity for MDC industrial technologies, such as steel and automobiles, to be capital intensive, and to create relatively few jobs. Moreover, such technologies tend to become less labor intensive over time and are often picked up by LDCs only when they are far advanced. All of this has led to calls for intermediate technology (normally simply older MDC technology) or "appropriate" technology (new but labor intensive) to be developed and transferred. Again, this is very similar to the neotraditionalist perspective within MDCs, which, however, also stresses the "human-scale," the personally fulfilling nature, and the environmentally "friendly" character of "appropriate" technology (Dorf and Hunter 1978; de Moll and Coe 1978; Schumacher 1973).

Classical liberals and radicals are far less ambivalent about technology. Some classical liberals would argue that the market is capable of selecting the "appropriate" technology: a relatively capital-intensive technology is chosen only if it is the most economically efficient. Wages could be too high relative to skill levels, perhaps because of government action that distorts the labor market. Some radicals are also likely to be reluctant to see anything but the most advanced technology adopted by LDCs for fear that "intermediate" or "appropriate" may be euphemisms for noncompetitive (as classical liberals suggest) and may help hold the LDCs in an internationally subordinate position. If, in fact, "intermediate" technologies should be adopted in spite of their higher costs, because of the employment and income equality benefits they offer, then the LDCs may need to cut themselves off from the MDCs in order to do so (they could not trade competitively) and pursue autarkic development paths.

To this point we have been looking in general terms at how the impact of technology on other aspects of global development is perceived and how world views organize such perceptions. Clearly we would like to be able to move to a more detailed level with respect to a discussion of impact— looking at individual technologies and specific implications. In the next section I do turn to specific technologies, both recent developments and possible future ones. It is appropriate now, however, to consider the ways in which experts try to estimate or evaluate the impact of technologies on the broader global development system.

The U.S. government has established the Office of Technology Assessment (OTA) and governments around the world have recognized the desirability of anticipating consequences of the introduction of new technologies (Teich 1972). Increasingly, assessments are performed, and increasingly they have become quantitative and "scientific." For instance, studies of the impact of seeding hurricanes or snow clouds, of building the Alaskan oil pipeline, and of converting automobiles to alternative power systems have been undertaken (Coates 1974). Some of these have used a "tree decision structure." That is, consequences of introducing or not introducing the technologies are listed, probabilities of consequences and costs (or benefits) defined, and probable overall costs and benefits computed.

Another approach to technology assessment involves the Delphi technique, also used in estimating the probabilities of technological development itself. This involves asking experts for their estimates of the probability of a particular impact and their evaluation of it. When the experts provide their responses individually, they are given those of other experts (anonymously) and asked to reconsider their own (Gordon and Ament 1972). This naturally leads, with more iteration, to greater convergence.

Such approaches, although an important step in technology assessment, obviously have two limitations. First, they tend to be more specific than we might like, forecasting the particular year of a potential discovery or the cost of a particular process. Thus, Delphi approaches prove difficult to use in investigation of more general issues, such as the relative future potential of solar and coal technologies. Second, and more importantly, they tend to codify the biases and world views of the participants: they are much more collections of opinions than explanations of causality.

It should be noted in passing that it has also been suggested that technological change is related to the long waves, or Kondratieff cycles, discussed earlier. Economist Christopher Freeman argued, as Schumpeter had earlier, that the timing of long waves and major technical innovations was related, with innovations like the internal combustion engine, railways, and electricity having broad repercussions on the economic and social systems (Freeman 1978). The mechanisms of the impact have not been specified very clearly, but employment levels and investment rates are probably the most important. Unfortunately, as we shall see in the next section, it is very difficult to make specific judgments in advance concerning the employment or investment implications of a given technology.

FORECASTING: THEORIES AND MODELS

It has been suggested that there are two ways of looking at the bases of technological change: "ontological" and "teleological" viewpoints (Ayres 1969, 29). The *ontological* view is that technology has its own dynamics. Thus, discoveries or innovations can partially be explained in light of their sequence, with a natural building, or cumulation, although, in fact, there is a strong randomness and unpredictability involved. The particular genius and mentality of individual scientists and inventors adds an important idiosyncratic element. Major inventions, such as the plow, the stirrup, or the transistor, may have been "inevitable" in a broad sense, but their timing was far from predictable.

The *teleological* view is that technological and scientific advance is more derivative from the social, military, and economic needs of the time. In fact, inventions that arrive too early, like Babbage's calculator (invented in 1880), appear to fail and need to be revived later. This view is, of course, also consistent with "planned" innovation, such as the development of the atomic bomb in the Manhattan Project or the development of lunar spacecraft in the U.S. rush to the moon.

This is an important philosophical difference because it has obvious ramifications for perspectives on the issues addressed here. If one holds a teleological view, then one believes that the need to produce more food for a growing global population, the need to develop alternative energy sources to replace conventional oil and gas, and the need to discover production and consumption patterns to protect the environment will result in appropriate innovations. This is not true from an ontological viewpoint, which emphasizes the more fortuitous character of innovation. Clearly, the modernist is more likely to hold a teleological view.

The distinction between the two views on technology is largely untestable, subject primarily to anecdotal evidence on both sides. A more productive approach for us in examining technological change here may be a combination of simple extrapolation and "expert" judgment. More specifically, it should be useful to review recent technological innovations and possible future direction in three areas widely recognized to have tremendous potential: semiconductors and associated electronic and communications technologies; newer energy technologies; and biological technology, especially recombinant DNA and genetic engineering. As we shall see, these technologies are of fundamental importance to other elements of the global development system. It should be noted that other technologies could also have been selected. For instance, a "materials revolution" is now occurring with the development of super strength and very lightweight synthetic materials and alloys. Drucker (1969) argues that this revolution, and the implications for steel, glass, and wood replacement, is of especially great significance.

Semiconductors

The general history of semiconductor technology is increasingly familiar, as writers retrace the revolution (see, for example, Ide [1982]). In 1946 ENIAC (Electronic Numerical Integrator and Calculator) was constructed with 18,000 vacuum tubes. It is often called the first electronic computer. The next year, the transistor was developed. A transistor is made of semiconductor material, usually silicon, to which minute quantities of impurities are added. Thus, it will conduct when a sufficiently large current is applied and can act as a switch, as did vacuum tubes in ENIAC. Individual transistors still needed to be wired together.

In the late 1950s, transistors were produced in batches and cut apart. In 1959 Texas Instruments and Fairchild decided to wire the transistors together while on a single slice and later simply deposit tiny aluminum conductors on a semiconductor surface. Thus, integrated circuits, or chips, were born. By 1980, about 64,000 (64K) bits of information could be stored on a single silicon chip 5 millimeters square; the chips sold for under ten dollars. Such a chip would have approximately 128,000 components. Although currently the 16K chip is the workhorse, the Japanese had by early 1980 prototypes of a 256K chip and by 1990 chips will most likely be produced with 1,000,000 components (note that this suggests some leveling of the growth rate shown in figure 8.4).

Most chips are designed for a specific purpose, such as keeping time or storing information in a computer, and then mass produced. In 1971 Intel brought out an integrated circuit that was configured specifically as a computer's central processing unit—a microprocessor. In effect, the 18,000 vacuum tubes of ENIAC had been reduced to a single chip. Integrated circuits are now a $10 billion per year industry, growing at 30 percent per year. The industry based on it (watches, calculators, computers, video games, etc.) is about $100 billion and projected by 1990 to be $400 billion, about the size then of the global auto industry, now the world's largest (Norman 1980). Although the Japanese have taken the lead in semiconductors, the United States retains the edge in microprocessors.

Although consumer products, such as calculators, watches, and, increasingly, personal computers, are the most obvious beneficiaries of the technology, they are not alone, and applications on the production side of the economy will almost certainly have greater short and mid-term impact. In industry, semiconductor technology has been used for sensing devices (vision and touch), for measuring instruments (temperature, size), for information processing, and for controllers on elements of the production process (assemblers, welders). Robots represent the fusion of these functions (sensing, measuring, information processing, and control). According to a Carnegie-Mellon study, the U.S. robot work force in 1980 was thirty-five hundred strong. These are not the human appearing (android) intelligent robots of science fiction. General Motors had three-hundred robots in 1980 and may have fourteen-thousand by 1990. The market in Japan, now one-half of all the world's robots, could be worth $1.3 billion by 1985.

The advance in robots depends in part on progress in computer intelligence. The Japanese Ministry of International Trade and Industry (MITI) is now backing a ten-year project to build what is called the fifth-generation computer, to be characterized by a considerable degree of artificial intelligence. In the United States, the government has decided to encourage a group of domestic computer manufacturers to pool R&D resources in the development of a "super computer." Computing speed and functions can be expected to continue to advance rapidly, while costs simultaneously decline.

The potential impact of computerization in services is at least as great as that in manufacturing. Whereas the typical factory worker uses twenty-five-thousand dollars of equipment, the typical office worker has two-thousand dollars at his disposal. Word processors, a very close relative of the personal computer, are changing the balance. So are new copiers and distributed computers for calculation and, perhaps more important, information storage and retrieval. The communications industry is being both shaken by and linked to the changes based on semiconductor technology. Besides the largely user-transparent changes in switching systems, from electromechanical to digital, the communication of data is benefitting from an interface of semiconductor and other technologies (e.g., microwaves, lasers) in several areas, such as satellites and optical fibers. Dick Tracy wrist-sized communicators seem to be inevitable, given that wrist televisions are already available commercially. Electronic mail systems and facsimile transmitters are already in growing use.

It is impossible not to return to speculation as to probable impact of these developments. Much of the speculation in print centers on labor force implications. Studies, such as one in England and one in Germany, on the employment implications of semiconductors come, as we might expect, to strikingly different conclusions (Morehouse 1981, 247). Nevertheless, the general consensus is that semiconductor technology represents a significant threat to employment levels. Most technological innovations affect a single industry or a small set of industries. Labor displaced can migrate to other industries. Semiconductors appear to be having a labor-saving effect in a very broad range of industries, and perhaps more significantly, in services as well.

Some have suggested that changing demographic patterns in the global North—namely, fewer young people entering the labor force from the baby-boom bubble, a slowing of female entry to the labor force as their participation rate approaches that of males, and a growing number of retirees, including early ones—could lead to a labor shortage in the next few years. Microelectronics seems at least a potentially strong counter-force. In the Third World countries the problem may be much more severe. Faced with rapidly growing labor forces and existing high underemploy-ment, labor displacing technology poses a dangerous potential problem. Yet if the Third World does not accept the technology, it may weaken its competitive position (Morehouse 1981).

Whether or not this is true depends in part on other aspects of the technology. For instance, is it capital saving as well as labor saving, or is it, as much technology has been, a substitution of capital for labor? What about energy implications? These issues are less often addressed than labor repercussions of semiconductor technology. Much of semiconductor tech-nology is, however, not highly capital demanding. The enormous capital requirements of the American auto industry retooling to robots are atypical. More gradual retooling—often simplifying machinery in terms of moving part numbers and size—can be capital saving. With respect to energy, the evidence seems even clearer. Much of semiconductor tech-nology is energy saving. For instance, applications within automobiles, within machinery, and within both commercial and residential heating and cooling systems are often directly for the purpose of energy saving. The miniaturization of equipment normally yields automatic energy savings. In fact, the rapid adoption of semiconductor technology is already being assisted by higher energy prices and that adoption in turn is contributing to slackened energy demand growth rates. All of this implies that the Third World, both capital and energy short, might also benefit significantly from the new technology.

Energy

Like the field of semiconductors and related developments in the com-puter and communications industries, the energy industry is experiencing major technological changes. Unlike semiconductors, however, there is no single technology easily identified as central to the changes. In fact, a very broad range of technological developments in energy are of importance to the future of the global development system—too broad a range to be more than touched on here.

Debates over energy technology, like those concerning semiconductors, do not hinge only on technological feasibility. Most important to these debates is economic cost. Also critical, however, are environmental implications (insofar as they are recognized) and the range of social and political implications of alternative technology discussed in Chapter 6.

Because of the absence of a single centrally important energy technology, I shall organize this brief review by primary energy type. I want to look first at the traditional fossil fuels (oil, gas, and coal) and then move to the "eternal" energy forms: nuclear, geothermal and solar energy. A reader wanting a readable but comprehensive review of current and probable future energy technology could productively turn to the study of *Energy in Transition, 1985–2010* by the National Research Council (National Academy of Sciences 1979).

Although no one disputes the transition from oil and gas to other energy forms, as we have seen, the speed of the transition and the target of it are very much open issues. The speed depends not only on the size of the conventional oil and gas resource base but also on the proportion of that which can be extracted and on unconventional resources not heretofore used in significant quantities. Higher oil prices and improved technology have combined to boost the extraction rate of oil in place considerably, a factor not yet much captured in figures on oil reserves. Secondary and tertiary recovery methods can more than double recovery rates and thus the lifetime of the resource. Similar methods could even open up whole new resource areas, such as the heavy oil belt of Venezuela, which contains more oil than all known global conventional reserves. Potentially more important, and certainly more controversial, however, are the unconventional hydrocarbons, such as oil shale and tar sands. Denis Hayes, an advocate of solar power, has estimated the global recoverable oil shale resource base as 200 billion barrels or less—that is, about 10 percent of most conventional oil resource estimates (Hayes 1977, 44). In contrast, Herman Kahn presents a U.S. Geological Survey estimate of total oil in shale as a figure for "potentially recoverable resources," which it is not, and arrives at a figure equivalent to more than 200 trillion barrels—one hundred times the conventional oil resource (Kahn, Brown, and Martel 1976, 63); see table 6.5.

In fact, hardly any oil is now being recovered from shale, and the technologies are essentially in test phases, so even with very similar estimates of the oil in global shale deposits, dramatically different recoverability figures are possible. The uncertainty is reflected in cost estimates for oil shale recovery. Shortly after the 1973–74 oil shock, many pundits were saying that oil shale and tar sands were economically usable resources at prices then prevailing—$11.50 per barrel. In fact, a 1970 estimate of tar sand oil put the cost at $2.90 per barrel (Science and Public Policy Program 1975, 5–15). More recent estimates put oil shale recovery costs between $21.50 and $27.50 per barrel in 1978 dollars (National Academy of Sciences 1979, 138). Even that may be optimistic given the near collapse of the Colorado oil shale industry in the face of global oil prices well within that range. The constant increases in estimated recovery costs must prompt some skepticism about the future of oil shale.

Coal has been touted by many experts (e.g., Wilson) as the bridge fuel during the transition to some "eternal" energy form. And, in fact, the resource base supports such claims. Globally recoverable coal resources are at least ten times those of oil in energy equivalent. There have historically been problems associated with coal's use that have made it less desirable than oil or gas, especially pollution. I shall address some of these issues in the next chapter. Several new technologies, however, could replace much or all of the traditional burning of coal for electricity, with major environmental improvements. For instance, fluidized-bed combustion (burning pulverized coal in a mixture with limestone, suspended in a stream of combustion air) might greatly reduce ash, sulfur oxides, and nitrogen oxide emissions. For relatively small scale plants it is a working technology. Interestingly, the country which has perhaps moved fastest is China, where over two thousand fluidized-bed boilers operate (*Compressed Air,* Sept. 1981, 8). Its use in large central power stations appears to be about ten years off (Wilson 1980, 185; National Academy of Sciences 1979, 169).

Fuel cells (converting fuel to electricity electrochemically, rather than thermally) have been around a few years, but not at a size and cost competitive with thermal generating plants. Their likely time of introduction varies with the expert cited, but they could be important commercially by the end of the century. Magnetohydrodynamic (MHD) technology (the production of electricity directly from combustion gases rather than the use of those gases to drive steam or gas turbines) is still another fossil fuel stretching and enhancing technology, but is not likely to be available commercially before the end of the century.

Most attention recently has been focused on synthetic oil and natural gas from coal, both more proven technologies. South Africa has had a working commercial-size coal liquefaction plant (SASOL) since the mid-1950s, economically acceptable only because of the political isolation of South Africa from the major international oil producing countries. Coal liquefaction and gasification plants are now being constructed elsewhere in the world, including the United States. Present oil and gas prices appear to make present technologies marginally viable.

Turning to nuclear technology, we must distinguish three categories: fission burner plants, fission breeder plants, and fusion plants. Each cate-

TABLE 8.3. *Status of Nuclear Technology*

Reactor Type	Development Status	Possible Commercial Introduction in the U.S.
Light water (LWR)	Commercial in United States.	1960
Light water breeder (LWBR)	Experiment running.	1990; fuel cycle 1995 or later
Heavy water (CANDU or HWR)	Commercial in Canada, some U.S. experience.	1990
High temperature gas-cooled (HTGR)	Demonstration running; related development in Germany.	1985; fuel cycle 1995 or later
Molten-salt breeder (MSR or MSBR)	Small experiment run; much more development needed.	2005
Liquid metal fast breeder (LMFBR)	Many demonstrations in the United States and abroad.	1995
Gas-cooled fast breeder (GCFBR)	Concepts only; borrows LMFBR and HTGR technology.	2000

Source: National Academy of Sciences, *Energy in Transition, 1985–2010* (San Francisco: W. H. Freeman, 1979), 197.

gory has a number of actual or potential competing technologies. These technologies and their status for the fission plants are summarized in table 8.3.

Fusion technology has been demonstrated only in the form of the hydrogen bomb. The major problem has been the heat required for the process— about ten times that of the sun's core (because of the lesser pressures obtainable on earth). Such heat must be achieved and maintained long enough for fusion of atoms, and must moreover be confined in order to be useful as energy. Since traditional containers are hardly feasible, magnetic confinement (e.g., the Tokamak reactor) or inertial confinement (pellets dropped into a vacuum and irradiated by lasers) are two approaches being developed. Such reactors must achieve scientific feasibility (more energy out than in), technological feasibility (continuous operation), and commercial feasibility (acceptable costs). Scientific feasibility is probable soon, technological feasibility is possible by the end of the century, and commercial feasibility is not likely before 2020 (National Academy of Sciences 1979, 388–94). The fuel cycle and waste disposal problems of fission power are not expected to be as severe for fusion power.

Geothermal technology does, of course, now exist, although its use is minuscule. Currently, only deposits of hot water or steam near the surface of the earth are usable, and they are somewhat limited. In the long term, dry rock formations may be usable. Overall, however, geothermal energy appears to most experts to have much less potential than either nuclear or solar energy.

Solar energy represents a collection of technologies even more diverse, if generally much less complex, than nuclear energy. Many people think automatically of one of the most sophisticated, namely photovoltaic (the direct conversion of sunlight to electricity). Already in use in space and remote areas, photovoltaic cell arrays produced power in 1977 at about twenty dollars per peak watt, and in 1982 at ten dollars (Flavin 1982, 14), or about ten times residential electricity costs. This was a drop from fifty dollars in 1975. The Department of Energy once sought costs of fifty to seventy cents by 1986, which would make photovoltaic cells competitive with other electricity. More recent goals established by the European Economic Commission and Japanese governments are five dollars in 1985 and two dollars in 1990. Many variations of the technology are being investigated and global investment reached $500 million in 1982 (Flavin 1982, 6). Production has been growing at almost 50 percent per year in the last five years, but annual production is still only about the equivalent of one hundredth of the output of a single modern nuclear plant.

Other high-technology approaches to solar energy include the use of ocean thermal gradients for electric generation, i.e., ocean thermal-electric conversion (OTEC), and the use of waves. Also considered are advanced forms of windmills and solar power plants (like the ones France and the United States already have in operation) using many mirrors and a central boiler. The most science fiction-like idea is an array of solar collectors in space (perhaps five miles square), and equally large microwave collector stations on ground to receive the power.

Within the field of solar power there is an important distinction between the high technology approaches (especially the large centralized ones) and the simple, decentralized ones. Among the most important of the latter is passive solar, the decentralized direct collection of sunlight for heating or cooling. One estimate is that in the United States the combination of energy-conserving design with passive solar design could reduce energy use in buildings by at least one-half and possibly as much as two-thirds (National Academy of Sciences 1979, 359).

Among the other relatively decentralized and low-tech solar technologies are the the use of biomatter—for instance, the burning of municipal waste for electricity or the production of alcohol from farm wastes, or even from plants grown specifically for fuel. Solar energy advocates believe that a combination of such technologies has more potential and much less environmental cost than nuclear energy.

No overview of energy technologies would be complete without a mention of conservation. Increasingly it has been recognized that conservation technologies have the potential to reduce energy use for a variety of functions at lower cost than additional supply can be produced (Stobaugh and Yergin 1979, 233). For instance, U.S. transportation efficiencies can probably be doubled in twenty-five to thirty-five years with less than a 10 percent increase in manufacturing costs (National Academy of Sciences 1979, 84–85). Nearly comparable efficiency improvements in building energy use appear possible.

In spite of a variety of technological feasibility, cost, and environmental concerns, it is possible to see from the above listing of technological options or potential options why modernists downplay the long-term energy issue. Many of the neotraditionalist concerns are environmental; I turn to those in the next chapter.

The Genetic Revolution

Many technologies with roots in biology and chemistry are of importance to the issues of global development addressed in this volume. Among them is hydroponics, or the growing of plants in a nutrient solution without soil. This is already a commercially competitive technology now in use for crops like lettuce (*Forbes,* Mar. 2, 1981, 90–94). Among them also are improved surgical techniques, including organ transplants and, increasingly, artificial limbs and organs. So, too, are artificial insemination and embryo transplants, both of which have had major impacts on animal breeding.

But very probably that technology with widest ramifications is biological engineering, or the manipulation of the genetic code in microorganisms, plants, and animals. Recognition of this is the basis for the high market value of Genentech, Inc., or Cetus Corporation shares, and those of other newly formed companies, even though they presently can market few, if any, commercial products.

The history of the field is fairly short. In the 1920s practical manipulation of unseen genes was leading to improvement of corn seed, but we knew relatively little about genes. In 1921 American geneticist Hermann J. Muller summarized our knowledge in writing: "Genes are definite, but small and unknown substances (connected with the chromosomes in the nuclei of cells) which can mutate and thereby lie at the root of evolution" (*Science News,* Mar. 13, 1982, 180–82). In 1944 evidence was first presented that the substance of genes is deoxyribonucleic acid (DNA). In 1953 James D. Watson and Francis H. C. Crick announced the double-helix model of DNA, taking a large step in our understanding of its structure. The search for the code that links specific genetic structures to the amino acids of protein (that allow genes to specify biological structure) was first partially rewarded in 1961. The code proved identical for organisms from bacteria to humans. In 1973 recombinant DNA technology began with the discovery that it is possible to use enzymes to cut DNA molecules, to use other enzymes to rejoin pieces, and then to introduce the sliced material into a cell.

The ramifications of these advances appear enormous, and agriculture will be a principal beneficiary. Already the new knowledge has allowed the much faster and more precise tailoring of plant characteristics—for instance, resistance to specific diseases. One of the biggest hopes for the future is the development of hybrids of plants or the soil microorganisms on which they depend that can obtain nitrogen directly from the atmosphere. This could potentially replace millions of tons of nitrogenous fertilizers (Brill 1981, 199). Plants may also be tailored to saline or highly acidic soil. Closer in time than nitrogen fixing plants are probably a number of microbiologically produced hormones and vaccines for animals (using genetically tailored microorganisms), including some not now available at all. Animal growth hormones may well be licensed within three years (*Business Week*, June 21, 1982, 130). In late 1982 mice almost twice normal size were produced by transfer of the gene for rat growth hormone into fertilized mouse eggs—the first such success in mammals. The mice can pass on the increased size characteristic to offspring.

The implications of all this for agriculture are staggering. The implications for human health are, of course, also major. More than two-thousand human genetic diseases have been described. Currently some can be treated but none can be cured. In 1982 it was announced that this barrier may have been crossed with the development of techniques to activate dormant genes in sufferers from sickle cell anemia. Some hope of cures can now be held (Anderson and Diacumakos 1981, 106). Already prenatal screening and diagnosis is increasing rapidly, including that for Down's Syndrome. And it is already possible to tailor microorganisms to produce pharmaceuticals. Successes with insulin and interferon have received recent attention (Aharonowitz and Cohen 1981, 152). Perhaps the most successful medical use of the technology to date lies in the creation of monoclonal antibodies through fusion of mouse tumor cells and other mouse cells that produce antibodies (the malignant cell produces clones indefinitely in the lab). The antibodies are used in clinical tests. The Food and Drug Administration has already approved twenty clinical tests using monoclonal antibodies, including one for prostate cancer (*Science News*, May 7, 1983, 296–98).

Other Technologies

This brief review has focused on three technological areas with very obvious relevance to the future of the global development system. Technologies often surprise us, however, and many others may well prove to be of equal or greater importance. For example, in nuclear physics, progress in mapping the universe of subatomic particles continues to be made. Among recent accomplishments is the theoretical unification of two basic forces: electromagnetism and the weak, or Fermi, interaction. The search continues for a grand unified theory (GUT) tying these together with gravitation and the nuclear, or strong, force (also called chromodynamic interaction). The particle called a ''boson'' was discovered in early 1983 (thought to transmit the weak force), and the search is under way for the ''graviton.'' We cannot be far from understanding the Whippoorwillian effect. At the other extreme, our cosmology, our understanding of the universe, continues to expand. And the plate tectonic theory of the earth's crust, which can be traced back only to the 1960s, is still shaking up geology. Some writers refer to a ''materials'' revolution being structured in metallurgy and organic chemistry. In medical technology, new generations of artificial organs and limbs extend and improve life. And by no means least, the recent advent of reusable space shuttles may mean that space technology is just now taking off. By one estimate, manufacturing revenues from space will reach $10 billion by 2000 (Hamrin 1980, 114).

Interestingly, one of the most recent and most widely publicized global futures studies, *The Global 2000 Report to the President,* devoted only 15 of its seven hundred pages to a discussion of technology. In contrast, 220 pages were given to the environment. Of the 15 pages on technology, the majority said in effect that the report's projections in various areas were based on existing technology or on fairly conservative assumptions of change. It is interesting, but not surprising, in a neotraditionalist report. Modernists often reverse the proportions, and that, too, is easy to understand. Any reviews of recent or nearly developed technology inevitably suggests that tools are available to deal with the problems of the global development system.

9. The Environment

Within the set of issues I have labeled the global development system, the future of none is more controversial than the quality of the environment, our physical and biological surroundings. We shall see that attempts to forecast it have much in common with those for technology.

BACKGROUND: HISTORY AND FORECASTS

It is easy to make the case that the environment is deteriorating under the assault of human population and economic systems. We read regularly of the growing local problem of chemical dumps and the more general problem of persistent chemicals in the environment. We know that forests are disappearing globally and that the level of carbon dioxide in the atmosphere is steadily climbing. The concern with acid rain continues to grow, as does that over nuclear waste disposal and soil erosion.

Environmentalism has only recently emerged as an issue of major importance to a wide public. Attention to it was given a dramatic boost in 1962, with the publication of Rachel Carson's *Silent Spring*. Her book documented the dangers of chemical pesticides. The forecast implicit in the title is of increasing damage to animals, including birds. Her warning helped found the environmental movements of the late 1960s and 1970s.

Surprisingly, at least to neotraditionalists, the argument is often made that environmental issues are very manageable. Although some aspects of environmental quality have deteriorated, such deterioration is reversible. Examples can be given like Lake Erie, long given as a prime example of worsening pollution and described as a "dead" lake. Lake Erie's water quality has improved in recent years as a result of treatment plants for waste disposed of in the lake, and both commercial fishing and recreational use of the lake have increased. Similarly, DDT and some other chemicals recognized as harmful after the publication of *Silent Spring* have been

168

banned in the United States and elsewhere. There has actually been a reduction in pesticide residues measured in humans (*Denver Post*, May 27, 1982, D1). Air quality in the United States has improved in most cities since the passage of automobile emissions control legislation.

Modernists are likely to argue that we can have the quality of environment for which we decide to pay. For many LDCs, as for the MDCs over the last century, the need for economic growth is perceived to be so great that they are willing to pay some environmental price for it. Smokestacks belching black remain a symbol of achievement and progress in many places. With increased affluence, however, we can turn attention to environmental issues and the MDCs are increasingly doing so: increased affluence need not mean increased effluents. We can trade slightly lower growth in national product, as a result of pollution control legislation and government spending, for improved environmental quality. The cost of doing so, according to modernists, is not all that great. For instance, Leontief argues that very conservative pollution abatement standards could be met with expenditures of less than 2 percent of GNP (Leontief et al. 1977, 7). By another calculation, expenditures have already gone from .4 percent in 1970 to an expected 3.1 percent of GDP in 1984 (Hamrin 1980, 54–55).

Moreover, we have illustrated that pollution control capability already. According to a 1982 report by the Council on Environmental Quality (supported slightly earlier by one by the Conservation Foundation), the level of suspended particles in the air of U.S. cities declined on average by 55 percent from 1970 to 1980 (*Denver Post*, July 21, 1982, 1–A). The deterioration of stream quality was halted, although not reversed in the decade. These examples can be attributed to the simple decision to do something about pollution.

One of the greatest problems of the economic approach to environmental issues, however, is achieving agreement on costs and benefits of action or inaction. A 1982 study argued that the Clean Air Act had provided $21.4 billion in benefits compared to $17 billion in costs (*Science News*, July 24, 1982, 58). But manufacturers often claim greater costs and fewer benefits, while environmentalists argue the opposite.

Business economist and futurist Julian Simon also takes an economic approach to the question, agreeing that we can have the quality of environment we can afford and choose to have. He goes considerably further than most modernists would by arguing that the regular upward trend in life expectancy is an appropriate indicator of improving global environmental quality. He even labels diseases such as pneumonia and tuberculosis "environmental pollution" based, effectively arguing that their lesser incidence should be attributed to improved environmental quality (Simon 1981, 130). Unless one considers modern medicine a part of the "environment"—greatly stretching the common definition—this argument makes no sense. It is possible, however, to point to the atrocious quality of water, "preserved" food, and sanitation facilities in many LDCs and conclude that, in fact, economic advance has brought the MDCs greatly improved environmental quality in many areas.

Modernists face, however, essentially the same problem with respect to the environment that neotraditionalists do with respect to technology, that is, the diffuseness of the issue. With respect to technology, a neotraditionalist arguing that we will experience growing energy scarcity must contend with a vast array of possible energy sources. In response to it being noted that oil shale did not prove economically viable at $15 per barrel oil prices, and appears not to be viable at $34 per barrel, the technological enthusiast simply falls back on the declining prices of photovoltaic cells or the advances being made in fusion energy, or the "certainty" of a viable shale industry at $45 per barrel. Similarly, an environmental pessimist confronted with evidence on the improved water quality in Lake Erie can still point to global desertification rates or increases in carbon dioxide as the ultimate problem. It is little wonder that modernists are generally as loathe seriously to address environmental concerns as neotraditionalists are to consider technological options.

The similarities of the two issues extend even further. The environment also poses similar measurement and conceptual problems. It is about as easy to measure micrograms of lead in the Greenland ice cap or parts per million of carbon dioxide in the atmosphere as to measure costs of semiconductors. And the lead and carbon dioxide measures provide no more useful a picture of environmental quality than does the cost of semiconductors a picture of the technology. Mercury could be as important a pollutant as lead, and availability of adequate sensing devices may be a bigger bottleneck for robot technology than semiconductor cost. Just as the issues are diffuse, so are the measures and basic concepts.

And, of course, there is the problem of tying change in the measures to changes in other variables. There are discontinuities, or thresholds, in technological change, that make either the technology itself or its impact hard to predict. Similarly, there are discontinuities in environmental quality change. The introduction of a nuclear waste disposal problem could hardly have been anticipated fifty years ago. And there appear to be thresholds for many toxins below which no (measurable) impact appears, but above which major damage is done. A good example in another environmental area is grazing. Up to a point, intensification of grazing causes no degradation of pasture quality; after a point, it degrades quickly. This may also be the case with respect to increases in atmospheric carbon dioxide and global temperature increase: at a certain point melting of polar ice packs may initiate major climatic changes with their own dynamics.

Another characteristic to some extent shared by technology and the environment, but of special importance for the latter, is that of delays. A technology, like the assembly line, may be around for many years before the pervasiveness of its impact is felt. Environmentalists draw our attention strongly to the importance of delays. Among the most important are those caused by the progressions of toxins through the food chain. For instance, studies of DDT suggest that after its application rate drops, its ingestion by small animals and fish continues to increase its concentration in them for perhaps a decade. Ingestion by humans of the animals and fish would further delay its greatest impact on humans for several years. This phenomenon of considerably delayed impact, coupled with the threshold phenomenon noted already, means that action must be taken long before a problem really begins to appear. In actuality, however, action tends to be delayed, even after initial problems become obvious.

These then are some of the elements of environmental issues which make neotraditionalists suspicious of modernist statements about taking a cost-benefit kind of approach to the environment. As hard as it might be to define the environmental costs of a practice currently and to weigh those costs against benefits, anticipating the costs once a threshold has been crossed, understanding the delays, and taking appropriate societal action in advance may pose an impossibly demanding sequence.

Finally, there is the issue of reversibility and again there is a parallel to technology. It may be impossible to put the genie back in the bottle, to decide not to use a technology such as nuclear power once it is known. Similarly, there may be environmental areas where reversing the direction of change could be extremely difficult, if not impossible. Once soil is lost to erosion, for example, rebuilding it can be done, but only gradually and at great cost. This point is missed by Simon (1981) in his ''economic'' approach to land use and soil loss. It may well be, as he suggests, that decisions to build on agricultural land are made rationally, on the basis of calculations with respect to the value of the land for agriculture and for commercial use, highways, etc. Similarly, farmers may make rational decisions concerning acceptable loss of soil in light of food prices, fertilizer, remaining soil, and so on.

The rationality assumption itself does not always appear appropriate, for example, farmer behavior with respect to tree planting and plowing practices immediately prior to the U.S. dust bowl days. The rationality assumption must be qualified by the availability of critical information. Neotraditionalists build on this argument concerning information availability. They feel that in some not too distant future, the value of agricultural land and soil is likely to be much greater than it is now, because of population pressures and the increasing scarcity of areas that can be brought under cultivation for the first time. If those higher future land values were correctly perceived, the agricultural land and soil would, in fact, be valued more highly now and longer-term rational choices might be made. But they are not. And most importantly, once the cost structure changes, it will involve great expense to reverse the earlier processes. It costs little to remove land from agriculture in order to build an office building, shopping center, or freeway; it would cost a great deal to prepare the land again for agriculture by destroying the construction on it while that construction still has a useful life. Similarly, it costs much less to prevent soil from eroding than it does to rebuild it.

Other examples abound in which the cost of ecological restoration far exceeds the cost of ecological preservation, and may, in fact, be infinite. Careful storage of chemical wastes and prevention of subsequent land use around dumps is expensive. But it is cheap compared to relocating the residents of the Love Canal area or compensating them for health problems. Most health damage is irreversible. Another example is climate change. If we do, in fact, have an impact on climate, we may be incapable of reversing it. Both of these examples suggest that the fairly simple economic model of many modernists may be inappropriate. A supply function for the production of many goods is a simple curve, such that if price falls and production drops, a subsequent price increase will bring supply back to the earlier level (capacity can be simply idled and then brought back into production). Thus movement along a supply function has a reversibility in the abstract of economic theory which may not exist in the real world. For instance, if lowered food prices result in less attention to soil and thus erosion, raising the prices to earlier levels may be incapable of returning production to former levels.

FORECASTING: THEORIES AND MODELS

There is obviously no way to make blanket statements about the future of the environment. It is also very difficult to decide how to subdivide the issue so as to narrow the focus and intelligently approach aspects of the environment. One might be tempted to make a physical or biological division. Clearly it could not be a clean one—the two interact too much. Land quality affects grasslands and water quality affects fisheries. Chemical pollutants have a range of biological system impacts. One might be tempted to divide by general type of environment, e.g., land, air, and water. But pesticides and other chemicals affect land and water; coal burning affects air and water; soil erosion affects air, water, and land.

It is not surprising, then, that the approaches most often taken to environmental issues do not depend on typologies. Once again there is a parallel to the study of selected technologies. Most authors focus on environmental problems in a fairly ad hoc manner, relying on their own and others' perceptions of the importance of issues. I shall do the same here.

Specifically, I shall review briefly what experts are saying with respect to five issues: atmospheric carbon dioxide, persistent chemicals, nuclear waste, land use, and key biological systems.

Carbon Dioxide and the Greenhouse Effect

Since 1850 human activities have resulted in an increase in atmospheric carbon dioxide from 290 parts per million to more than 330 parts per million (Woodwell 1979, 34). There remains considerable debate over how much of this increase should be attributed to the burning of fossil fuels and how much to clearing of forests, the major biological sink of carbon globally. There also continues to be uncertainty as to how quickly the oceans can absorb atmospheric carbon dioxide—an important issue since they are the major physical sink globally.

In spite of the uncertainties, the global trend for atmospheric carbon dioxide seems very clear (figure 9.1). Simple extrapolations of the curve and more complex models based on fossil fuel useage projections suggest that a doubling of carbon dioxide relative to the 1850 value is likely by about the middle of the next century.

The feared impact of increased carbon dioxide is known as the "greenhouse effect." Carbon dioxide allows shortwave solar radiation (light) to pass through while retarding the re-radiation of infrared longwave radiation (heat), just as does the glass in a greenhouse. The effect is long-term warming. According to theory, the greenhouse effect already should have caused warming of about 0.5 degrees centigrade; in fact, we experienced global cooling between 1940 and 1965 (Kellogg and Schware 1982, 1082). Although this has made some observers skeptical about the greenhouse effect theory, most scientists believe the cooling is explicable (e.g., increased atmospheric dust from other human activities and volcanoes) and is temporary.

By 2000–2020 the global average temperature may well be one degree centigrade warmer than the long-term average, with considerably greater changes toward the poles, especially in the Northern Hemisphere, where there is less ocean area to moderate changes. While the more catastrophic effects of the warming, for example, ice cap melting, might well take thousands of years, rainfall patterns could change very quickly. In figure 9.2 we see one rather speculative estimate of which global areas would be drier and which wetter. Among other changes, the breadbaskets of both the United States and the USSR could be drier, not at all desirable changes.

As speculative as the greenhouse effect is, it is widely accepted among climatologists. And given the low probability that fossil fuel use will decline significantly before the end of the next century, there is virtual certainty that the theory will be tested. Two reports released late in 1983—one by the National Research Council (part of the National Academy of

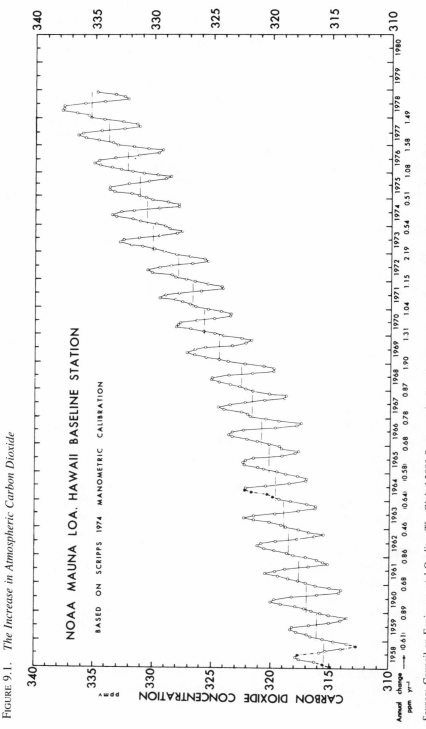

FIGURE 9.1. *The Increase in Atmospheric Carbon Dioxide*

Source: Council on Environmental Quality, *The Global 2000 Report to the President* (Washington, D.C.: CEQ, 1981), 258. Reprinted with permission.

Note: Monitored at the National Oceanic and Atmospheric Administration's Mauna Loa Observatory, Hawaii.

FIGURE 9.2. *The Possible Impact of Global Warming on Soil Moisture*

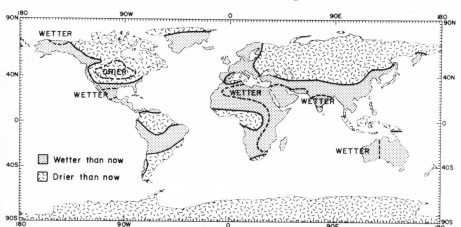

Source: William W. Kellogg and Robert Schware, *Climate Change and Society* (Boulder, Colo: Westview Press, 1981), 49.

Sciences) and one by the Environmental Protection Agency (EPA)—concluded that temperature rises of nearly five degrees centigrade are likely to occur by 2100. Sea levels might rise two feet. Neither report suggested that cessation or even significant slowing of fossil fuel use is feasible; both concluded that adaptive action held most hope.

Other atmospheric issues have been raised. For instance, destruction of upper atmospheric ozone by chlorofluorocarbons used as refrigerants and propellants in some aerosol cans (no longer used in the United States) could increase the ultraviolet radiation reaching the earth's surface (Schneider 1976, 182). Atmospheric methane, from cattle and other ruminants and other sources (including termites), is apparently increasing at about 2 percent per year and also can affect atmospheric chemistry (*Science News,* July 3, 1982, 5). Methane, too, can cause a greenhouse effect. Recent evidence from ice in Greenland suggests that global levels began to increase about four-hundred years ago, presumably as a result of expanded human agriculture (*Science News,* Dec. 11, 1982, 375).

Chemicals

The introduction of chemicals into the environment continues to increase and there is little or no reason to believe that the trend will be reversed. As we increasingly bring infectious diseases under control, environmental agents come to pose the most difficult medical problems. Prior to World War II, U.S. production of synthetic materials was less than 1 billion pounds annually; by 1978 production had reached 172 billion pounds per year (CEQ 1981, 254). The growing use of many synthetic substances is tied directly to the need for higher agricultural production. For instance, the growth trend in fertilizer application suggests that by the year 2000 we shall be globally fixing more nitrogen for agriculture than is fixed by natural systems (CEQ 1981, 27). Fixed nitrogen is a relatively benign chemical, primarily increasing growth rates of vegetation. But it also increases the decomposition rate of organic matter in the soil, thus degrading soil quality and engendering a dependence on its continued use. Its runoff into streams and standing water increases plant growth and often helps create "blooms." When accelerated algae growth reaches the higher limits to its growth provided by the additional nutrients and begins to die off, its decay in the water removes oxygen, promoting eutrophication. The full effects of such considerable increase in fixed nitrogen availability are not well understood.

Also associated with the increased intensity of global agriculture are higher levels of herbicide and pesticide applications. Both are expected to grow at about the same rate as fertilizer use, that is, to double by 2000 (CEQ 1981, 286), and to increase fourfold in LDCs. Herbicide use in developed countries has also accelerated as a result of adoption of no-till and minimum-till techniques. These techniques eliminate deep plowing and thus conserve energy and soil moisture. Seeds have even been sown by air. The techniques have spread to nearly one-fourth of U.S. cropland. They require, however, greater use of both herbicides and pesticides.

Although much of the industrialized world has recently banned DDT and other persistent insecticides, their use in Third World countries is about half of all pesticide use, and is growing at about 9 percent per year. Moreover, pests continue to develop immunity to the chemicals, leading to more frequent applications and higher dosages. Twenty-four species of malarial mosquitoes are now immune to DDT. In the United States, cotton attracts several insects immune to all currently available insecticides.

Agriculture is, of course, by no means alone in adding chemicals to the environment. Industry has been responsible for the release of PCBs— stable, insoluble, organic chemicals with much similarity (including persistence) to DDT. Although their sale was banned in the United States after 1979, they will almost certainly be discovered in unexpectedly lethal concentrations for years. Heavy metals, such as mercury and lead, have become another problem, especially in marine environments, where they can become concentrated by organisms. Mercury poisoning has remained a local phenomenon, while lead concentrations in the ocean have been increasing more generally. A major ultimate source of environmental pollution has been lead additives to gasoline, which have come under some control but which still contribute lead to the air and ultimately to the oceans. In 1982 about ninety-thousand tons of lead were emitted into the air (*Science News,* June 5, 1982, 373). Another source is paint, sometimes ingested by children. Although also increasingly controlled, it remains a problem in older dwellings, including U.S. inner city environments, where it is especially likely to be flaking and available for children to ingest.

As this example indicates, one of the major problems with environmental control is that substances that no one questions for many years—or that are actually perceived to be beneficial—may subsequently prove to be hazardous. An excellent recent example is asbestos, used as a fire retardant in schools across the U.S. Recently (1982) it was reported that asbestos in flooring may also pose a serious health hazard as floor wear releases it to the air; no action has been taken in this area. Another example is the use of nitrates as a preservative in meat, such as bacon.

The modernist might point to the regulation concerning many of these chemicals as proof that they can be controlled. The neotraditionalist would retort that overall chemical use keeps increasing, that control over specific areas often comes only after considerable damage has been done, and that we shall almost certainly continue to uncover new problems, most likely at an accelerating rate. Indeed, our recognition of the persistence of many of these chemicals is contributing very rapidly to a growing chemical waste disposal crisis. Around the country instances of ultimately unsafe disposal continue to surface (often literally). Among the most famous was the Love Canal incident in New York, where residences were built over a chemical dump, leading to significant health problems for residents and relocation of them in 1978. Elsewhere disposal sites have been closed down because of discoveries that wastes were leaking into ground water; a recent example is the Lowry landfill in Denver. Loss of long-term disposal sites and tightening of regulations on temporary storage has unfortunately led in some areas to even more dangerous and indiscriminate "midnight dumping" of wastes by companies not having other options they consider viable. In 1980 the U.S. Congress established a $1.6 billion "Superfund" to clean up hazardous waste sites. In late 1982 the EPA selected 418 locations for top priority (*Denver Post,* Dec. 21, 1982, 3A).

Another chemical problem—one related to the energy system—is acid rain. Fossil fuel combustion, particularly increased coal use, has led to increased emissions of sulfur oxides (SO_x) and nitrogen oxides (NO_x). Emissions of these compounds have been high for some time. Whereas "pure" rain has a level of acidity (pH) near 5.6, in every Eastern state and province of North America average rain pH is 4.6, or ten times as acidic (*Science News,* June 5, 1982, 373). This has caused the elimination of fish from many lakes in Upstate New York, as it has in Scandinavia (in the shadow of the Ruhr). It has increasingly clear economic costs in reduced growth rates of timber. In fact, evidence has begun to build of timber kills related to acid rain. The Germans now believe that every second tree in the

Bavarian National Forest is dead or dying as a result of acid rain and general air pollution (*Der Tagesspiegel,* July 28, 1983).

Nuclear Waste

Nuclear waste is one of the most difficult environmental topics upon which to form a judgment because of the bitter controversy over the dangers and techniques involved. Some modernists argue that the problem has been technically solved. Temporary storage until the wastes can be concentrated is the first step, now divided between a short stay at the reactor and a longer one at centralized temporary storage sites. "Permanent" storage in deep salt formations, or other sites considered to be geologically stable and free of water over a very long period, is the second step. According to its proponents, the risks associated with such storage are negligible. Among the most sanguine supporters is the modernist Simon. He cites at length a physicist arguing that a family could safely store its share of nuclear waste from an all nuclear economy at home in a metal-wrapped, orange-sized ball, inside a cubicle with three feet thick walls (Simon 1981, 122–26).

The difficulties of any serious storage plan are numerous. In the short term there are significant amounts of high-level nuclear waste which must be held for ten years or so before being processed for the longer term. In the United States such waste is now being generated at the rate of about one thousand tons per year (*Science,* Nov. 1977, 591). The temporary storage sites have been found to leak, threatening to contaminate ground water. The citizens of the states with the three commercial dumps (South Carolina, Washington, and Nevada) have reacted by attempting to restrict dumping. In 1980 Congress decreed that each state must be responsible for its own low-level waste (*Congressional Quarterly* 1981, 81). Until 1970, much low-level waste was put in metal barrels and dumped into the ocean. The EPA has said that by 1980 one-fourth of those receptacles were leaking.

Plans for long-term storage in salt mines near Lyons, Kansas, were abandoned when it was discovered that they had been penetrated by oil and gas exploration drilling. In spite of intensified efforts to resolve the long-term disposal issue, no final decisions have been made in the United States. In late 1982 Congress passed an act requiring the Department of Energy to nominate future sites for permanent storage and in 1985 to recommend three to the president. The president is to pick a site in 1987 and it is to be ready by 1998 (*Denver Post,* May 14, 1983, 5A). Although the National Academy of Sciences has expressed confidence in our ability safely to dispose of wastes for ten thousand years, past delays make one less than completely confident that we shall have prepared a site before the end of the century. The Department of Energy is already suggesting that the 1982 timetable may not be met.

Land Use

Competing demands for land use continue to intensify. Agricultural requirements have led to land being cultivated which was at one time forest or which was earlier considered too marginal to be economical. Among the results has been deforestation. On a global basis, closed forests now cover about one-fifth of all land surface, but will shrink to one-sixth by the year 2000 (CEQ 1981, 318–19). In some local areas the situation is worse. For example, in Haiti forests cover only 9 percent as much of the country as they originally did, and the watersheds are no longer protected. Erosion is rapid (CEQ 1981, 280).

Pressure from grazing upon grasslands has damaged them as well. In large part as a result of overgrazing, desert areas are spreading. The United Nations has projected that sufficient area has a high or very high probability of desertification to triple global desert area by 2000 (CEQ 1981, 277). The losses are greatest in Africa, especially the Sahel, and in Asia.

Other related problems associated with the extension and intensification of agriculture include soil loss. There is considerable debate over the amount of soil lost to wind and water erosion relative to annual soil formation. Lester Brown, citing primarily USDA sources, estimates a loss of 2 billion tons in the United States annually, compared to 1 billion tons newly formed (Brown 1981, 18; see also Brown [1978]). This is the equivalent of 781,000 acres of cropland. Outside the United States estimates are scarcer. By one calculation, deforestation and new cultivation in the Ethiopian highlands has led to a soil loss rate of 1 billion tons per year.

In addition, some irrigated land is lost to production each year from waterlogging, salinization, and alkalinization (CEQ 1981, 279). Globally, it is a very small percentage (about 0.06) of irrigated land. The more severe problem is depletion of ground water where it is relied on for irrigation. This poses a significant threat to agriculture in much of the Western United States.

Key Biological Systems

The central issue raised by all of these land use concerns is the carrying capacity of the physical environment for the biological systems central to human survival. Lester Brown has argued that on a per capita basis we may well have already reached the upper limits (table 9.1). Wood production per capita peaked in 1964 and has declined steadily since (although net deforestation continues). Fish production peaked in 1970 (table 9.2). Total freshwater and marine catch was stable from 1970 through 1978 and has increased relatively little since then. It appears that we may be very near the limits of sustainable global fish catch.

In addition, per capita yields from grasslands appear to be declining.

That is clearly true for mutton and, although it is a bit early to be certain, may well be true for beef. That leaves cropland as the single major biological system from which per capita yields are still rising. I discussed in Chapter 7 the issue of whether such growth is sustainable.

The concept of carrying capacity is one used often by neotraditionalists in consideration of the environment. It is, of course, linked directly to the "tragedy of the commons," discussed earlier. Unfortunately, individuals pursuing their own goals have no incentive to cease exploiting the commons when the carrying capacity is reached. This is the principal reason to fear overexploitation, degradation, and an eventually reduced carrying capacity. A common non-human example is that of deer on the Kaibab Plateau north of the Grand Canyon. When predators were reduced by bounty hunting, the deer population rose above its estimated sustainable level of forty thousand. At fifty thousand the herd destroyed vegetation to the point where massive starvation occurred in 1925–26; forty years later

TABLE 9.1.   *Global Production per Capita of Biological Resources, 1950–1981*

Year	Wood (in cubic meters)	Fish (in kilograms)	Beef (in kilograms)	Mutton (in kilograms)	Wool (in kilograms)
1950	—	—	4.69	.74	0.65
1955	—	—	8.49	1.62	0.70
1960	—	13.2	9.18	1.88	0.83
1961	0.66	14.0	9.62	1.90	0.84
1962	0.65	14.9	9.85	1.89	0.85
1963	0.66	14.7	10.74	1.88	0.83
1964	0.67	16.1	10.06	1.84	0.80
1965	0.66	16.0	9.92	1.79	0.78
1966	0.66	16.8	10.20	1.77	0.78
1967	0.64	17.4	10.38	1.89	0.78
1968	0.64	18.0	10.67	1.89	0.79
1969	0.64	17.4	10.70	1.85	0.78
1970	0.64	19.1	10.55	1.86	0.75
1971	0.64	18.9	10.60	1.90	0.73
1972	0.63	17.4	10.52	1.88	0.70
1973	0.64	17.3	10.23	1.79	0.65
1974	0.63	17.9	10.58	1.33	0.64
1975	0.61	17.3	10.85	1.34	0.65
1976	0.62	18.1	11.04	1.34	0.63
1977	0.61	16.3	11.12	1.29	0.61
1978	0.61	16.4	10.98	1.29	0.61
1979	0.60	16.4	10.52	1.29	0.63
1980	0.60	16.3	10.18	1.32	0.64
1981	—	16.6	10.10	1.33	0.63

Sources: Lester R. Brown, *Building a Sustainable Society* (New York: W. W. Norton, 1981), 51; Food and Agriculture Organization, *Production Yearbook* (Rome: FAO 1951, 1956, 1961, 1966, 1971, 1973, 1976, 1979); Food and Agricultural Organization, *Yearbook of Fishery Statistics* (Rome: FAO, 1977 and 1981), United Nations, *Demographic Yearbook* (New York: UN, 1981).

TABLE 9.2. *Total World Fish Catch, 1953–1981 (in millions of metric tons)*

Year	Marine Fish	Crustaceans and Mollusks	Mollusks	Total
1953	19.1	2.6	—	—
1954	20.3	2.9	—	—
1955	21.3	2.8	—	28.9
1956	22.7	2.9	—	30.8
1957	22.8	3.0	—	31.7
1958	24.1	3.0	—	33.3
1959	26.8	3.3	—	36.9
1960	29.2	3.6	—	40.2
1961	32.2	3.5	—	43.6
1962	35.6	3.8	—	44.8
1963	36.4	4.1	—	46.6
1964	40.9	4.0	—	51.9
1965	39.6	4.1	2.9	53.3
1966	43.0	4.3	3.0	57.3
1967	45.9	4.5	3.2	60.4
1968	48.7	5.0	3.5	63.9
1969	47.2	4.7	3.2	62.6
1970	52.7	5.1	3.4	69.6
1971	52.5	5.1	3.4	70.9
1972	47.2	5.3	3.6	66.2
1973	47.1	5.4	3.5	66.8
1974	50.8	5.5	3.5	70.4
1975	49.3	5.8	3.8	69.7
1976	55.2	6.9	4.4	69.5
1977	53.5	7.9	5.1	68.7
1978	55.0	7.7	4.8	70.4
1979	55.3	8.4	5.3	71.3
1980	55.7	8.5	5.2	72.4
1981	57.6	8.5	5.2	74.8

Sources: Council on Environmental Quality, *The Global 2000 Report to the President* (Washington, D.C.: Government Printing Office, 1981), 105; Food and Agriculture Organization, *Yearbook of Fishery Statistics, Catches and Landings* (Rome: FAO, 1981), 41.

the plateau could still sustain only ten thousand deer (Webb and Jacobsen 1982, 7). It may well be that the erosion of soil and overgrazing of range land in the United States is currently reducing our own carrying capacity.

Other biological environment issues have been raised. One issue that has rather uncertain implications is the accelerating extinction rate of species or subspecies. By one estimate we now lose about one or two species or subspecies per year in the United States, compared to one each thirty years prior to 1600 (Harrington and Fisher 1982, 124). Globally the problem is much more severe. Some experts believe species are disappearing at the rate of one thousand per year and that the rate may reach ten thousand by 1990 (globally there are about three to ten million species). These losses—due overwhelmingly to the reduction in forest area—obviously reduce the genetic variety available for agricultural or pharmaceutical purposes. For instance, about three-thousand species, 70 percent in the tropics, are known to have anticancer properties, and species in the tropics are disappearing fastest. Besides such economic costs, there is a much more subjective element in the value that almost all of us place on the preservation of distinct life forms.

Genetic engineering recently raised still another biological issue. At Harvard a team of medical scientists won federal approval to use deadly diptheria toxin in gene-splicing experiments. It will be spliced with a common intestinal bacterium (E. coli) and other scientists have voiced concerns that a lethal new disease might result and eventually escape from the laboratory (Denver Post, Jan. 1, 1983, 3A).

Products of genetic engineering now exist which will be purposefully released. For instance, in the fall of 1983 release of genetically engineered bacteria was planned in northern California. The bacteria were to compete with and ideally replace cousins that cause ice to form on potato leaves at temperatures below freezing. Researchers had excised the gene that gives natural bacteria that characteristic, and the new bacteria might allow plants to survive temperatures of minus six to eight degrees centigrade for several hours (Newsweek, Aug. 15, 1983, 63). The plan is to develop a virus that will attack and destroy the natural bacteria. However, similar bacteria exist in the upper atmosphere and they may now help precipitate rain and snow. Should the altered bacteria replace them, global climate might change (Science News, Aug. 27, 1983, 132). Jeremy Rifkin, a neotraditionalist (1980) and environmental activist, led an unsuccessful effort to stop such experiments. The appropriate government regulatory body has now approved several others (Business Week, Oct. 3, 1983, 44–45).

The impact of human activities on the physical and biological environment is clearly in some way proportional to our numbers and to the scope of our economic activity. By no means all of the impact is to be condemned; much of it—for example, the elimination or vast reduction of disease-producing microorganisms or disease carrying insects, or the development of global transportation and communication networks—can be lauded. The focus here has been on the problem areas, or at least those areas perceived as problems by many observers. We have seen that the selection of evidence and the interpretation of information is strongly shaped by a larger world view. In the case of environmental issues, however, the very decision to emphasize or de-emphasize consideration of them is often a more fundamental derivative of world view.

10. Values and Political Structures

Organizationally, the chapters of this volume have taken us gradually down the layers, or strata, of the global development system presented initially in Chapter 1 (see figure 1.1). Now we jump back to the top layers, those that provide controlling, directing, or steering mechanisms for all lower layers but are in turn constrained and shaped by the lower layers. Because of the closeness of the linkages between the value and social/political layers, I treat them jointly.

VALUES

Throughout this volume one recurring theme that transcends world view differences is that human beings, individually and collectively, can influence their future. There may be major disagreements over the degree to which the influence is pernicious or benign, intentional or serendipitous, but not over the fact of influence. That agreement is what makes the value issue so important. Among the large set of alternative world futures, which do we want to see evolve?

Universal Values

There have been many attempts to develop lists of values that are universally held. At the individual level, the best known of such efforts is the need hierarchy of Abraham Maslow (Maslow 1970, 35–47). Maslow posited a ranking of needs, the most basic of which are physiological: food, shelter, sex. Once these most basic needs are relatively satisfied, humans turn to safety or security needs, then to belongingness and love, to self-esteem, and finally to self-actualization. These five levels can also be grouped into three: self-preservation, community, and self-determination.

Maslow never presented his ranking as an absolute hierarchy but instead as a pattern of emphasis. He wrote:

> In actual fact, most members of our society who are normal are partially
> satisfied in all their basic needs and partially unsatisfied in all their basic
> needs at the same time. A more realistic description of the hierarchy
> would be in terms of decreasing percentages of satisfaction as we go up
> the hierarchy of prepotency. For instance, if I may assign arbitrary
> figures for the sake of illustration, it is as if the average citizen is
> satisfied perhaps 85 percent in his physiological needs, 70 percent in his
> safety needs, 50 percent in his love needs, 40 percent in his self-esteem
> needs, and 10 percent in his self-actualization needs. (Maslow 1970, 53–
> 54)

The Maslow hierarchy has relevance in at least two quite different respects
to this discussion of alternative world futures. First, it provides some
context for the differences in approach of MDCs and LDCs to the issues.
The overwhelming emphasis on growth by LDCs, even at the expense of
the environment or the future availability of resources, can be seen as a
translation of the low physiological need satisfaction of citizens in those
countries into national policy. Second, and less obviously, the hierarchy
may provide a value basis for the choice among paradigms. Neotraditionalists differ from traditional peoples in one important respect—they are
usually affluent. They direct our attention to community needs or the
importance of self-actualization at least in part because their lower level
needs are satisfied. This is the basis for an important criticism of them by
modernists, who might go one step farther and argue that their needs for
self-esteem have driven them to efforts to pull the ladder up after them. On
the other hand, neotraditionalists might well characterize modernists as
"fixated" at the physiological level—seeking ever more economic
growth, even in rich countries.

Going beyond psychological name calling, it is obvious that the kinds of
values I am talking about here shape the structure of society and political
institutions in very major and fundamental ways. It has often been argued,
for example, that democratic institutions are much more likely to flourish
in an environment in which basic physical needs have been met (Lipset
1959; Cnudde and Neubauer 1969). Marx made the same argument with
respect to socialism—in fact, he viewed the improved production and
consumption potential generated by advanced capitalism as a precondition
for the attainment of socialism. Explicit forecasts were that socialism
would first be attained in advanced capitalist countries, most likely the
United States, England, and Germany. If Marx would call the eco-
nomic/political form now existing in the USSR, China, and Albania socialist (as opposed to his category of Asiatic), his prediction would rank
among the worst forecasts reviewed in this volume.

The forecast implicit in the Maslow need hierarchy is not altogether
clear. One could argue that if the world were to succeed in continuing to
improve average well-being, a growing proportion of the world's popula-

tion should shift primary attention to higher levels of need, and desires for greater production and consumption of goods should weaken. That conclusion, however, would not hold if, as many suggest, satisfaction of self-esteem needs implies a position of *relative* wealth.

Cultural Distinctions

It has often been argued that values are much less universal than implied in Maslow's hierarchy and much more easily shaped by the culture into which an individual is socialized. For instance, paralleling distinctions many others have made, sociologist Pitirim Sorokin has outlined three major logically integrated cultures, two of which differ profoundly from each other. For members of the *Ideational* culture, reality is hidden and what they sense is illusory. Reality lies instead in God, Nirvana, or some other spiritual concept. The needs of individuals are mainly spiritual and "the method of their fulfillment or realization is self-imposed minimization or elimination of most of the physical needs" (Sorokin 1937, 73). In contrast, in the *Sensate* culture, reality is what the senses say it is—needs and aims are primarily physical, and the method of attaining them is "modification or exploitation of the external world." The third logically integrated culture is a mixed form, the *Idealistic*. Sorokin, as have many since him, identified the Ideational culture as that historically dominant in much of the Orient and the Sensate as a modern, Western phenomenon. The distinction, and the desirability of an Idealistic balance, have become popular in concepts such as yin (feminine, passive) and yang (masculine, active) from Chinese cosmology and in literature such as *Zen and the Art of Motorcycle Maintenance* (Pirsig 1974).

The Western Sensate culture has, of course, been relatively stronger and more aggressive in the last several centuries and the world is increasingly dominated by it. Thus, an extrapolative forecast rooted in this cultural perspective might well be the opposite of that based in Maslow's need hierarchy. Neotraditionalists are, of course, much more likely to point favorably to the Ideational culture (e.g., Schumacher's work on Buddhist economics, 1973). Only a rather ironic future—and not one normally proposed—would integrate the need hierarchy and culture clash perspectives—a future in which the "counter-culture" (generally Ideational) groups in the developed West had succeeded in achieving dominance and the Sensate culture had swept the Orient.

The importance of this distinction between a universal need approach and a culturally or socially determined value approach should be emphasized. As Amitai Etzioni has noted, it pervades much of social/political thinking:

> The central point at which the prevailing theories of social action of both the Meadian and Parsonian traditions differ from *both* the Marxist and the

Weberian perspectives is that the former assume, in effect, that human needs are almost completely pliable within very broad limits set primarily by physiological tolerance, such as the need for heat, sleep and food. Social needs—e.g., for affection—are recognized by these theories, but it is emphasized that such needs may be satisfied by a large variety of institutional arrangements . . . it is assumed, in principle, that there are very few if any limits to socialization and social control. The best indication of this assumption is the presence in these theories of conceptions of deviant individuals, sub-cultures, and even social movements, *but never of a deviant society*. (Etzioni 1968, 623)

Politically Specific Values

On the whole, however, universal need hierarchies or general cultural categories may be a bit too removed from specific social and political institutions to offer much assistance in any discussions of the future of the latter. Interestingly, when we begin discussing values in the context of specific institutions, a whole different set of concepts normally emerges, such as freedom or equality—a set of concepts difficult to link to discussions of universal needs or cultural categories. Among the best efforts to develop a comprehensive list of these political/social values is that of Dahl and Lindblom (1953). They list seven "basic ends for social action":

1. Freedom—the absence of obstacles to the realization of desires (economic, political, social)
2. Rationality—the designing of action so as to maximize goal achievement (many would say efficiency)
3. Democracy—the political equality of preference weighting
4. Subjective equality—the making of decisions, whenever possible, favoring the greater, not the lesser, number (many would prefer the concept of equity, in order to emphasize process, not outcome)
5. Security—the maintenance of freedom across time
6. Progress—the continuing increase in freedom
7. Appropriate inclusion—the drawing of the social boundaries with respect to whom the other values should apply

As useful as such a listing of political/social goals or values might be, they do not, of course, provide a rigorous framework for talking about the future of political/social institutions or the global development system. The first problem is that their definitions are sufficiently vague as to mean different things to different people. Is freedom increased by the legalization of abortion? More basically, does a minimal government provide greatest freedom, because it limits interference in the lives of individuals, or does a more activist and "socially conscious" government provide greater freedom, because it equalizes opportunity through education and health programs?

As suggested by these examples, the values often take on meaning through the institutions and policies with which they are identified. The mapping between values and institutions is confusing at best. With respect to rationality or efficiency, does a centralized government "make the trains run on time"? Or does such a government normally imply a bureaucracy which is uncaring, inefficient, and unmotivated? Turning to the future, and to the linkage of values and a different aspect of the global development system, namely technology, there are similar differences in perception. To many scholars, continued technological progress will mean increases in freedom, as defined in terms of increased choice or elimination of obstacles to realization of desires. Other critics fear the development of a technological elite (as suggested in references to a nuclear "priesthood") at the expense of freedom for the majority.

Values and World Views

It is sometimes argued that an approach to the study of the global development system is or can be value free. In particular, classical liberals portray their work as rational, scientific analysis of society. Ludwig von Mises stated: "Liberalism is derived from the pure sciences of economics and sociology, which make no value judgments within their own spheres and say nothing about what ought to be and about what is good and what is bad, but, on the contrary, only ascertain what is and how it comes to be" (von Mises 1962, 88–89; cited in Hamrin 1980, 189).

Unfortunately, this is not true. Even if world views were only descriptive, value judgments would be reflected in the aspects of the global development system which were selected for study and for report to the public. In addition, there are prescriptive elements in each world view in which value judgments become explicit.

One of the important trail maps through this forest of value definitions, linkages of values to other aspects of the global development system, and preference weightings of values proves to be world view distinctions. There are fairly consistent differences in the emphasis placed on values in the Dahl-Lindblom list by different paradigms. Generally, classical liberals place especially great emphasis on efficiency, or rationality, and freedom. Radicals are most likely to emphasize equality and democracy. Classical liberals would, of course, normally question the radical commitment to democracy, or view it as hypocritical. Radicals return the compliment with respect to classical liberals and freedom. In both cases, definitional issues lie at the root of disagreements—radicals argue that democracy grows out of participation in ownership of the tools of production and is impossible if that ownership is concentrated, while classical liberals view it more in terms of political processes, such as party formation or candidate selection. Classical liberals view freedom as the elimination of interference or control, often especially by government: radicals see it in terms of the positive provision to individuals of means to realize their desires. Radicals are also likely to argue for an especially wide definition of appropriate inclusion.

Neotraditionalists often emphasize security in terms of the maintenance of the system over time. For instance, in an explicit rank ordering of her values, Dana Meadows placed "survival of the total social and ecological system" at the top, material welfare (up to a basic level only) second, and equity, freedom, and efficiency explicitly lower (Meadows 1975, 29). Although in one sense this ranking and the weight it places on survival is simply an attempt to extend Maslow's need hierarchy to a societal level, the emphasis on survival also grows out of a perception on Meadows's part that it is threatened. In general, paradigms emphasize values perceived to be threatened or inadequately satisfied—there would be considerable agreement on the overall list of Dahl and Lindblom. Modernists place especially great emphasis on progress, especially defined materially.

World Views and Institutional Preferences

This selective emphasis on values also translates into differences with respect to institutional preferences. Classical liberals, of course, often emphasize minimal government as illustrated by the old saw, "That government governs best which governs least." Government should maximize freedom by not interfering with citizens, and should maximize efficiency by leaving as much as possible to the market. Protection of property and enforcement of contracts are two areas of legitimate governmental action. Radicals perceive collective control of the real fount of social and political power—namely, economic power—as a legitimate, in fact, basic responsibility of government. Only after control is made collective can true political and more general equality or equity be possible and true democracy exist. There is also a strain of thinking among radicals emphasizing the importance of societal value change, for instance, the creation of a "socialist man." There are similarities here to the arguments made by neotraditionalists.

Neotraditionalists are much more divided on the political/social implications of their values and their perceptions of the global development system. One group explicitly concludes that an expansion of governmental power into new areas is necessary. This inevitably involves some coercion. For instance, Daly recommends three new institutions: a *distribution institution* placing maximum and minimum limits on income in recognition of the importance of the distributional issue in the absence of a growing economic pie; *transferable birth licenses* to limit strictly population size (first proposed by Boulding [1964, 135–36]); and *depletion quotas,* to restrict use of nonrenewable resources (Daly 1980, 330–48). Garrett Hardin is even stronger in his recommendation of coercion. And, as we saw in Chapter 1, many neotraditionalists, like Heilbroner, forecast the unfortunate inevitability of more authoritarian institutions in a harsher world.

The second strain of thought among neotraditionalists emphasizes value change. In the tradition of thought that values are highly pliable and greatly influenced by institutions and culture, many neotraditionalists stress the importance of the "counter-culture" in the creation of new environment-friendly values and eventually environment-friendly institutions. This group is especially vulnerable to the charge that if culture and current institutions do in fact shape values, it will be exceptionally difficult to change the values from within the current culture (anthropologists and students of ancient civilizations often emphasize the importance of outside shocks, like an invasion and long occupation, as prerequisites to cultural change). Nor can they fall back on an argument based on a Maslow-type need hierarchy, that there will be an inevitable shift of attention to higher levels—if that were true, they need not bother sounding the alarm. The frequent argument of neotraditionalists, and perhaps the only one consistent with their beliefs, is that the growing scarcity of resources and damage to the environment does constitute the kind of shock necessary to change the values of a culture. They hope that, given intelligent leadership, the events of the 1970s will have provided sufficient warning to set such change in motion; they fear that it will require more.

In fact there is some evidence to suggest that just the kind of value change proposed by neotraditionalists is occurring. A Harris poll in 1977 found that 79 percent of Americans would prefer to emphasize "teaching people how to live more with basic essentials" rather than "reaching higher standards of living" (Hamrin 1980, 87). Without similar results from an earlier period it is impossible to be certain, but this attitude most likely reflects a significant change in values.

It is especially difficult to characterize political institutions associated with the values and development system preferences of modernists. They are often effectively those of classical liberals or radicals, more often classical liberals. Obviously, institutions which support technological advance, whether *laissez innover* or government directed research, are essential.

POLITICAL FUTURES

There are several possible approaches to speculating about political futures. One can focus on major institutional structures that provide formal shape to political systems and behavior. Or one can look at the output of the political systems. Finally, one can attempt to characterize the process

of policy-making and political behavior generally. In this section I devote
some attention to each approach. Because less attention is given within
political ecology perspectives to political institutions and processes, this
discussion will rely more on political economy perspectives.

Background: Trends in Political Institutions

My interest here is obviously not in detailed analysis of institutions
(formal or informal) but in very broad tendencies. In particular, I wish to
focus on political institutions as they interact with other aspects of the
global development system. The central issues are the degree and nature of
that interaction.

One generalization of importance is that the degree of interaction has
been increasing—both the influence of lower layers of the development
system hierarchy (see figure 1.1) on government and the control exercised
by government over the lower layers have grown. We can see this by
reviewing government policy directions in the issue areas already
discussed.

Before looking at policy, however, it would be useful to make some
general remarks with respect to three major categories of political and
economic institutions that figure prominently in any discussion of the
global development issues: nation-states, international organizations, and
multinational (or transnational) corporations. Although the third of these
can hardly be considered a true political institution, the MNCs' power
internationally has led to frequent treatment of them as if they were.

The Nation-State. It is often suggested that there is an inevitable conflict among these three types of institutions with respect to an implicitly
limited amount of policy authority. In particular, the argument periodically
surfaces that international organizations and multinational corporations are
undercutting or gradually limiting the jurisdictional authority of nation-
states. Although it is not my purpose to investigate such claims—and there
is without doubt some validity to them—the subsequent discussion suggests that they are considerably exaggerated. The root of the exaggeration
lies in the implicit (and erroneous) constant-sum assumption that the power
of one can grow only at the expense of the others. As already noted, an
important generalization of this discussion is that the extent of efforts from
the political layer to shape and control lower layers of the global development system has grown sharply. As a result, the power of all three types of
institutions has grown.

Several years ago it was more common than it now is to suggest that
nation-states were an increasingly anachronistic institution. For instance,
John Herz published in 1957 an article titled "The Rise and Demise of the
Territorial State" in which he argued that just as gunpowder had made the

feudal unit an indefensible one and given rise to the nation-state, nuclear weapons had now rendered nation-states incapable of self-defense and we would see a movement towards globalism. Herz himself revised and weakened the argument considerably in 1969; but belief in the original argument persists.

The 1970s and 1980s have led many to conclude that the earlier rumors of the demise of the nation-state were, indeed, greatly exaggerated. International resource issues, especially oil, have taken on an importance not perceived in earlier decades, and given birth to a whole new school of geopoliticians and power politics enthusiasts. The breakdown of key international economic institutions in the early 1970s (discussed below), coupled with adjustment problems in the face of the shocks, or crises, of the decade, have rekindled economic nationalism. The resurgence of the cold war in the early 1980s also suggests the limits on the supposedly powerful forces undercutting nation-state maneuverability.

A prime example of the refurbished image of the nation-state comes in the area of energy. Prior to the events of the early 1970s it appeared that the international oil companies had both oil producer and consumer nations under their strict control. The oil companies were clearly the largest and most powerful of the multinational corporations. Concessions extracted from OPEC and other producers (generally with the help of the companies' home base countries) gave them virtually complete control over production and pricing. The home base countries were able to exercise little authority over the far-flung company empires, and, as in the U.S. case, often provided generous tax relief. In less than a decade—and primarily in the first three or four years of that period—the producer countries stripped the companies of almost all production and pricing control, made them largely international distributors, and acted to limit even that role. Consumer countries have taken away many tax benefits and have intervened strongly in domestic distributional activities and down-stream pricing.

Even though the nation-state thus shows no clear sign of losing its status as the world's dominant political institution, we should not lose sight of its vulnerability in the longer run. Marx was correct in pointing out the intimate relationships between fundamental economic and political structures, just as Herz rightly pointed to the importance of military technology. It is not impossible that we live in an era like that of the pre–World War I European empires, and are as blind to imminent change as were their monarchies.

Within the radical political economy perspective, the dominant political institution serves an integral role in the global economy. When that economy was largely agricultural, city-states were institutions in which a single city could extract surplus from agricultural hinterlands. Empires were the subjugation of other cities by a dominant one. With industrialization, the nation-state, containing multiple cities but often with a clearly dominant one, evolved as an appropriate political institution to help structure a more complex territorial division of labor. While serving the economic power of domestic producers, it simultaneously facilitates economic competition globally and rewards economic efficiency (Chase-Dunn and Sokolovsky 1983, 359–60). The state and domestic producers (often controlling and always sharing state power) are in constant conflict with other states, and one or more hegemonic states use their economic power (and military power, as necessary) to retain hegemony. War generally has an economic purpose, as in Germany's efforts in World War I to gain access to raw materials and markets in a global economic system dominated by Great Britain. A movement away from the nation-state as the dominant institution would be a logical consequence of changing global production technology. For example, centrality of services and information sectors might change market needs for manufactures (and even needs for raw materials) and have fundamental political ramifications.

Internationalist and classical liberal perspectives tend to separate the nature of political institutions from economic structures to a greater degree. However, the interaction of technology and political/social structures does receive attention. Thus, for instance, the emphasis by Herz on military technology. And since technology and economic forms are intricately linked, these thoughts bring us back to economic system/political system relationships, but with a perspective quite different from that of the radicals. Human society based on hunting and herding was well served by tribal structures often tied together in loose networks (e.g., Indian Nations). Fixed agriculture, especially that based on irrigation, depended on broader and more stable political institutions. And territorial defense took on an even more critical importance once fixed investment became important. Empires with stable, hierarchical political structures proved quite durable. But they alternated with smaller feudal or city-state units, also serving local agricultural economies and defense needs. W. W. Rostow, who argues that there are stages of political development associated with those of economic development, portrays a pattern of Malthusian political cycles prior to the industrial revolution:

> Although we know less than we would wish to know about population movements in the ancient empires, the mechanism of technological constraint appears to be more complex than a simple shortage of food in the face of an expanding population: the devastations of war and the attractions of the city pull men off the land; the limits of agricultural technology prevent an adequate increase in production; the limits of industrial technology prevent full and productive employment in the cities, throwing welfare burdens on the state which become increasingly burdensome in the face of simultaneous and enlarging claims of security

policy; the struggle for Eisenstadt's "free economic resources" leads to levels of taxation so high that they accelerate rather than stem the tide. (Rostow 1971b, 52)

Some neotraditionalists would argue that this description might fit today's nation-states as well as ancient empires.

In some cases, views on international relations take on lives of their own, largely divorced from specific economic and technological structures. For instance, the "realist" school sees a constant struggle for territorial control and security as goals in and of themselves. One variant of this is an identification of hierarchical global structures, like those of the radicals, dominated by a single power. It suggests cycles of world leadership of roughly one hundred years, and argues that global leadership passed in turn from Portugal to The Netherlands to Great Britain and then to the United States (Modelski 1978; Thompson 1983). Within this general perspective are also those who see such nation-state struggles largely as increasingly anachronistic remnants of the gradual evolution of human political structures from tribal to global structures and who feel that we can now move to more universal institutions.

International Organizations. While nation-states still appear to have a dominant role in the international system, and while any threat to that dominance appears relatively weak, the growing interdependence of nation-states constitutes an indisputable trend. International trade grew half again as fast in the 1950s and 1960s as did world production. As a result, U.S. dependence on the world economy (imports plus exports divided by GDP) rose from 10 percent to nearly 20 percent. Foreign investment grew as rapidly, in both directions. The increasing ability of U.S. and USSR militaries to destroy not just each other but humanity has provided impetus for increasing (albeit periodically interrupted) international communication. These kinds of factors support the growth of international organizations (IOs).

There are two major types of IOs: those with government members, called intergovernmental organizations (IGOs), and those with private individual or group members, called international nongovernmental organizations (INGOs). Both have grown enormously in numbers. Prior to World War I there were 49 IGOs and 170 INGOs (Kegley and Wittkopf 1981, 131); by the mid-1970s the totals had grown to 300 and 2,400, respectively. Of course, numerical growth does not necessarily indicate growth in power. Nevertheless, growth so far in excess of population or economic activity does strongly suggest increased power, and review of the actual activity levels (like that later in this chapter) of these organizations confirms it.

There is a consensus among students of IOs that their numbers and/or their role will continue to grow. Such organizations often have developed to perform specific functions; a basic theory with respect to their continued evolution is called functionalism (Plano and Riggs 1967, 381). Functionalists argue that several fundamental forces—among the most important of which is technology—underly the continually growing need for more IOs. That is, IOs are needed to control transport, communications, and so on. Increasingly, functionalists have identified resource problems or environmental issues as additional areas requiring functional organizations. Over time, many functionalists argue, the very actions of IOs create international activities requiring still additional IOs, as when the increased post–World War II global trade facilitated by organizations like GATT lead to not yet satisfied pressures for domestic economic policy coordination.

Of perhaps greatest significance is the fact that global international organizations devoting some of their attention to common security issues are a phenomenon of this century. Only with the League of Nations between the two world wars did membership in such organizations become effectively universal. Pessimists will point out that the United Nations merely extends in geographic membership the character of the nineteenth century Concert of Europe, which began with the Congress of Vienna and ended in World War I, or of the League of Nations, which ended during World War II. Optimists, combining hope with arguments based on our own interests in self-preservation (perhaps another form of hope), suggest that perhaps we have finally crossed the threshold to a central political institution that will persist and grow in ability to dampen conflict.

Most students of international organizations and proponents of variants of functionalism fall into the internationalist world view. The perception of international organization growth as benign and perhaps inevitable derives from that view. Radicals argue that many of the post–World War II international organizations are effectively tools of the dominant global powers, especially the United States. For instance, radicals suggest that the important economic organizations established in the late 1940s, such as the International Monetary Fund, the World Bank, and the General Agreement on Tariffs and Trade (all to be discussed later), have in common the objective of maintaining a liberal global trade order, that is, freedom for goods and capital to move across national boundaries. Such an order always benefits most the technologically and economically dominant powers. It is no coincidence that the United States and Great Britain, the dominant power prior to the U.S. assumption of that role, collaborated after World War II to establish these institutions. Their future evolution or destruction will depend in large part on the global economic power pattern.

Multinational Corporations.   Multinational corporations (MNCs) have grown numerically at least as quickly in the last two to three decades as have IOs, but definitional problems make it difficult to get reasonable counts. In 1977 at least 10,373 business firms had at least one foreign affiliate. This figure may overstate the number of MNCs, however, since some definitions require an MNC to have at least four overseas affiliates (Kegley and Wittkopf 1981, 131).

The largest MNCs are truly huge. The biggest fifty MNCs collectively account for about 10 to 15 percent of non-Communist industrial production and perhaps one third of international investment (Modelski 1979, 45). It has become common to see tables in which MNC annual sales are compared with nation-state GDPs. On that basis, Exxon in 1982–83 was the world's twenty-second largest economic unit (table 10.1).

The future of MNCs and their relationship to nation-states have been subjects of much speculation. Gilpin outlines three models of their future (1979): *sovereignty-at-bay, dependencia,* and *mercantilist.* The *sovereignty-at-bay* model, named for Raymond Vernon's book by that title (1971), predicts a gradual erosion of nation-state economic power as MNCs achieve more and more of it. Nation-states cannot retard the development, it is argued, because they increasingly need the efficiencies, technology, marketing power, and capital of the MNCs. The trend will be generally benign, because it will increase the overall efficiency of the economic system (classical liberals generally like this model) and will even assist the LDCs in their own development. The *dependencia* model grows out of radical thought and portrays the MNCs as tools of the developed countries from which they arise, one more instrument of Third World exploitation. Even when manufacturing activities are located in LDCs by MNCs, the "higher-level" functions, management and research, continue to be performed in the developed countries. The *mercantilist* model picks up a theme developed earlier, the resurgence of the nation-state and international economic competition. It predicts the economically developed nation-states bringing the MNCs to heel in their competition with each other. Although it is unlikely that this model has been elaborated by neotraditionalists, it would seem to be quite consistent with their thought on global economic futures.

Background: Trends in Policy Areas

Population. Active attempts by governments to influence population growth rates were, until recently, very infrequent. The surge in LDC government programs is really almost a post-1965 phenomenon. Of the largest LDCs, India has the oldest program, dating from 1952; the seeming lack of success by that dean of programs has been a major factor in the conclusion drawn by many policy analysts (see Chapter 4) that such programs are ineffective. Most programs are, however, still quite young, and many LDCs have recently adopted them. One estimate is that sixty-five

TABLE 10.1. *Economic Size of Countries and Multinational Corporations*

Rank	Economic Entity	GNP or Annual Sales (in billions of dollars)	Rank	Economic Entity	GNP or Annual Sales (in billions of dollars)
1	United States	2946.0	51	Colombia	36.4
2	USSR	1259.9	52	STANDARD OIL (CA)	34.4
3	Japan	1185.4	53	IBM	34.4
4	West Germany	829.9	54	DUPONT	33.3
5	France	658.3	55	Kuwait	31.4
6	United Kingdom	510.2	56	Pakistan	29.6
7	Italy	391.2	57	ENI	29.4
8	People's Republic of China	297.4	58	Chile	29.4
9	Canada	275.9	59	GULF OIL	28.4
10	Brazil	267.5	60	Hong Kong	28.4
11	Spain	214.3	61	Egypt	28.2
12	India	179.5	62	STANDARD OIL (IND)	28.1
13	Netherlands	167.4	63	Malaysia	27.3
14	Australia	165.1	64	GENERAL ELECTRIC	26.5
15	Mexico	160.2	65	ARCO	26.5
16	Poland	153.2	66	Libya	26.2
17	Sweden	123.4	67	Portugal	24.7
18	East Germany	121.7	68	New Zealand	24.3
19	Belgium	118.0	69	UNILEVER	24.1
20	Saudi Arabia	117.2	70	FRANCAIS DES PETROLES	22.8
21	Switzerland	111.5	71	Hungary	22.5
22	EXXON	97.2	72	Israel	22.4
23	Czechoslovakia	86.4	73	Peru	21.5

24	ROYAL DUTCH SHELL	82.3	74	KUWAIT PETROL	20.6
25	South Africa	81.7	75	SHELL OIL	20.1
26	Indonesia	79.2	76	Morocco	19.9
27	Austria	77.6	77	ELF-AQUITAINE	19.7
28	Nigeria	76.2	78	PETROLEUS DE VENEZUELA	19.7
29	Argentina	72.2	79	FIAT	19.6
30	Turkey	70.1	80	PETROBRAZ	18.9
31	Denmark	66.9	81	PEMEX	18.8
32	South Korea	66.1	82	Ireland	18.7
33	Venezuela	65.0	83	US STEEL	18.4
34	Yugoslavia	62.8	84	OCCIDENTAL	18.2
35	GENERAL MOTORS	60.0	85	PHILLIPS	17.1
36	MOBILE	60.0	86	VOLKSWAGEN	16.8
37	Norway	57.7	87	DAIMLER-BENZ	16.3
38	Romania	57.2	88	NISSAN	16.3
39	BRITISH PETROLEUM	52.2	89	RENAULT	16.2
40	Finland	51.2	90	SIEMANS	16.0
41	TEXACO	47.0	91	ITT	16.0
42	Taiwan	44.6	92	MATSUSHITA	15.7
43	Greece	42.9	93	TOYOTA	15.7
44	Algeria	41.9	94	PHILLIPS PETROLEUM	15.7
45	Bulgaria	39.3	95	HITACHI	15.5
46	Philippines	39.2	96	SUN	15.5
47	United Arab Emirates	38.5	97	HOECHST	15.3
48	FORD	37.1	98	TENNECO	15.2
49	Thailand	37.0	99	NIPPON	15.2
50	Iraq	36.7	100	BAYER	15.0

Sources: World Bank, *World Development Report 1983* (New York: Oxford University Press, 1983), 148–49; *Fortune 500* (May, 1983); Sumner Levine, *The 1983 Dow-Jones Irwin Business and Investment Almanac* (New York: Dow-Jones, 1983), 216.

countries had programs by 1976 (Population Reference Bureau 1976, 11) while another estimate claims thirty-five countries had such programs by 1978 (Birdsall 1980, 60). Programs are difficult to count because they rely on very different measures (sterilization, distribution of contraception-prevention aids, or public education), because they dispose of greatly varying levels of resources, because their location in the bureaucracy differs substantially among countries, and because they can be given considerably increased or decreased emphasis when governments change.

Developed countries, where fertility is low, have supported fertility reduction programs in LDCs. The United States has been the most actively involved in such programs since a 1965 decision by President Johnson to make it a high priority effort within the overall U.S. aid program. Between 1965 and 1975, the United States disbursed a total of $732 million in aid for population control programs; other developed countries boosted the collective total to $1,054 million.

There has been close cooperation (rather than competition for turf) between nation-states and IOs in this area. Most of the nation-state aid has been channeled through the United Nations Fund for Population Activities (UNFPA), founded in 1967. By 1979 its annual pledges had increased more than five-fold to $112 million (UNFPA 1979, 15). These funds are used for health, education, and research activities, as well as to direct efforts to reduce fertility.

The population issue had clearly gained international attention and recognition as a collective problem by 1974, when the World Population Conference met in Bucharest. Despite much North-South rhetoric (even charges by some in the South that the Northern emphasis on population control amounted to genocide) and the irony of locating the conference in a country with a very low birth rate and a pronatalist policy, 135 nations approved the recommendation that they "encourage appropriate education concerning responsible parenthood and make available to persons who so desire advice and means of achieving it" (Population Reference Bureau 1976, 11). Positions at the 1984 World Population Conference in Mexico City show the difference that ten years can make; more universal and considerably stronger support for family planning characterized the conference.

Population issues have also attracted the attention of at least two important INGOs. The International Planned Parenthood Federation (IPPF) has taken a leading informational and propaganda role for antinatalist policies (Marden, Hodgson, and McCoy 1980). The most important pronatalist, or at least anti-antinatalist organization, is the Catholic Church. The relatively slow fall in fertility in Latin America—even at levels of income elsewhere associated with quite rapid fertility decline—testifies to the Church's impact, in spite of somewhat reduced efforts by the Church to influence childbearing decisions.

It hardly need be repeated that the neotraditionalist world view is the most strongly antinatalist. Modernists are not, however, generally pronatalist, although some modernist writers are (e.g., Simon 1981). The policy direction of the last two decades clearly supports neotraditionalists quite strongly, although most of them would urge even greater efforts.

Economics. No issue illustrates the growth of institutional influence better than economics. All three of the institutional types discussed here— MNCs, nation-states, and IOs—have dramatically expanded their economic roles over the last half century. The economic importance of MNCs was documented earlier in terms of their growth in sales and control of production. Here I want to sketch the growth of the nation-state and especially of the IO roles.

The economic role of national government has grown steadily since at least the Great Depression, in large part because of the post-Depression acceptance of economic doctrine (i.e., Keynesian economics) associating government spending with strong demand and high economic growth rates. For industrial countries as a whole, public consumption grew from 17 percent of GDP in 1960 to 19 percent in 1980. Over the same period in low-income countries, public consumption rose from 9 percent to 11 percent; in mid-income countries, the figure grew from 11 to 13 percent of GDP (World Bank 1981, 143). Although it is difficult to obtain extensive data from the Depression period (much of national economic accounting was developed then), U.S. national income originating in government grew from 12.5 percent in 1929 to 14.8 percent in 1941 (Denison 1974, 19).

These percentages of national income or of consumption accounted for by government actually understate considerably the growth in government control over the economy. Legislation, often in areas related to the issues addressed here, has mandated the expenditure of much additional money. For instance, in the United States, the Council on Environmental Quality has estimated that in 1984 nongovernmental expenditures of $40 billion (in 1975 dollars) will be needed to comply with environmental legislation—1 to 2 percent of the GDP (CEQ 1976, 175). In addition, transfer payments merely channeled through the government are now very significant portions of the economy, but do not show up in government consumption figures.

Whether the trend toward an increased governmental role can or will continue is a hotly debated issue, with governments in Great Britain under Thatcher and in the United States under Reagan arguing that it cannot. In general, a reaction against the increased economic and other roles of government dominates the times and may stop the trend, although that is far from clear.

Turning to the international economic role of national governments, growth has been less spectacular. The expenditures of developed countries on foreign aid have been a roughly constant percentage of their GDP over the last two decades, although that fact conceals a drop in U.S. percentage contributions (from nearly .5 percent of GDP in 1965 to under .3 percent in the 1970s) and an offsetting increase among other developed countries. Table 10.2 shows the total flows from developed to developing countries, including private flows. The achievement of total flows of over 1 percent in the late 1970s is ironic because that was the target set by LDCs in the context of the New International Economic Order. However, the LDCs had asked for .7 percent from governments and .3 percent from private flows, government funds being much less often in the forms of loans or direct investment and more often in the form of outright gifts. The actual percentages have proven to be almost the reverse, with much more rapid private flow growth. Much of the private flow is, of course, a result of MNC activities, although the role of bank lending since the first oil shock has grown enormously (see Chapter 5).

Multilateral institutions have also increased their share of international spending much faster than have governments or the private sector (table 10.2). National contributions channeled through such organizations increased twentyfold from the mid-1960s to 1981. It is to the role of such institutions that I want to turn next.

Much of the current basic international economic machinery grew out of the Depression and World War II experiences. In July, 1944, representatives of forty-four nations gathered at Bretton Woods to lay the institutional foundations of an order which might help nations avoid further economic and political collapses like those of the previous decade and a half. The emerging global economic power, the United States, teamed with the historic one, Great Britain, to push for a "liberal" trading system, that is, one in which international trade and investment faced the fewest possible restrictions. Classical liberals see such a system as the most economically efficient one, capable of generating the greatest global economic growth; radicals see it as a natural expression of the desire of economically dominant nations to apply their power abroad with the fewest restrictions.

The conference provided for the establishment of the International Monetary Fund (IMF) to promote currency stability (for many years at fixed exchange rates) and to oversee a system of multilateral payments to overcome short-term foreign exchange restrictions. Its role has since increased. It frequently imposes requirements on domestic economic policy as a prerequisite for access to foreign exchange. It also issues Special Drawing Rights (SDRs), a form of international currency. The second major institution established at Bretton Woods was the International Bank for Reconstruction and Development (IBRD), or World Bank. The Bank lends money subscribed to it by nation-states and increasingly also lends funds raised

TABLE 10.2. *Net Foreign Assistance and Private Grants to LDCs (in millions of dollars)*

Source of Aid	Average 1964–66	1970	1975	1981
Official	6,147	7,929	16,609	32,243
	(.46)[a]	(.39)	(.43)	(.44)
Bilateral	5,550	5,667	9,815	18,283
Multilateral	363	1,124	3,770	7,353
Other	224	1,139	3,024	6,607
Private investment	3,928	6,875	22,428	53,780
	(.29)	(.34)	(.58)	(.74)
Voluntary agencies	n/a	858	1,342	2,018
		(.04)	(.03)	(.03)
Total	10,075	15,662	40,378	88,040
	(.75)	(.78)	(1.05)	(1.21)

Sources: Organization of Economic Cooperation and Development, *Development Co-operation: Efforts and Policies of the Members of the Development Assistance Committee* (Paris: OECD, 1975, 1977, and 1982).
[a]Figures in parentheses are percentages of donor GNPs.

in the world capital markets by issuing long-term debt (bonds). Its lending has recently grown rapidly, from $3 billion in 1972 to over $12 billion in 1981 (World Bank 1981b, 10).

A third important post–World War II liberal institution is the General Agreement on Tariffs and Trade (GATT), established in 1947. GATT has grown from twenty-three to eighty members, although LDCs still complain of MDC domination of all three institutions. Seven rounds of negotiation have been held under GATT auspices to lower tariffs and other barriers to trade, the most recent round being the Tokyo round. Although by no means all progress in lowering tariffs has resulted from GATT—and much has preceded GATT—U.S. tariffs dropped from an average of 60 percent in 1934 (Smoot-Hawley was passed in 1930) to 25 percent in 1945 and to 8.3 percent by 1971, about the same average level as other industrialized countries have attained. Post–World War II trade exploded: global exports were $60 billion in 1950, $310 billion in 1970, and $2,000 billion in 1980, approximately 15 percent of global GDP. In the 1970s the multi-fold increases of world oil prices contributed much numerically (in terms of value, rather than volume) to the increase in world trade. There are important reasons to doubt that world trade value can continue to be fueled by such price increases. In fact, the disruptions in trade balances they have caused now support a mini-resurgence of protectionism. Partly because of agreements reached under GATT, the manifestations of new protectionism have increased non-tariff barriers to trade, such as quotas, orderly marketing agreements (OMAs), and bilateral bartering agreements.

LDCs have pointed out that commodity groups of special interest to them, such as primary agricultural goods, face tariffs two to four times the average 10 percent level of MDCs, and that they also face health restrictions, or special quotas, that they view as discriminatory. LDC share of global exports was, in fact, down from 31.9 percent in 1950 to 17.2 percent in 1970.

The perception of the liberal trading order and its institutions as discriminatory has led LDCs increasingly to establish their own institutions and to push for changes in the dominant ones. Much of this activity has been associated in one way or another with the United Nations. After 1955 a compromise between the United States and the Soviet Union facilitated the admission of many LDCs. Already in 1955 the Bandung Conference of fifty LDCs began to indicate an increased international political role. The movement of the cold war to LDCs (the Soviet-Egyptian Aswan Dam Agreement was also signed in 1955) further presaged their new role.

In 1964 the first United Nations Conference on Trade and Development (UNCTAD) met in Geneva; every four years these conferences have become major LDC forums. The first Secretary-General of the permanent UNCTAD organization was Raul Prebish, an important subscriber to the school of thought which believes structural distortions in the world economy have led to deteriorating terms of trade for LDCs and to continued economic inferiority. In 1974 the UN General Assembly adopted the Declaration and Action Programme on the Establishment of a New International Economic Order. Among its demands upon the developed countries were aid at .7 percent of GDP per annum, renegotiation of LDC debt, the right of expropriation of foreign investment, improved technology transfer, nonreciprocal MDC tariff reductions, and an integrated commodity program to support the prices of several basic commodities. By 1975 with the adoption of the U.S. Trade Reform Act, all MDCs did have some preferential tariff scheme, or Generalized System of Preferences (GSP), however weak. Some action has been taken on many other of these demands, although MDCs, especially the United States, are generally resistant to the introduction of non-liberal elements into the global economic system.

To get a very complete picture of the evolution of either national or IO economic policy-making, one has to step back and look at two important global economic trends of recent years: the declining role of the United States and the emergence of a group of LDCs called Newly Industrializing Countries (NICs).

With respect to the U.S. role, after World War II the United States accounted for about 50 percent of global goods and services. This dominant economic position, since eroded to about 20 percent, and the related World War II devastation of Europe, led to an international economic role. In 1947 the new post–World War II institutions were not doing well;

Western Europe itself experienced real economic hardship. From 1947 until 1960 the United States stepped in to manage the system almost unilaterally, beginning with the $17 billion Marshall Plan in 1948–52 (compare that with total MDC aid to LDCs from 1950–55 of $2 billion per year).

The United States effectively sought balance of payments deficits to provide international liquidity for the recovery of Europe and Japan. The gold supply provided inadequate liquidity for the rapidly expanding global trade volume and the dollar became an international currency. But by 1960, foreign dollar holdings exceeded U.S. gold volume for the first time, throwing doubt onto the equivalency of dollars and gold; in November, 1960 the first run on the dollar occurred. In spite of actions to slow the dollar outflow, including the cutbacks in aid (as a percentage of GDP) mentioned earlier, by 1971 the U.S. gold stock was down to $10 billion (from $24.2 billion in 1948) and dollars abroad were up to $80 billion. The United States also ran a balance of trade deficit in that year for the first time since World War II. In 1971, President Nixon unilaterally took the United States off the gold standard (suspended convertibility) and readjusted the U.S. currency value. By 1973 the fixed exchange rate system had collapsed and floating rates replaced them. The special (de Gaulle had said "privileged") place of the United States in the global economic system was no more.

It may appear that events associated with the declining role of the United States (including the introduction of floating exchange rates) and with the turbulence of the 1970s (including two oil shocks and two major global recessions) have shaken certain international institutions. However, the IMF and World Bank are now stronger than ever, and their functional roles seem more critical.

The growth of the NICs—including South Korea, Hong Kong, Singapore, Taiwan, Brazil, and Mexico—has been as spectacular as the fall of the United States. Other countries in the NIC category, as identified by the OECD, are Greece, Portugal, Spain, and Yugoslavia. Between 1967 and 1977 average exports for NICs grew at 24 percent per year, compared to 18 percent for MDCs. The growth in global economic importance of this ten-country group can also be illustrated by their share of OECD imports, which rose from 2.6 percent in 1963 ($1.2 billion) to 8.9 percent in 1979 ($55 billion) (OECD 1981, 7). The dependence of the NICs on export-led economic growth has called into question the sustainability of their rapid growth in the 1980s. However, high rates of capital formation also characterize these countries and suggest that their strength may have a more solid base.

This very brief review of recent international economic developments suggests both trends and uncertainties. Among the dominant trends are the increased IO and private economic roles; the elevated position of some LDCs, and the decline, if not elimination, of U.S. dominance. Among the greatest uncertainties are the longer-term impact of the economic shocks of the 1970s, the initial impact of which on LDC inflation, debt, and growth were noted in Chapter 5.

Agriculture. Agriculture illustrates strong and seemingly increasing roles for all three major institutional categories. Nation-states throughout the world have refused for various reasons to allow a free market to reign in agriculture. During the years of considerable surpluses in the 1950s and 1960s—and renewed again in the late 1970s and early 1980s—the major intervention pattern for Western developed countries has been price supports. Some of the post–World War II sensitivity to the plight of agriculture and farmers can be traced to the period preceding the financial crash of 1929 and the "official" onset of the Great Depression. A global depression in agriculture preceded other events, with prices falling by 30 percent from 1925 to 1929 and stocks, or inventories, of agricultural goods rising by 75 percent (Kindleberger 1973, 86). Among the new economic policies growing out of the Depression period were farm price supports. The most recent reincarnation of such supports in the United States is the payment-in-kind (PIK) program, whereby farmers are provided the surpluses of past years as incentive to reduce acreage planted.

In Europe the political compromises necessary to secure French participation in the European Community resulted in a Common Agricultural Policy with especially strong protection for farmers. Although the result for Europe has quite consistently been the government purchase and holding of huge quantities of butter, powdered milk, poultry, and alcohol and high external tariffs on food, the European surpluses have generally not matched those of the United States. U.S. surpluses gave rise also to the Food for Peace program, facilitating disposal of surpluses to LDCs.

As much as classical liberals decry such market intervention policies by developed countries, they also disparage LDC policies, often almost the mirror image. Partly to protect the growing urban populations, with their high unemployment rates, and to insulate governments from the unhappiness of the unemployed, many LDCs have adopted price subsidies and price controls. Partly because of the belief, held especially in the 1950s and 1960s, that industry is the key to economic development, government investment programs have consistently favored industrial projects. Low prices and investment levels have combined to retard growth in LDC agricultural production and to increase dependence on imports or food aid. As both classical liberals and radicals would agree, food aid may well have been another structurally distorting factor, decreasing the incentives (prices) and abilities of local LDC farmers. LDCs have found it very difficult to break out of the low production/high consumption "trap" of subsidized food prices, as riots in Egypt and elsewhere have shown when attempts have been made. Although the events of the 1970s pushed many LDCs towards a greater commitment to agriculture, it is not yet clear whether the basic patterns of the prior two decades have been broken.

There is near consensus among all world views discussed here that increased investment in LDC agriculture is badly needed and also has high payoff potential relative to investment in MDC agriculture. The debate is over where it should come from and how it should be organized. Classical liberals often feel it can be self-generated by market prices (Johnson 1980). Neotraditionalists normally see massive infusions of outside capital needed even to keep up with population growth. Radicals frequently direct attention to the income aspects of the issue and argue that only redistribution of income will provide the food purchasing power needed by the poor—it is a demand, not a supply problem (Christensen 1978). Modernists look to the advances in agricultural technology as the key factor, and one which often will actually reduce investment requirements.

Multinational corporations (MNCs) also play an important part in the global food system. Analogous in terms of trade control to the Seven Sisters of petroleum are the five great international grain trading houses: Cargill, Continental, Bunge, Louis Dreyfus, and André (Morgan 1979). The analogy does not extend, of course, to the control of production levels or pricing, over which the petroleum MNCs had at least some influence. Nongrain and food processing companies, such as Nestlé and General Foods, and agricultural product suppliers, such as Ralston-Purina and Deere and Company, have been important as well, and are growing quickly.

Among these are the United Nations Food and Agriculture Organization (FAO), a Rome-based body largely dedicated to collection and exchange of information. The World Bank has increased its emphasis on agriculture quite steadily. Prior to 1968 only 8 percent of total lending went to agriculture and rural development, compared to 32 percent by 1981 (World Bank 1981b, 13). It has been estimated that 40 percent of all external funding for food and agricultural development in LDCs now is channeled through the bank (Hopkins, Paarlberg, and Wallerstein 1980, 35).

Among very important fairly recent developments in agriculture has been the formation of an international research network. Starting with the establishment in the Philippines of the International Rice Research Institute in 1960, this network has grown to nine bodies (table 10.3). Increasing international attention to agriculture was also demonstrated in 1974 by the World Food Conference, held in Rome; the establishment at that conference of the World Food Council; and the creation by the FAO in 1974 of a Global Information and Early Warning System.

TABLE 10.3.   *The International Agricultural Research Network*

Year Founded	Headquarters	Center	Program
1960	Philippines	International Rice Research Institute	Rice, multiple cropping
1966	Mexico	International Maize and Wheat Improvement Center	Wheat, maize, barley, triticale
1968	Nigeria	International Institute of Tropical Agriculture	Maize, rice, cowpeas, soybeans, lima beans, cassava, yams, sweet potatoes, and farming systems
1969	Colombia	International Center of Tropical Agriculture	Beans, cassava, beef and forages, maize, rice, and swine
1972	Peru	International Potato Center	Potatoes
1972	India	International Crops Research Institute for the Semi-Arid Tropics	Sorghum, millets, peanuts, chickpeas, pigeon peas
1974	Kenya	International Laboratory for Research on Animal Diseases	Blood diseases of cattle
1974	Ethiopia	International Livestock Centre for Africa	Cattle production
1976	Lebanon, Syria, Iran	International Center for Agricultural Research in Dry Areas	Wheat, barley, lentils, broad beans, oil-seeds, cotton, and sheep farming

Source: Sterling Wortman and Ralph H. Cummings, Jr., *To Feed This World* (Baltimore: Johns Hopkins University Press, 1978), 130–31.

Energy.   Nation-state energy policies have historically been largely determined by a country's own energy position. We may distinguish among self-sufficient or net exporter nations without control over their own resources; self-sufficient nations with control; and net importers. The major transition of the last decade was of the OPEC countries from the first to the second category. Prior to 1970 the major oil companies effectively controlled the production levels and pricing of oil produced in the OPEC countries. This should not be overemphasized in importance, however, since global prices were quite steadily falling in the face of dramatic expansion of Persian Gulf production—hardly indicative of very meaningful production or price control. It might be more accurate to say that prior to the 1950s the companies had considerable pricing and production control, and that the period between the mid-1950s and 1970 was an aberrant one for producers, companies, and countries, in general, none of which could easily control the market (Odell 1974, 198). OPEC was founded in 1960 by thirteen LDC producers as an attempt to gain such control and to stop the price slide. By 1980, those countries had in fact reduced the company role to management and distribution and reasserted producer control over the market.

The second category, that of self-sufficient countries with control over their own resources, consisted prior to 1970, almost exclusively of the United States in the western world, and of the Soviet Union in the Communist world. As OPEC moved into the category, the United States moved out, becoming a net importer. In fact, the United States was an importer prior to 1970 but had made the decision to restrict its oil imports to a fairly small fraction of domestic oil production (12 percent of that east of the Rockies), and therefore to an even smaller fraction of domestic energy consumption. By the early 1970s these import quotas were no longer sustainable (domestic production was inadequate) and in 1973 they were removed. The two sets of category changes were not unrelated. The earlier U.S. voluntary abstinence from the world market—justified on the basis of national security and called by its opponents the ''drain America first'' policy—had forced Mideast oil to other markets and depressed world prices. U.S. entry into the world market had the reverse effect.

The third category of nation-states, net importers, consists of countries which have had reason to be concerned about their dependence on outside energy sources. Western Europe heavily taxed petroleum, giving rise to gasoline prices about $1 per gallon when those in the United States were still $.30 per gallon. Since the volatility of supply was proven in 1973–74, these countries, now including the United States, have moved to diversify supply sources domestically and abroad and to increase the efficiency of energy systems. Domestically this has resulted in a growth of new institutions. The United States established the Federal Energy Administration in 1974, when it appeared that the interruption of supply was a transitory phenomenon. In late 1974 steps were taken to create an Energy Research and Development Agency (ERDA), because it appeared the problem of high prices might be around a while. By 1977 the Department of Energy was proposed, illustrating a growing belief that the energy issue was long-term and very fundamental. Reagan's desire to eliminate the Department of Energy, expressed repeatedly during his 1980 campaign, was not translated into action, in part because of widespread belief that energy problems will persist.

It would be a mistake to dismiss the MNCs as only an historical influence in energy. The so-called Seven Sisters, or oil majors, are Exxon, Mobil, Standard Oil of California, Texaco, Gulf, Royal Dutch Shell, and British Petroleum. In 1972 they jointly produced 75 percent of all non-North American and non-Communist area crude; in 1952 these companies had produced 90 percent of the total (Hughes, Rycroft, and Sylvan 1980, 50). A glance back at table 10.1 will show that the Seven Sisters were in 1982 still all *individually* among the largest sixty economic entities in the world—Exxon was number twenty-two. They have all recognized the inevitability of the transition from oil and gas to other energy forms and are transforming themselves into that which they already call themselves: energy companies. There is no reason to believe that the economic power held by virtue of sheer size will in the near future significantly erode for them or for the considerable number of other energy companies following them closely on the list of table 10.1.

Turning to IOs, the two key actors are the representatives, respectively, of producer and consumer countries: the Organization of Petroleum Exporting Countries (OPEC) and the International Energy Agency (IEA). There is still no real evidence that OPEC can impose pricing and production discipline on its members; so far its success has resulted almost entirely from the forces unleashed by the early stages of the transition from oil and gas.

In 1974, seventeen oil-importing countries, basically the nations of the OECD except France, established the IEA. Agreements have been reached on joint energy research. Overall the energy R&D budgets of IEA countries surged from $2.1 billion in 1974 to $4.9 billion by 1977 (Hughes, Rycroft, and Sylvan 1980, 101). They have also agreed to share supplies in the event of oil market disruptions.

Further indications of IO interest in energy include an increase in World Bank lending from 1 percent of its total prior to 1968 to 5 percent by 1981 (World Bank 1981b, 13), and the holding in 1981 of a United Nations Conference on New and Renewable Sources of Energy. Among the suggestions made was one for a network of global energy technology research centers like those now in place for agriculture. The IMF has also established special facilities to assist those countries most severely affected by oil prices.

World view positions on energy issues resemble those on agricultural issues in basic respects. Classical liberals look to the market and uncontrolled prices as key forces; neotraditionalists look to major conservation efforts and life-style changes; radicals look to assistance for the Third World and the poor of the West in the face of high energy prices; and modernists look to the variety of new technologies available.

The Environment.   Although LDCs have been less concerned about particular types of environmental damage than MDCs—especially direct side-effects of industrialization, such as noise, air pollution, and chemical pollution—there are no areas of the world which have not striven for improvements in some aspects of the environment. An especially large emphasis for LDCs has been water quality, namely the provision of potable water. Other emphases include basic sanitation and hygiene. MDCs, having largely conquered such problems have gone on to the problems associated with industrialization.

The activities and institutions established to address environmental issues in MDCs are far too numerous even to enumerate. Among the most important in the United States was the 1969 National Environmental Policy Act, that established the Council on Environmental Quality, mandated environmental impact statements, and set many air and water quality standards.

Much environmental activity has occurred at the international level, with a real surge in activity during the early 1970s. In the early 1970s it was believed that the decade would be one of intensive effort and considerable progress in the area—it was perceived as an environmental, not an energy decade. The first and second oil shocks and the stagflation of the period greatly reduced efforts and expectations.

In 1970 the OECD established an Environmental Committee and in 1971 the Economic Commission for Europe set up the Senior Governmental Advisers to the EC Governments on Environmental Problems (Dahlberg, Hetzel, and Soroos 1980, 81). In 1973 Western European action probably helped elicit an Eastern European response: the Council of Mutual Economic Assistance (CMEA) established a Council for Environmental Protection.

Action moved to a global level in 1972 with the United Nations Conference on the Human Environment in Stockholm. In 1973 the United Nations created its Environment Programme (UNEP). This permanent organization has headquarters in Nairobi, the first UN global body located in an LDC. Most activities are information gathering and environment monitoring, including a Global Environment Monitoring System (GEMS) and an International Register of Potentially Toxic Chemicals (IRPTC). It undertakes some project funding, principally education, training, and technical assistance (UNEP 1979).

The issue of environment covers so much that it is difficult to draw the boundaries on related activities. Clearly related are the 1972 Ocean Dumping Convention and the 1975 Endangered Species Convention. Also related are the activities related to the Law of the Sea. The First Law of the Sea Conference began in 1958, the Second in 1960, and the Third in 1974 (Swing 1976, 529–31). By 1974 the last major global commons had already shrunk through national territorial water extension to 65 percent of ocean space, and it is estimated that the 35 percent already expropriated by countries contains almost all of the world's oil and gas and 95 percent of all harvestable living resources (Swing 1976, 531). Nevertheless, high stakes remain in the area of deep-sea mining. The major issues dividing the United States from effectively all other countries of the world who have signed the Law of the Sea Treaty are the nature of a global authority and the extent of required technology sharing (Oxman 1980; Richardson 1980). The United States, as the global leader in technology for ocean exploitation, is reluctant to be bound by a global authority or to share its technology with other countries.

Technology. There is no question that nation-states have steadily increased their efforts to sponsor technology. In 1940 total U.S. government support for research and development (R&D) was only $74 million (Norman 1979, 15). By 1980 it was close to $30 billion, about 50 percent of which went to defense. As a percentage of GDP, Japan and West Germany now spend as much as the United States. Among the most aggressive national institutions with respect to technology has been Japan's Ministry of International Trade and Industry (MITI), which has sought both to purchase technology from abroad and to encourage its local development (Leonard and Gilpin 1981, 108).

Corporations have also aggressively sought new technology. Already by 1975 several MNCs had annual R&D budgets near $1 billion (Norman 1979, 33). These included General Motors and IBM.

Many IOs have technology development or transfer functions. Among them are the United Nations Institute for Training and Research (UNITAR), the World Health Organization (WHO), the agricultural research network noted earlier, and the network proposed for energy. Two newer ones (actually nationally based) have been established to facilitate R&D in LDCs and technology transfer to them: Canada's International Development Research Center (IDRC) and the Swedish Agency for Research Cooperation with Developing Countries.

Comment. In addition to highlighting the growing role of three types of institutions in global development issues, this brief review should have shown that claims that nothing is being done in response to the concerns of the neotraditionalists are incorrect. In each area, institutions have been established and actions have been taken. That statement does not allow, however, a corollary conclusion of response adequacy or appropriateness. Neotraditionalists see much activity as too little, and often too late. Classical liberals, of course, conclude that the actions of nation-states and IOs are misguided and may well create problems rather than resolving them. Radicals point out that the real root of many of the problems—maldistribution of wealth and income—are not addressed by most programs. Modernists sometimes see R&D response as inadequate, but are generally the most sanguine about its prospects.

To repeat, however, the trend towards strengthening of interactions between the political layer of the global system and the lower layers (see figure 1.1) appears unmistakable. Continuation of that trend seems a very reasonable long-term forecast.

Forecasts: Social/Political Futures

The above historical review concentrated heavily on formal political and economic institutions. Social forecasters have broader aims. They are interested more generally in patterns of interaction, including the cooperative and the conflictive, the hierarchical (centralized) and the nonhierarchical (decentralized). Formal institutions, especially political ones, are only a part of that. Before I turn to some forecasts, I should point out how poorly past prophets have often done.

Sociologist Seymour Martin Lipset has reviewed a number of failures in social and political forecasts (1979, 8–14). In the 1950s much sociological literature attempted to explain the growing pressures for conformity in American society. David Riesman introduced the concept of "other-directed" as one of many similar notions. The growth of big labor, big government, and big business all seemed to conspire to produce varieties of the man in the gray flannel suit. Yet the 1960s and 1970s, marked by social tension across age, race, ideological, and even sex boundaries, directly contradicted most such extrapolations.

Also in the earlier post–World War II years, many sociologists, especially on the left, foresaw the decline of social mobility and opportunity as economic growth and geographical expansion slowed or stopped. Eventually this was expected to lead to fixed class lines, not earlier known in the United States, with a large segment trapped across generations in unskilled positions. Instead, the rapid growth of the middle class has changed the social structure from pyramidal to diamond-shaped, and the number of menial jobs has decreased.

Marxist and non-Marxist sociologists agreed that industrialization, urbanization, and mass education would break down traditional ethnic society; assimilation was a matter of time. Yet we seem to be faced with a resurgence of national and ethnic cultural identities. The Soviet Union may fear it as much as any other threat. In 1982 previously military-exempt college students from Russia were drafted in order to help maintain non-Asian dominance in the army (*Business Week,* Aug. 2, 1982, 38). It is hard to argue that there has been significant assimilation of important ethnic minorities in Ireland, Belgium, Canada, Lebanon, and Spain, to note only a very few examples.

In political analysis, many explained McCarthyism in terms of "status politics": those falling in status in a highly competitive society were attracted to racist or hate movements. Yet such movements have not continued to prosper in the face of ongoing social mobility. Many young people with high social status purposely chose downward mobility in the 1960s and 1970s, creating peaceful groups preaching love.

For many years the end or decline of ideology was touted. Even before the economic disruptions of the 1970s, the emergence of the New Left in the 1960s began to weaken such forecasts.

Lipset has pointed out that Marxists might attribute such predictive failures to the inadequacy of bourgeois social science. Yet, in addition to Marxist concurrence with many of the faulty forecasts noted above, they have repeatedly foretold economic breakdown in the West and lack of growth in LDCs. Among the all-time worst forecasts, however, must be that the United States, as the most advanced capitalist country, would be the first socialist country, and that socialism could not develop in economically backward countries.

Having undertaken this kind of review of unmet expectations, we should now be sufficiently wary of social/political forecasts to look at some additional ones. I noted earlier that social forecasts tend to focus on patterns of interaction in terms of degree of hierarchy (or centralization) and the level of conflict (either overt or imbedded in social structures). Social futures—portrayed by academics, or scholars, but also by journalists, popular novelists, and science fiction writers—not surprisingly reveal the possibility of nearly every imaginable extreme. Almost all of these futures combine prescriptive and descriptive statements.

Centralized, Conflictive Futures. This category of futures is a large one and is generally characterized by an image of the future society dominated by one interest or elite. For example, the interest might be the military, as in Lasswell's garrison state (1962). In this example, the domestic conflict is limited by the channeling of hostilities towards an outside enemy. The image is clearly an intensified cold war extrapolation. It has similarities to George Orwell's *1984* (1949). In this latter, highly popular vision of today's world, external conflict is again used to divert public attention from the totalitarian control of society by a political/military elite. The international conflict resembles more the traditional power politics of a classical balance of power world, however, than Lasswell's bipolar image. The necessity for simultaneous domestic repression and violence, whenever propaganda or domestic consensus-building activities fail, is captured by Orwell.

Still another variation is domination by an economic elite. In Dwight Eisenhower's farewell address he identified a growing military-industrial complex. C. Wright Mills saw it as a much stronger and more pervasive *Power Elite* (1956). An extreme extrapolation of these notions, and the growing power of MNCs, provided the concept of the movie *Rollerball*. In that film, corporate wars had already occurred and conflict was now being channeled into the violent roller games. Marxist images (descriptive) of the current and near-term future would fall into this category.

Aldous Huxley portrayed the dominance of still another elite, a technocratic one, in *Brave New World* (1932). Although the Orwellian vision involved totalitarian use of modern technology for control, that theme is even more central to Huxley's anti-utopia. Principles of advanced medicine are used to tailor humans genetically, and psychology and sociology are used to shape their behavior. When modernists talk of the societal necessity to "override" local concerns about nuclear plant siting, neotraditionalists see a shadow of the technocratic elite.

In science fiction a recurring theme is a future society run by a religous or theocratic elite, often under a single religious leader, who could be an extrapolation of the Ayatollah Khomeini. (See, for example, Herbert's *Dune* [1965].) A return to monarchism is perhaps an even more common social order in much science fiction.

Centralized, Cooperative Futures. There is often a fine line between this category and the prior one. The implied presence of some elite in any centralized society may only mean that if there is no overt conflict, the noncoercive mechansims for maintaining order are simply very effective. In essence, the mechanisms work to shape values and not just to direct behavior. A case can be made that such mechanisms are as coercive— some would say "violent"—as overtly violent direction of behavior.

The inevitability of an elite in a centralized society was the point made by Djilas in trying to expose the Communist party leaders as *The New Class* (1957) of the supposedly classless Communist society. The point with respect to implicit violence is often made by other non-Marxist critics of Communist society, for whom the effort to shape a socialist man is seen as brainwashing. The same could be said with respect to the creation of "true Christians."

Because of the general reaction against centralization, it is hard for most in our age to picture attractive centralized futures, even if they control conflict. It might help to remember that the writing of Huxley (1932, 1937) and of Orwell (1946, 1949) was very much a reaction against centralized socialism and National Socialism, both of which promised just such features. Huxley argued forcefully that the ends, no matter what quality of socialist man or ideal society was promised, could not justify repressive means, and that, in fact, the means shape strongly the character of the ends.

One fairly popular attempt to create a positive image of such a cooperative, peaceful, but still quite centralized society (on a small scale) was B. F. Skinner's *Walden Two* (1948). Behavior of society members was to be shaped by principles of operant conditioning, especially positive reinforcement. The necessity of having at least one individual play God was addressed by Skinner and clearly a concern to him. In fact, the gap between *Walden Two* and *Brave New World* is not large, and might appear even smaller were it not for the portrayal by Huxley of negative reinforcement techniques in his society's childhood training. Skinner used only positive reinforcement for behavior modification.

The differences between the two images of centralized society, one conflictual and one cooperative, hinge to a considerable degree on the extent of shared or homogeneous values. Plato's image of *The Republic* is a peaceful society in which everyone accepts birth into his own social hierarchy rank. In 1898 Edward Bellamy produced *Looking Backward,* a socialist view of an ideal world. It, too, appears highly regimented to contemporary readers, although the society portrayed relies heavily upon instilling a sense of mutual responsibility in order to maintain cooperative behavior.

Obviously, centralization/decentralization and cooperation/conflict are matters of degree and my dichotomization here greatly oversimplifies positions. For instance, Falk (1975) put forward a prescriptive global political future involving a set of global institutions (including a World Assembly) which seems to strike something of a balance between calls for world government and autonomy. There is a considerable community of world federalists and others who prescribe such generally centralized and simultaneously cooperative futures, based on a community sharing a commitment to liberal democratic (or democratic socialist) values.

Decentralized, Cooperative Futures. This point with respect to shared values is critical to many neotraditionalist prescriptions of the future that tend to emphasize decentralization of power, simultaneously with voluntary behavior modification (e.g., simpler lifestyles, lower levels of competition). That which makes this a credible future, for those who portray it, is a belief in the possibility of very extensive value change. This can be seen in the work of Hazel Henderson (1978, 1981), E. F. Schumacher (1973), and the Club of Rome project directed by John Richardson (1982). Other writers, also in the neotraditionalist world view, seriously question the credibility of this kind of voluntarism on a wide scale. Herman Daly (1980), Dennis Pirages (1977), and William Ophuls (1977) suggest that institutions at least as centralized and coercive as current ones are likely to be necessary to enforce neotraditionalist values; Garrett Hardin (1980) feels that stronger ones may be necessary. Thus, the neotraditionalists straddle this category and the previous one in their definitions of preferred futures.

The centrality of shared values in any image of a decentralized, cooperative society is, however, undeniable. Even the decentralized *Utopia*

(1516) of Sir Thomas More depended on shared basic religious values, including the belief in God, a requirement for citizens.

There have been many technocratic images of decentralized, cooperative futures. Perhaps the first was that of Sir Francis Bacon, *New Atlantis* (1627). Bacon's New Atlantis is an island discovered by sailors. Like More's vision, that of Bacon was held together by religion. But science, working through a gigantic laboratory on the island, provided the progress, comfort, and even luxury missing in *Utopia*. Bacon was clearly one of the earliest modernists. Secularization of the technocratic *Utopia* was complete by the time of H. G. Wells's *Things to Come* (1936). However, in this vision, shared values within the "brotherhood of science" saved the world from warfare and, through the constant quest for knowledge, provided abundance.

Interestingly, the futures of Toffler in *The Third Wave* and of Naisbitt in *Megatrends* both seem to fit best into this category. Although neither writes at length about probable political institutions, both emphasize general decentralizing trends. Among Naisbitt's ten trends are a movement in the United States to (1) a "bottom-up" society (an increasing movement of ideas from the local level to the national one), (2) a "participatory" rather than "representative" democracy, (3) self-help rather than institutional help, and (4) informal communications networks rather than chain-of-command forms. Both authors appear to see such decentralization without an increase in overt conflict, and both focus on the United States to the near exclusion of the rest of the world.

It is curious that many neotraditionalists and modernists either foresee or prescribe decentralized, cooperative futures. The obvious attractiveness of such futures to the values of most Americans (and perhaps to deeper human values generally), and thus a certain amount of wishful thinking, probably plays a role along with more serious analysis in defining such images. In general, those whose thinking is dominated by the political ecology dimension tend seldom to focus on specific political structure issues. That must make us wonder if many have fallen prey to that against which Thucydides (chronicler of the Peloponnesian War) warned us two thousand years ago, when he wrote, "The usual thing among men is that when they want something they will, without any reflection, leave that to hope, while they will employ the full force of reason in rejecting what they find unpalatable" (reported in Augustine 1982). We can hope that the wish has not fathered the thought for so many modernists and neotraditionalists.

Decentralized, Conflictive Futures. Futures in this category are images of reversion to anarchy, in the pejorative sense of that term (anarchists would put their own images of desired futures in the previous category). One classic image was that in Nobel Prize winner William Golding's *Lord of the Flies* (1954), in which well-bred English schoolboys, marooned on a tropical island, begin to be ruled by superstition, ritual, and primal instincts. In spite of possible shared values (or because of the wrong ones), the absence of central authority led quickly to conflict and violence.

This is the image of international society which has led to proposals for a wide variety of global governments. Golding makes the analogy clear by marooning the boys as a result of nuclear war and having them picked up by a naval cruiser. It is also a common portrayal of adult futures after a nuclear war or a global natural catastrophe.

The Forces at Work

In seeking a basis for assessing the relative likelihood of movement in any of the above directions, it is useful to review the forces at work, especially those with respect to centralization and decentralization.

The wave of the past, at least, has been quite clearly increased centralization, explaining in part the relative popularity of work in the vein of Orwell and Huxley. The industrial era has been one of centralization in political units, including the creation of nation-states, and in economic units, including large corporations.

Politically the reasons for centralization include that posited by Herz, namely the military indefensibility of smaller units. In addition, improved communications and transportation technology has allowed a centralized government to communicate its will and to enforce it upon peripheral areas. Ancient empires had considerable extent, but to maintain it armies were practically always in motion (see, for example, Caesar's account of his conquest of Gaul). Advanced communications and transport technology, combined with the advent of mass education, also have made it possible to socialize people as members of the nation-state political unit. And political centralization has been a reaction to economic centralization, with the government often seen by modern liberals as the only force capable of resisting concentrated economic power.

In economics, continued refinements in the divison of labor and the appearance of highly complex technology have been powerful forces for both bigness in economic institutions and for hierarchy. And many modern industries, such as steel, railroads, or automobiles, require large scale. The capital intensity of the dominant energy forms of the last thirty to forty years, oil and gas, has reinforced these tendencies.

And the pressure of problems in the issues discussed here seems often to suggest the need for even greater centralization. Environmental issues often cannot be addressed at the national level, much less at the local ones—not when contaminants from one area can drift in air or water around the world. Food and energy issues are also often unresolvable locally when large volumes of trade are needed to sustain the systems.

Yet an extrapolation of more of the same for the future may not be warranted. Many major systemic changes seem to be occurring: we are moving into dramatically different eras with respect to population, energy, North-South relations, and technology. Many commentators (e.g., Daniel Bell [1973]) have written of the post-industrial era. Henderson (1981, 7) calls this "rearview mirror thought"—defining the future too much in terms of the past. The dominant forces may increasingly be decentralizing.

This is a major theme of Toffler's work, both *Future Shock* and *The Third Wave*. In an extension of the notion that modern society fosters pluralism, or the existence of many competing interest groups, Toffler emphasizes that the need for identity and a sense of belonging (Maslow's community value) in the face of rapid social and economic change, leads to the creation of small subcommunities.

Politically, not long ago it was common to read about how modern society had become "mass society" (Kornhauser 1959)—the authors' reaction to mass political movements such as National Socialism or Communism, or to the depersonalizing forces of mass production and mass consumption. Or, society was perceived in terms of the clash of major classes. Now we are more likely to read of the clash of specialized interest groups: pro-choice and anti-abortion (or pro-life); pro-guns and anti-guns; pro-smoking and anti-smoking; pro-nuclear and anti-nuclear; pro-solar, pro-space, anti-high rise buildings, and so forth.

There appear also to be economic and technological forces at work for decentralization. The most important factor may be the relative decentralization of increasingly dominant service and information sectors of the economy. Even within heavy industry the scale of plants seems to have nearly stopped growing. We no longer read frequently of the "world's largest" factory being constructed. In fact, new steel and automobile plants are increasingly dispersed geographically in modern societies and are smaller than they once were. Even if they remain constant in absolute size, the growth of population and economy size make them relatively smaller in impact. And new technologies such as robot production may facilitate a decline in production scale—at the very least they increasingly allow the tailoring of products to individual customer desires. An important force at work earlier in industrial societies was called the "backwash" effect. When there exist limited supplies of capital, knowledge, or skilled labor, these factors often tend to move towards a common geographical center in order to attain the threshold levels necessary for their effective utilization. Thus, for many years the "North" of various industrial countries (in, for example, the United States, France, Italy) drained the "South"; such centralization still goes on in many LDCs. With increasingly plentiful supplies of all production factors, however, we can see the effects of the reverse, or "spread," effect. "Silicon Valley" (Palo

Alto, Menlo Park, Los Altos), California, may still dominate semiconductor technology creation and manufacture, as Pittsburgh once did steel or Detroit automobiles, but all such dominations appear to be weakening (not least importantly, the role of the United States in the world economy). Already important high-technology centers in semiconductors have arisen in Massachusetts, and to lesser degrees in Minnesota and Colorado, and are growing quickly in other countries.

Although some of the issue area problems addressed in this volume, like the environment, seem to call for centralized decision-making, some do not. Neotraditionalists would even argue that solutions to most environmental problems begin with changes in local behavior, as do those to energy problems. Increasingly, local communities are mobilizing to utilize local energy resources, for example, geothermal reservoirs in Idaho, wood in Maine, or solar potential in Florida. In the longer term, the transition away from oil and gas in energy will almost certainly decentralize the global energy system. With the exception of proposals for satellite solar collecting stations or huge floating nuclear "parks" on the oceans—two highly speculative dominant technologies—most alternatives would disperse global energy production relative to its current concentration in the Mideast. With respect to agriculture, global concentration is already much lower than it is in energy, and both the greater potential and need for many importing regions to increase production suggest that the system may become even less concentrated.

As important as any of these forces of decentralization is the increasingly prevalent rejection of "bigness" in modern societies. Attitudes are supportive of increased international "functional" cooperation, as documented earlier, but not necessarily of global centralized government. Similarly, national interests increasingly organize on "functional" or narrow interest bases while simultaneously decrying "big government." This segmentation and functional division help reconcile the increasing scope of control of nation-states and IOs in various areas with the pervasive public gut reaction against centralization (see also Brzezinski [1970]).

11. What Are We to Think?

n this book I have tried to outline the competing views concerning the future of the global development system. In looking at them by issue area, I have not outlined them without comment—counter arguments have been presented frequently and reliance by advocates on extreme or not widely accepted data has been noted. My biases have undoubtedly shown through, in spite of efforts to be generally even-handed.

Those readers labeled "believers" in Chapter 1 most likely still believe, and very possibly feel, that this book has been biased against their world view (with some luck that is equally true for each world view). Those readers who were earlier labeled "confused" now have additional information, concepts, and theories, but certainly still would like to have a clearer image of what the future is likely to be. What can be said in conclusion to this volume?

First, recognition of values and world views helps us understand much better the basis of the work of futurists. Henderson (1981) proposed an information quality scale like that of figure 11.1 as a way of organizing our perceptions of the interaction of values, world views, models, and data. Like the multilevel, hierarchical image of the global development system (figure 1.1), its organization is hierarchical—values shape goals and purposes, which determine in large part our world views and paradigms, which direct our choice of models, which lead us to select or emphasize particular bits of data or information. Lower levels do assist us in reorganizing higher ones, even in ultimately changing world views and values. Once values are identified or world views formed, however, for most people they change slowly and often very little.

The complexities of value systems and world views are simply too great for me to have provided tidy diagrams or charts. Organization via the two dimensions of political economy and political ecology proves very useful.

219

FIGURE 11.1. *Information Quality Scale*

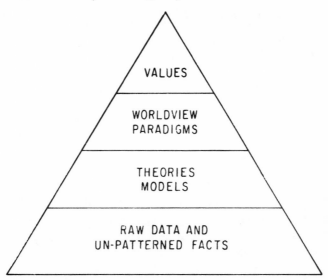

VALUES

WORLDVIEW
PARADIGMS

THEORIES
MODELS

RAW DATA AND
UN-PATTERNED FACTS

Source: Adapted from Hazel Henderson, *The Politics of the Solar Age* (Garden City, N.Y.: Doubleday, 1981), 349.

Again and again we have seen how general acceptance of a world view shapes the choice of concepts, of models and theories, and of "facts."

One important question left largely unanswered is how values and world views are determined. Clearly, childhood socialization and formal education are critical, as are social position, rank, class, and life experiences, which serve as a "reality test" for our belief systems. In fact, one could view the future as a grand experiment with respect to world views. If at the turn of the century global shortages of energy and food have become severe, if environmental problems have intensified, neotraditionalists will be vindicated; if humans almost everywhere are more affluent, healthier, and happier, modernists will be shown correct. If new categories of NICs have emerged and North-South income gaps are closing, classical liberals will have support; if the condition of the global poor remains basically unchanged, radical viewpoints will gain credence.

But such an experimental perspective has at least two weaknesses. First, world views are resilient. Studies even of religious cults forecasting the end of the world at a specific time show the ability of many members to recover mentally and to explain and discount the failure of the event to occur. Ideologies adapt to changed circumstances. Believers continue to believe. In social affairs they can point to appropriate adjustments having been made to avoid their worst-case scenario or to inadequate effort having been undertaken to attain the rosier future promised. Second, the world in the year 2000 is unlikely to be like that portrayed by any of the world views. Forecasters have repeatedly illustrated the tenuousness of their understanding of the forces at work. Moreover, human action is part of the system and does react to problems and opportunities. Predictions often do have either a self-denying (a problem is foreseen, so we fix it), or self-fulfilling (an opportunity is perceived, so we grasp it) character.

This leads to the second conclusion that can be drawn. The world views portrayed here are somewhat extreme, certainly in relation to each other. The future often, of course, does prove to be extreme. The royal families of Continental Europe immediately prior to World War I failed to comprehend the strength of the forces that would overthrow them; the extremists who said that a new world order was at hand were proven correct. Even science fiction has often failed to keep up with the speed of technological change in the last fifty years. Yet, in a high percentage of cases the future tends to be bracketed by expectations. Forecasts like those reviewed here can be treated a little like a Delphi panel; the "confused" should look seriously at the central tendency and not be embarrassed by indecisiveness in the face of the strong world view images of the believers.

The argument presented here—that none of the major world views will necessarily become dominant—contradicts many futurists. Adherents to each of the world views presented here feel that their arguments will ultimately prevail. Those who consciously think in terms of world view, or paradigm, clash—and many do—look to history for evidence that one paradigm vanquishes another. Copernican astronomy defeated the Ptolemaic order. Round earth proponents defeated flat earth believers. But I have shown that each world view has weaknesses as well as strengths. And the global development system is so complex that students of it are in the position of the blind men with the elephant that was described differently by each because each touched a different part of it.

An alternative to dominance by one world view is synthesis of several world views. Synthesis, too, has historic bases in paradigm clash. Einstein's physics did not vanquish Newtonian physics—it extended and encompassed it. Moreover, unlike students of the solar system or the nature of the atom, students of the global development system are studying a rapidly changing phenomenon. Hence, all world views must be adaptive. It is probable that in twenty years all of the world views presented here will be discernible in somewhat evolved form throughout contemporary writing, but that a greater synthesis will be apparent.

In addition, surprises will occur, and some will reshape the future, as well as our images of the world. This leads to the third conclusion. The next twenty to fifty years are especially likely to be surprising. Perhaps that conclusion is based partly in a natural human desire to see ourselves as

unique in terms of our position in time, as well as relative to other individuals, nations, etc. As Daniel Bell wrote in 1973, ''Every seer has a
sense that an age is ending (how many 'crises,' oh Lord, have we experienced), but there is little agreement as to what may be ahead'' (1973, 51).
Little did Bell know of crises in 1973, just prior to the food, energy, and
economic crises of the 1970s. There are many bases for concluding that
this is indeed an era of major transition; and when directions are changing,
our normally extrapolative-based forecasting tools are especially weak.

The concept of major transition, or turning point, has in fact become
one cutting across all world views. Many ''sub-transitions'' have been
identified here. We are, for example, in the middle of a demographic
transition. It can be viewed as a surge of global population from a level
supportable by pre-industrial societies to one supportable by industrial or
post-industrial societies. We have reached or passed the mid-point of the
transition and population growth rates are slowing. Further slowing could
occur voluntarily or because of limits.

We have entered a period of energy transition. Although at a fairly early
stage of it, there can be little doubt that transition is occurring. There is
much uncertainty as to the kind of energy system this transition will take us
to. Eventually it must take us to ''eternal'' energy sources, such as solar,
nuclear, or geothermal energy. With a re-emphasis on coal, unconventional oil, and gas that ''eventually'' might be quite a long time away.

We are in a period of economic transition. The LDCs are industrializing; the MDCs are now dominated by service and information sectors.
Whether or not the LDCs catch up with the MDCs, and whether we will
attain a new ''steady-state'' or face indefinite change, might not be clear.
But the fact of transition is.

As difficult as it might be to lay out its scope, a technology transition
also engulfs us. Much has been made of the accelerating pace of technology change over the last two centuries. Some observers see an imminent deacceleration; other observers believe that continued acceleration in
the pace of technological advance can be expected.

We are in the midst of a transition in our relationship with our environment. Our ability measurably to shape it can no longer be in doubt.
Whether we will use such power to alter it dramatically or whether we use
it to preserve its condition is a matter of doubt.

We are undergoing a value transition. Perhaps that can best be described
in terms of a natural movement up Maslow's hierarchy of values. Perhaps
it is better seen as a result of social choice. What is clear is that values are
changing and that they will help reshape institutional structures and less
formal social relationships.

All of this leads to a fourth, and final, conclusion. We do stand at a
unique point in time in still another sense, that is, in the sense of having

effective choice. Historically, transitions like those described here have occurred, but often almost without significant debate. Certainly people did not argue about the implications of the global population explosion ten-thousand years ago. Nor did they seriously ask about the broader consequences of the transition from firewood to coal. Even if society had recognized such transitions, the social and political institutions would have been incapable of directing or significantly influencing the change.

Today we recognize and even increasingly understand the transitions before us. Our political, social, and economic institutions have grown powerful in their abilities to influence global development subsystems. In other words, we now have more effective choice than ever before. Battle lines have been drawn on many issues, and alternative proposals (futures) have been sketched for us. We may not have control over our future, but we have more conscious influence than ever before. It is increasingly up to all of us to examine our value systems and our world views and to decide what kind of global future we want.

Bibliography

Adelman, Irving, and Cynthia T. Morris. 1973. *Economic Growth and Social Equity in Developing Countries.* Stanford, Calif.: Stanford University Press.

Adelman, M. A. 1972. *The World Petroleum Market.* Baltimore: Johns Hopkins University Press.

Aharonowitz, Yair, and Gerald Cohen. 1981. The Microbiological Production of Pharmaceuticals. *Scientific American* 245 (September): 140–53.

Ahluwalia, Montek S. 1976. Inequity, Poverty, and Development. *Journal of Development Economics* 3: 307–42.

Ahluwalia, Montek S., Nicholas G. Carter, and Hollis B. Chenery. 1979. *Growth and Poverty in Developing Countries.* World Bank Staff Working Paper No. 309, Revised. Washington, D.C.: World Bank.

Anderson, W. French, and Elaine G. Diacumakos. 1981. Genetic Engineering in Mammalian Cells. *Scientific American* 245 (July): 106–21.

Augustine. 1947. *The City of God.* Edited by R. V. G. Taylor. New York: Dutton.

Augustine, Norman R. 1982. *Augustine's Laws.* New York: American Institute of Aeronautics and Astronautics.

Ayres, Robert U. 1969. *Technological Forecasting and Long-range Planning.* New York: McGraw-Hill.

Bauer, P. T. 1981. *Equality, the Third World and Economic Delusion.* Cambridge: Harvard University Press.

Beenstock, Michael. 1983. *The World Economy in Transition.* London: George Allen and Unwin.

Bell, Daniel. 1973. *The Coming of Post-Industrial Society: A Venture in Social Forecasting.* New York: Basic Books.

———. 1982. *The Social Sciences Since the Second World War.* New Brunswick, N.J.: Transaction Books.

Birdsall, Nancy. 1980. *Population and Poverty in the Developing World.* World Bank Staff Working Paper No. 404. Washington, D.C.: World Bank.

Blake, David H., and Robert S. Walters. 1976. *The Politics of Global Economic Relations.* Englewood Cliffs, N.J.: Prentice-Hall.

225

Bogue, Donald J. 1980. "Policy Implications of the Changing Relationship Between Population and Economic Change." In *The Politics of Food,* edited by D. Gale Johnson, 124–39. Chicago: Chicago Council on Foreign Relations.

Boulding, Kenneth E. 1964. *The Meaning of the Twentieth Century.* New York: Harper and Row.

Brandt, Willy. 1980. *North-South: A Program for Survival.* Cambridge: MIT Press.

Breckling, John J. 1974. Affluence or Scarcity: A Perspective on the History of Political Ideas. Ph.D. diss. Case Western Reserve University, Cleveland.

Brill, Winston J. 1981. Agricultural Microbiology. *Scientific American* 245 (September): 199–215.

Brown, Lester R. 1978. *The Worldwide Loss of Cropland.* Worldwatch Paper 24. Washington, D.C.: Worldwatch Institute.

———. 1981. *Building a Sustainable Society.* New York: W. W. Norton.

Bruckmann, Gerhart. 1983. The Long Wave Debate. *Options* 2:6–9.

Brzezinski, Zbigniew. 1970. *Between Two Ages: America's Role in the Technetronic Era.* New York: Viking Press.

Bury, J. B. 1932. *The Idea of Progress.* New York: MacMillan.

Caesar, Julius. 1917. *The Gallic War.* Trans. by H. J. Edwards. Cambridge: Harvard University Press.

Central Intelligence Agency. 1977. *The International Energy Situation: Outlook to 1985.* Washington, D.C.: Government Printing Office.

Chase-Dunn, Christopher, and Joan Sokolovsky. 1983. Interstate Systems, World-Empires, and the Capitalist World-Economy. *International Studies Quarterly* 27: 357–67.

Chenery, Hollis, ed. 1971. *Studies in Development Planning.* Cambridge: Harvard University Press.

Christensen, Cheryl. 1978. "World Hunger: A Structural Approach." In *The Global Political Economy of Food,* edited by Raymond E. Hopkins and Donald J. Puchala, 171–200. Madison: University of Wisconsin Press.

Clarke, Arthur C. 1962. *Profiles of the Future: An Inquiry into the Limits of the Possible.* London: Victor Gollancz.

Cnudde, Charles F., and Deane E. Neubauer, eds. 1969. *Empirical Democratic Theory.* Chicago: Markham Publishing.

Coates, Joseph F. 1974. "Technology Assessment." In *Yearbook of Science and Technology.* New York: McGraw-Hill.

Cole, H. S. D., Christopher Freeman, Marie Jahoda, and R. L. R. Pavitt. 1973. *Models of Doom.* New York: Universe Books.

Commoner, Barry. 1976. *The Poverty of Power.* New York: Alfred A. Knopf.

Congressional Quarterly. 1979. *Energy Policy.* Washington, D.C.: Congressional Quarterly.

Congressional Quarterly. 1981. *Energy Policy.* 2d ed. Washington, D.C.: Congressional Quarterly.

Council on Environmental Quality (CEQ). 1976. *Environmental Quality.* Washington, D.C.: Government Printing Office.

————. 1981. *The Global 2000 Report to the President*. Washington, D.C.: Government Printing Office.

Cromwell, Jerry. 1977. The Size Distribution of Income: An International Comparison. *Income and Wealth* 23 (September).

Crosson, Pierre R., and Ruth B. Haas. 1982. "Agricultural Land." In *National Resource Policy*, edited by Paul R. Portney, 253–82. Washington, D.C.: Resources for the Future.

Dahl, Robert A., and Charles E. Lindblom. 1953. *Politics, Economics and Welfare*. Chicago: University of Chicago Press.

Dahlberg, Kenneth A., Nancy K. Hetzel, and Marvin S. Soroos. 1980. *Global Issues: Environment*. Columbus, Ohio: Consortium for International Studies Education.

Daly, Herman E. 1980. "The Steady-State Economy: Toward a Political Economy of Biophysical Equilibrium and Moral Growth." In *Economics, Ecology, Ethics*, edited by Herman E. Daly, 324–56. San Francisco: W. H. Freeman.

————. 1982. Review of the Ultimate Resource by Julian Simon. *The Bulletin of Atomic Scientists* 38 (Jan.): 39.

————, ed. 1980. *Economics, Ecology, Ethics*. San Francisco: W. H. Freeman.

de Moll, Lane, and Gigi Coe, eds. 1978. *Stepping Stones: Appropriate Technology and Beyond*. New York: Schocken Books.

Denison, Edward F. 1974. *Accounting for United States Economic Growth 1929–1969*. Washington: Brookings Institution.

DeVore, Paul W. 1980. *Technology: An Introduction*. Worcester, Mass.: Davis Publications.

Diesing, Paul. 1982. *Science and Ideology in the Policy Sciences*. New York: Aldine.

Djilas, Milovan. 1957. *The New Class*. New York: Praeger.

Dolan, Michael B., and Brian W. Tomlin. 1980. First World–Third World Linkages: External Relations and Economic Development. *International Organization* 34 (Winter): 41–64.

Dorf, Richard C., and Yvonne L. Hunter, eds. 1978. *Appropriate Visions: Technology, the Environment, and the Individual*. San Francisco: Boyd and Fraser.

Drucker, Peter F. 1969. *The Age of Discontinuity*. New York: Harper and Row.

Edelstein, Ludwig. 1967. *The Idea of Progress in Classical Antiquity*. Baltimore: Johns Hopkins Press.

Ehrlich, Paul R., and Anne H. Ehrlich. 1972. *Population, Resources, Environment*. San Francisco: W. H. Freeman.

Ehrlich, Paul R., Anne H. Ehrlich, and John P. Holdren. 1977. *Ecoscience*. San Francisco: W. H. Freeman.

Etzioni, Amitai. 1968. *The Active Society*. New York: Free Press.

Exxon Corporation. 1977. *World Energy Outlook*, New York: Exxon.

————. 1980. *World Energy Outlook*. New York: Exxon.

Falk, Richard A. 1975. *A Study of Future Worlds: Designing the Global Community.* New York: Free Press.

Ferkiss, Victor C. 1977. *Futurology: Promise, Performance, Prospects.* Beverly Hills: Sage Publications.

Flavin, Christopher. 1982. *Electricity from Sunlight: The Future of Photovoltaics.* Worldwatch Paper 52. Washington, D.C.: Worldwatch Institute.

Forrester, Jay W. 1971. *World Dynamics.* Cambridge: Wright-Allen Press.

———. 1977. "New Perspectives on Economic Growth." In *Alternatives to Growth I,* edited by Dennis L. Meadows, 107–21. Cambridge: Ballinger Publishing.

———. 1978. *Changing Economic Patterns.* Paper No. D-2891-1. Cambridge: MIT System Dynamics Group.

Fowles, Jim, ed. 1978. *Handbook of Futures Research.* Westport, Conn.: Greenwood Press.

Freeman, Christopher. 1978. "Holst Memorial Lecture" (December), as cited in Ward Morehouse, "Letting the Genie Out of the Bottle? The Micro-electronic Revolution and North-South Relations in the 1980s." In *Technology and International Affairs,* edited by Joseph S. Szyliowicz, 239–73. New York: Praeger.

Freeman, Christopher, and Marie Jahoda, eds. 1978. *World Futures: The Great Debate.* New York: Universe.

Fried, Edward R. 1976. International Trade in Raw Materials: Myths and Realities. *Science* 191 (20 February): 641–46.

Friedman, Milton. 1962. *Capitalism and Freedom.* Chicago: University of Chicago Press.

Fuller, R. Buckminster. 1981. *Critical Path.* New York: St. Martin's Press.

Fuss, M. S. 1977. The Demand for Energy in Canadian Manufacturing. *Journal of Econometrics* 5: 89–116.

Galbraith, John Kenneth. 1973. *Economics and the Public Purpose.* Boston: Houghton Mifflin.

Galtung, Johan. 1971. A Structural Theory of Imperialism. *Journal of Peace Research* 2: 81–117.

Gendron, Bernard. 1977. *Technology and the Human Condition.* New York: St. Martin's Press.

Gilpin, Robert. 1979. "Three Models of the Future." In *Transnational Corporations and World Order,* edited by George Modelski, 353–72. San Francisco: W. H. Freeman.

Golding, William. 1954. *Lord of the Flies.* New York: Capricorn Books.

Gordon, Theodore J., and Robert H. Ament. 1972. "Forecasts of Some Technological and Scientific Developments and Their Societal Consequences." In *Technology and Man's Future,* edited by Albert H. Teich, 5–20. New York: St. Martin's Press.

Goulet, Denis. 1977. *The Uncertain Promise: Value Conflicts in Technology Transfer.* New York: IDOC/North America.

Grant, Lindsey. 1982. *The Cornucopian Fallacies*. Washington, D.C.: Environmental Fund.

Hamrin, Robert D. 1980. *Managing Growth in the 1980s*. New York: Praeger.

Hansen, Roger D., and Contributors for the Overseas Development Council. 1982. *U.S. Foreign Policy and the Third World: Agenda 1982*. New York: Praeger.

Hardin, Garrett. 1980. "Tragedy of the Commons." In *Economics, Ecology, Ethics*, edited by Herman E. Daly, 100–114. San Francisco: W. H. Freeman.

Hardin, Garrett. 1982. An Ecological View of International Economics. *Africa Insight* 12: 30–31.

Hardin, Garrett, and John Baden, eds. 1977. *Managing the Commons*. San Francisco: W. H. Freeman.

Harman, Willis W. 1976. *An Incomplete Guide to the Future*. San Francisco: San Francisco Book Company.

Harrington, Winston, and Anthony C. Fisher. 1982. "Endangered Species." In *Natural Resource Policy*, edited by Paul R. Portney, 117–48. Washington, D.C.: Resources for the Future.

Hayes, Denis. 1977. *Rays of Hope: The Transition to a Post-Petroleum World*. New York: W. W. Norton.

Healey, Denis. 1979–80. Oil, Money and Recession. *Foreign Affairs* 58 (Winter): 217–30.

Heilbroner, Robert L. 1974. *An Inquiry into the Human Prospect*. New York: W. W. Norton.

Henderson, Hazel. 1978. *Creating Alternative Futures*. New York: Berkeley Publishing.

———. 1981. *The Politics of the Solar Age*. New York: Anchor Press/Doubleday.

Herbert, Frank. 1965. *Dune*. Philadelphia: Chilton Books.

Herrera, Amilcar O., Hugo D. Scolnik, Graciela Chichilnisky, Gilberto C. Gallopin, Jorge E. Harday, Diana Mosovich, Enrique Oteiza, Gilda L. de Romero Brest, Carlos E. Suarez, and Luis Talavera. 1976. *Catastrophe or New Society? A Latin American World Model*. Ottawa: International Development Research Centre.

Herz, John. 1957. Rise and Demise of the Territorial State. *World Politics* 9 (July): 473–93.

———. 1969. "The Territorial State Revisited: Reflections on the Future of the Nation-State." In *International Politics and Foreign Policy*, edited by James N. Rosenau, 76–89. New York: Free Press.

Hirsch, Fred. 1976. *Social Limits to Growth*. Cambridge, Mass.: Harvard University Press.

Hopkins, Raymond F., Robert L. Paarlberg, and Mitchel Wallerstein. 1980. *Global Issues: Food*. Columbus: Ohio State University, Consortium for International Studies Education.

Hopkins, Raymond F., and Donald J. Puchala, eds. 1978. *The Global Political Economy of Food*. Madison: University of Wisconsin Press.

Hudson, E. A., and D. C. Jorgenson. 1974. U.S. Energy Policy and Economic Growth, 1975–2000. *Bell Journal of Economics and Management Science* 5: 461–514.

Hughes, Barry B. 1980. *World Modeling.* Lexington, Mass.: Lexington Books.

Hughes, Barry B., Robert W. Rycroft, and Donald A. Sylvan. 1980. *Global Issues: Energy.* Columbus, Ohio: Consortium for International Studies Education.

Huxley, Aldous L. 1932. *Brave New World.* Garden City, N.Y.: Doubleday.

————. 1937. *Ends and Means.* New York: Harper.

Ide, Thomas Ranald. 1982. "The Technology." In *Microelectronics and Society: For Better or For Worse,* edited by Guenter Friedrichs and Adam Schaff, 37–88. Oxford: Pergamon Press.

International Energy Agency. 1981. *Energy Policies and Programmes of IEA Countries, 1980 Reveiw.* Paris: OECD.

International Labor Organization (ILO). 1977. *Employment, Growth, and Basic Needs.* New York: Praeger.

International Monetary Fund (IMF). 1983. *World Economic Outlook.* Washington, D.C.: IMF.

Jain, S. 1975. *Size Distribution of Income: Compilation of Data.* Baltimore: Johns Hopkins University Press.

Johnson, D. Gale. 1978. "World Food Institutions: A 'Liberal' View." In *The Global Political Economy of Food,* edited by Raymond F. Hopkins and Donald J. Puchala, 265–82. Madison: University of Wisconsin Press.

————. 1980. *The Politics of Food.* Chicago: Chicago Council on Foreign Relations.

Johnson, Stanley. 1972. *The Green Revolution.* New York: Harper and Row.

Kahn, Herman. 1979. *World Economic Development.* New York: Morrow Quill.

Kahn, Herman, William Brown, and Leon Martel. 1976. *The Next 200 Years.* New York: William Morrow.

Kegley, Charles W., Jr., and Eugene R. Wittkopf. 1981. *World Politics: Trend and Transformation.* New York: St. Martin's Press.

Kellogg, William W., and Robert Schware. 1982. Society, Science and Climate Change. *Foreign Affairs* 60 (Summer): 1076–1109.

Kindleberger, Charles. 1973. *The World in Depression 1929–1939.* Berkeley: University of California Press.

Kornhauser, William. 1959. *The Politics of Mass Society.* New York: Free Press.

Kravis, Irving B., Alan Heston, and Robert Summers. 1978. *International Comparisons of Real Product and Purchasing Power.* Baltimore: Johns Hopkins University Press.

Kuhn, Thomas S. 1970. *The Structure of Scientific Revolutions.* 2d ed. Chicago: University of Chicago Press.

Kuznets, Simon. 1963. Quantitative Aspects of the Economic Growth of

Nations: Distribution of Income by Size. *Economic Development and Cultural Change,* Part II, 11 (January): 1–79.

Lamb, Helen B. 1955. "The 'State' and Economic Development in India." In *Economic Growth: Brazil, India, Japan,* edited by Simon Kuznets, Wilbert Moore, and Joseph J. Spengler, 464–95. Durham, N.C.: Duke University Press.

Lasswell, Harold D. 1962. "The Garrison State Hypothesis Today." In *Changing Patterns of Military Politics,* edited by Samuel P. Huntington, 51–70. New York: Free Press.

Leonard, H. Jeffrey, and Robert Gilpin. 1981. "Industrial and Technological Policies of Western Economies." In *Technology and International Affairs,* edited by Joseph S. Szyliowicz, 98–128. New York: Praeger.

Leontief, Wassily, et al. 1977. *The Future of the World Economy.* New York: Oxford University Press.

Levy, Walter J. 1978–79. The Years that the Locust Hath Eaten. *Foreign Affairs* 57: 287–305.

Lipset, Seymour Martin. 1959. *Political Man: The Social Bases of Politics.* New York: Doubleday. Expanded edition, 1981. Baltimore: Johns Hopkins University Press.

Lipset, Seymour Martin, ed. 1979. *The Third Century: America as a Post-Industrial Society.* Stanford, Calif.: Hoover Institution Press.

Loehr, William, and John P. Powelson. 1981. *The Economics of Development and Distribution.* New York: Harcourt, Brace, Jovanovich.

Machiavelli, Niccolo. 1940. *The Discourses.* New York: Modern Library.

McLaughlin, Martin M., and Staff of the Overseas Development Council. 1979. *The United States and World Development: Agenda 1979.* New York: Praeger.

Macpherson, W. J. 1972. "Economic Development in India under the British Crown, 1858–1947." In *Economic Development in the Long Run,* edited by A. J. Youngson, 126–91. London: George Allen and Unwin.

Maddison, Angus. 1982. *Phases of Capitalist Development.* Oxford: Oxford University Press.

Malthus, Thomas R. 1916. *Parallel Chapters from the First and Second Editions of an Essay on the Principles of Population.* New York: Macmillan.

Marden, Parker G., Dennis G. Hodgson, and Terry L. McCoy. 1980. *Global Issues: Population.* Columbus, Ohio: Consortium for International Studies Education.

Markley, O. W. 1983. Preparing for the Professional Futures Field. *Futures* 15 (February): 47–62.

Marien, Michael. 1976. *Societal Directions and Alternatives.* LaFayette, New York: Information for Policy Design.

Marx, Karl. 1971. "Theories of Surplus Value." In *Marx and Engels on the Population Bomb.* 2d ed. Edited and translated by Ronald L. Meek, 13.

Marx, Karl. 1959. "Excerpt from 'A Contribution to the Critique of Political

Economy.' '' In *Marx and Engels,* edited by Lewis S. Feuer, 42–46.
Berkley, Calif.: Ramparts.

Maslow, Abraham. 1970. *Motivation and Personality.* 2d ed. New York:
Harper and Row.

McDermott, John. 1972. "Technology: The Opiate of the Intellectuals." In
Technology and Man's Future, edited by Albert Teich, 151–77. New York:
St. Martin's Press.

Meadows, Dana. 1975. "Making Value Sets Explicit." In *Making It Happen,*
edited by John M. Richardson, 28–29. Washington, D.C.: U.S. Association
for the Club of Rome.

Meadows, Dennis L., William W. Behrens III, Donella H. Meadows, Roger F.
Naill, Jørgen Randers, and Erich K. O. Zahn. 1974. *Dynamics of Growth in
a Finite World.* Cambridge: Wright-Allen Press.

Meadows, Dennis L. et al. 1976. *Toward Global Equilibrium.* Cambridge:
Wright-Allen Press.

Meadows, Donella H., Dennis L. Meadows, Jørgen Randers, and William W.
Behrens III. 1972. *The Limits to Growth.* New York: Universe Books.

Meek, Ronald M., ed. and trans. 1953. *Marx and Engels on Malthus.* London:
Lawrence and Wishart.

Mesarovic, Mihajlo D., and Eduard C. Pestel. 1972. A Goal-Seeking and
Regionalized Model for Analysis of Critical World Relationships—The
Conceptual Foundation. *Kybernetes* 1:79–85.

———. 1974. *Mankind at the Turning Point.* New York: E. P. Dutton.

———, eds. 1974b. *Multilevel Computer Model of World Development System.*
6 vol. International Institute for Applied Systems Analysis Symposium
Proceedings. Laxenburg, Austria: IIASA.

Miles, Ian. 1978. "Worldviews and Scenarios." In *World Futures: The Great
Debate,* edited by Christopher Freeman and Marie Jahoda, 233–78. New
York: Universe Books.

Mill, John Stuart. 1857. *Principles of Political Economy,* Vol. 2. London: John
W. Parker.

Mills, C. Wright. 1956. *The Power Elite.* London: Oxford University Press.

Modelski, George, 1978. The Long Cycle of Global Politics and the Nation-
State. *Comparative Studies in Society and History* 20 (April): 214–35.

———. 1979. "International Content and Performance Among the World's
Largest Corporations." In *Transnational Corporations and World Order,*
edited by George Modelski, 45–65. San Francisco: W. H. Freeman.

Morehouse, Ward. 1981. "Letting the Genie Out of the Bottle? The Micro-
electronic Revolution and North-South Relations in the 1980s." In
Technology and International Affairs, edited by Joseph S. Szyliowicz, 239–
73. New York: Praeger.

Morgan, Dan. 1979. *The Merchants of Grain.* New York: Viking Press.

Morgan Guaranty Trust Company. 1981. *World Financial Markets* (December).

Murdoch, William W. 1980. *The Poverty of Nations: The Political Economy of
Hunger and Population.* Baltimore: Johns Hopkins University Press.

Nachman, Gerald. 1982. Future Shuck. *Newsweek,* March 29, 9.

Naisbitt, John. 1982. *Megatrends.* New York: Warner Books.

National Academy of Sciences. 1979. *Energy in Transition 1985–2010.* San Francisco: W. H. Freeman.

National Commission on Supplies and Shortages. 1976. *Government and the Nation's Resources.* Washington, D.C.: Government Printing Office.

Nau, Henry R. 1978. "The Diplomacy of World Food: Goals, Capabilities, Issues, and Arenas." In *The Global Political Economy of Food,* edited by Raymond F. Hopkins and Donald J. Puchala, 201–36. Madison: University of Wisconsin Press.

Norman, Colin. 1979. *Knowledge and Power: The Global Research and Development Budget.* Worldwatch Paper No. 31. Washington, D.C.: Worldwatch Institute.

———. 1980. *Microelectronics at Work: Productivity and Jobs in the World Economy.* Worldwatch Paper No. 39. Washington, D.C.: Worldwatch Institute.

Odell, Peter R. 1974. *Oil and World Power.* 3d ed. Baltimore: Penguin Books.

Olson, Mancur. 1965. *The Logic of Collective Action.* Cambridge: Harvard University Press.

Olson, Mancur, and Hans H. Landsberg, eds. 1973. *The No-Growth Society.* New York: W. W. Norton.

Ophuls, William. 1977. *Ecology and the Politics of Scarcity.* San Francisco: W. H. Freeman.

Organization of Economic Cooperation and Development (OECD). 1979. *Interfutures: Facing the Future.* Paris: OECD.

———. 1981. *The Impact of the Newly Industrializing Countries.* Paris: OECD.

Orwell, George. 1946. *Animal Farm.* New York: Signet.

———. 1949. *1984.* New York: New American Library.

Oxman, Bernard H. 1980. The Third United Nations Conference on the Law of the Sea: The Eighth Session (1979). *American Journal of International Law* 74: 1–47.

Paddock, William, and Paul Paddock. 1976. *Time of Famines.* Reprint of *Famine* 1975. Boston: Little, Brown.

Page, William. 1973. "Population Forecasting." In *Models of Doom,* edited by H. S. D. Cole et al., 159–74. New York: Universe.

Pavitt, K. L. R. 1973. "Malthus and Other Economists." In *Models of Doom,* edited by H. S. D. Cole et al., 137–58. New York: Universe.

Paukert, F. 1973. Income Distribution at Different Levels of Development: A Survey of Evidence. *International Labour Review* (August): 97–126.

Peccei, Aurelio. 1977. *The Human Quality.* Oxford: Pergamon Press.

Pindyck, Robert S. 1977. *Interfuel Substitution and the Industrial Demand for Energy: An International Comparison.* Cambridge: MIT Energy Laboratory.

Pirages, Dennis, ed. 1977. *The Sustainable Society.* New York: Praeger.

————. 1978. *Global Ecopolitics: The New Context for International Relations.*
North Scituate, Mass.: Duxbury Press.

————. 1983. The Ecological Perspective and the Social Sciences.
International Studies Quarterly 27 (September): 243–55.

Pirages, Dennis, and Paul Ehrlich. 1974. *Ark II.* San Francisco: W. H.
Freeman.

Pirsig, Robert M. 1974. *Zen and the Art of Motorcycle Maintenance.* New
York: William Morrow.

Plano, Jack C., Milton Greenberg, Roy Olton, and Robert E. Riggs. *Political
Science Dictionary.* Hinsdale, Ill.: Dryden Press.

Plano, Jack C., and Robert E. Riggs. 1967. *Forging World Order.* New York:
Macmillan.

Platt, John. 1969. What We Must Do. *Science* 166 (November 28): 1115–21.

Plato. 1937. "Cratylus." In *The Dialogues of Plato,* translated by Benjamin
Jowett. New York: Random House.

————. 1956. *The Great Dialogues of Plato.* Translated by W. H. D. Rouse.
New York: Mentor.

Pohlman, Edward, ed. 1973. *Population: A Clash of Prophets.* New York:
Mentor.

Population Reference Bureau. 1976. *World Population Growth and Response.*
Washington, D.C.: Population Reference Bureau.

Ramesh, Jairam, and Charles Weiss, Jr., eds. 1979. *Mobilizing Technology for
World Development.* New York: Praeger.

Richardson, Elliot L. 1980. Power, Mobility and the Law of the Sea. *Foreign
Affairs* 58: 902–19.

Richardson, John M., ed. 1982. *Making It Happen.* Washington: U.S.
Association for the Club of Rome.

Rifkin, Jeremy. 1980. *Entropy.* New York: Viking.

Rostow, W. W. 1971. *The Stages of Economic Growth.* 2d ed. Cambridge:
Cambridge University Press.

————. 1971b. *Politics and the Stages of Growth.* Cambridge: Cambridge
University Press.

————. 1978. *The World Economy.* Austin: University of Texas Press.

Sagasti, Francisco R. 1979. Knowledge Is Power. *Mazingira,* No. 8.

Science and Public Policy Program, University of Oklahoma. 1975. *Energy
Alternatives: A Comparative Analysis.* Washington, D.C.: Government
Printing Office.

Schneider, Stephen H. 1976. *The Genesis Strategy.* New York: Plenum Press.

Schumacher, E. F. 1973. *Small is Beautiful.* New York: Harper Colophon.

Sealth, Chief. 1979. This Earth Is Sacred. *Technology Tomorrow* (April): 9.

Sewell, John, and the Staff of the Overseas Development Council. 1980. *The
United States and World Development: Agenda 1980.* New York: Praeger.

Simon, Julian. 1981. *The Ultimate Resource.* Princeton: Princeton University
Press.

Sinsheimer, Robert L. 1980. "The Presumptions of Science." In *Economics, Ecology, Ethics,* edited by Herman E. Daly, 146–61. San Francisco: W. H. Freeman.

Sivard, Ruth Leger. 1982. *World Military and Social Expenditures.* Leesburg, Va.: World Priorities.

Skinner, B. F. 1948. *Walden Two.* New York: Macmillan.

Smith, Adam. 1910. *The Wealth of Nations.* Vol. 1. London: Dent.

———. 1937. *An Inquiry Into the Nature and Causes of the Wealth of Nations.* New York: Modern Library.

Sorokin, Pitirim. 1937. *Social and Cultural Dynamics.* New York: American Book.

Spero, Joan Edelman. 1981. *The Politics of International Economic Relations.* 2d ed. New York: St. Martin's Press.

Sprout, Harold, and Margaret Sprout. 1971. *Towards a Politics of the Planet Earth.* New York: Van Nostrand Reinhold.

Stobaugh, Robert, and Daniel Yergin, eds. 1979. *Energy Future.* New York: Random House.

Stoker, H. Stephen, Spencer L. Seager, and Robert L. Capaner. 1975. *Energy: From Source to Use.* Glenview, Ill.: Scott, Foresman.

Swing, John J. 1976. Who Will Own the Oceans? *Foreign Affairs* 54 (April): 527–46.

Systems Analysis Research Unit (SARU). 1977. *SARUM 76 Global Modeling Project.* London: Departments of the Environment and Transport.

Teich, Albert H., ed. 1972. *Technology and Man's Future.* New York: St. Martin's Press.

Thompson, Louis M. 1980. "Climate Change and World Grain Production." In *The Politics of Food,* edited by D. Gale Johnson, 100–123. Chicago: Chicago Council on Foreign Relations.

Thompson, William R. 1983. Uneven Economic Growth, Systemic Challenges, and Global Wars. *International Studies Quarterly* 27: 341–55.

Thorner, Daniel. 1955. "Long-term Trends in Output in India," In *Economic Growth: Brazil, India, and Japan,* edited by Simon Kuznets, Wilbert E. Moore, and Joseph J. Spengler, 103–28. Durham, N.C.: Duke University Press.

Timmer, C. Peter, Walter P. Falcon, and Scott R. Pearson. 1983. *Food Policy Analysis.* Baltimore: Johns Hopkins University Press.

Toffler, Alvin. 1970. *Future Shock.* New York: Bantam.

———. 1980. *The Third Wave.* New York: William Morrow.

United Nations. 1973. *The Determinants and Consequences of Population Trends.* New York: United Nations.

United Nations Environment Programme (UNEP). 1979. *The United Nations Environment Programme.* Nairobi: UNEP.

United Nations Fund for Population Activities (UNFPA). 1979. *1979 Report.* New York: UNFPA.

U.S. Department of Commerce. 1977. *Social Indicators 1976*. Washington: Government Printing Office.
U.S. Department of Energy. 1981. *Energy Projections to the Year 2000*. Washington, D.C.: Government Printing Office.

Vernon, Raymond. 1971. *Sovereignty at Bay*. New York: Basic Books.
von Mises, Ludwig. 1962. *The Free and Prosperous Commonwealth: An Exposition of the Ideas of Classical Liberalism*. Translated by Ralph Raico. Princeton, N.J.: D. Van Nostrand.

Wädekin, Karl-Eugen. 1982. Soviet Agriculture and the West. *Foreign Affairs* 60 (Spring): 882–903.
Wallerstein, Immanuel. 1976. *The Modern World-System*. New York: Academic Press.
————. 1981. "Dependence in an Interdependent World: The Limited Possibilities of Transformation within the Capitalist World Economy." In *From Dependency to Development*, edited by Heraldo Munoz. Boulder, Colo.: Westview Press.
Watt, Kenneth E. F. 1974. *The Titanic Effect*. New York: E. P. Dutton.
Webb, Maryla, and Judith Jacobsen. 1982. *U.S. Carrying Capacity: An Introduction*. Washington, D.C.: Carrying Capacity.
Wildavsky, Aaron, and Ellen Tenenbaum. 1981. *The Politics of Mistrust*. Beverly Hills: Sage Publications.
Wilson, Carroll. 1977. *Energy: Global Prospects 1985–2000*. New York: McGraw-Hill.
————. 1980. *Coal-Bridge to the Future*. Cambridge: Ballinger Publishing.
Wittwer, Sylvan H. 1980. "Food Production Prospects: Technology and Resource Options." In *The Politics of Food*, edited by D. Gale Johnson, 60–99. Chicago: Chicago Council on Foreign Relations.
Woodwell, George M. 1979. The Carbon Dioxide Question. *Scientific American* 238 (January): 34–43.
World Bank. 1980. *World Development Report 1980*. Washington, D.C.: World Bank.
World Bank. 1981. *World Development Report 1981*. Washington, D.C.: World Bank.
————. 1981b. *World Bank Annual Report 1981*. Washington, D.C.: World Bank.
————. 1981c. *Agricultural Research: Sector Policy Paper*. Washington, D.C.: World Bank.
————. 1982. *World Development Report 1982*. Washington, D.C.: World Bank.
Wortman, Sterling, and Ralph W. Cummings, Jr. 1978. *To Feed This World*. Baltimore: Johns Hopkins University Press.

Index

237

The Johns Hopkins University Press

World Futures

This book was composed in Futura Book display and
Times Roman text type by The Composing Room of
Michigan, Inc., from a design by Susan P. Fillion. It
was printed on S. D. Warren's 50-lb. Sebago Eggshell
Cream paper and bound by BookCrafters, Inc.